String Fellows

String Fellows

A Cycling Odyssey into Cricket's Heartland

Colin Bateman

Matador
5 Weir Road
Kibworth Beauchamp
Leicester LE8 0LQ, UK
Tel: (+44) 116 279 2299
Fax: (+44) 116 279 2277
Email: books@troubador.co.uk
Web: www.troubador.co.uk/matador

ISBN 978 1848764 842

British Library Cataloguing in Publication Data.
A catalogue record for this book is available from the British Library.

Typeset in 11pt Palatino by Troubador Publishing Ltd, Leicester, UK

Matador is an imprint of Troubador Publishing Ltd

Printed in Great Britain by the MPG Books Group, Bodmin and King's Lynn

Dedicated to Brenda….
for her unwavering support for everything I do

CONTENTS

The Route   ix

Acknowledgements   xi

Introduction   xiii

Foreword By Angus Fraser   xv

The Challenge and the Peloton   1

The Pilgrims' Way   21

The Home Run   40

The Coastal Jaunt   55

High Plain Drifters   69

The Cider Classic   82

Border Patrol   104

The Ferryman Cometh   125

The Midland Miles   145

The Second Half   166

The Viaduct Velo   180

Top of the Country   201

The Long Haul   216

Industrial Industry   230

The Fox Chase   248

The Penultimate Push   263

Lords of the Road   277

Afterword   293

The 18 Counties Route

1. The Oval	7. Cardiff	13. Derby
2. Canterbury	8. Worcester	14. Trent Bridge
3. Hove	9. Edgbaston	15. Leicester
4. The Rose Bowl	10. Old Trafford	16. Northampton
5. Taunton	11. The Riverside	17. Chelmsford
6. Bristol	12. Headingley	18. Lord's

ACKNOWLEDGEMENTS

Above all, I have to thank my five cycling companions: Toddy, David, Alan, Tom and Jack (listed in order of age, not speed). The curious 1100-mile challenge we undertook would not have happened without them. They were great company, and when I came to write this book, they gave me their blessing to reveal the secrets of the *peloton*. Their excellent contributions and photographs have also enriched these pages.

We were greatly encouraged by our guest riders in the early days of the escapade, and this book contains sparkling articles from two of them: Angus Fraser and Steve James. Both former England cricketers, they have shone in their second careers as journalists. And it shows. Gus has since given up full time media work to return to the game as Director of Cricket at Middlesex, but his Foreword to this book reveals he has lost none of his wit and wisdom with the pen. Matthew Engel also played a major role in helping us to organise our charity fund-raising and in getting us drunk one night on the ride. He has written a moving piece for Chapter Eight.

There is special appreciation to my good friend and journalist colleague David Llewellyn for his encouragement, help and advice in getting this project off the ground, and to my son Rupert for his computer wizardry. Thanks also to

Sabina Gardner and David Llewellyn for copy-editing this book.

The ride around the 18 First Class cricket counties was made so much easier by the considerable help we received from within the game, particularly when it came to reducing our costs by providing free or cut-priced accommodation. Thanks go to Rebecca Trbojevich (Lancashire County Cricket Club), Yvette Thompson (Durham CCC), Shaun Callighan (formerly at the Headingley Experience), Carolyn Dunne (Kent CCC), Melinda Cooksey (Worcestershire CCC) and Rachael Mitchell (White House Hotel, Worcester). Thanks also to Nathan Ross (Surrey CCC), Jill Maxwell (BRIT Insurance), and, from the England and Wales Cricket Board, Colin Gibson, Medha Laud and Hugh Morris.

When we first mooted this strange venture, we received many sceptical looks from colleagues in the press box, who, like us, spend most of their working lives sitting on their backsides. When the project took shape, however, they were extremely generous in their support. There was special help from Paul Weaver of the Guardian and Phil Brown, a freelance photographer. Thanks to Daily Express cartoonist Graham Allen, who illustrated the cover of String Fellows so perfectly. Also to Dave Allen (Hampshire CCC historian), Cecil Hill (Tibshelf village historian), Martin and Gina Todd, Terence Compton at Troubador, and the many people along the way who supported us.

Also thanks to all those considerate drivers who gave us a very wide berth. That was a wise move.

My most loving thanks, though, go to my wife Brenda, for putting up with my ridiculous trips away from home without a word of complaint.

INTRODUCTION

This is the story of a curious journey made by a curious collection of companions. There was a serious point to our cycling odyssey, of course. That was the fund-raising for charity. But the main objective was to have fun. I hope that comes across in these pages. This book is very much my slant on our adventures and misadventures, but there are contributions from the other five members of the *peloton*. Two of our more famous guest riders also give their own accounts of their time in the saddle with us. You do not have to like cycling or cricket to enjoy this book – but by the end of it, I hope you do. CB.

FOREWORD

Angus Fraser MBE

Belief is an attribute few professional sportsmen lack. Many of us, whether we are current or former, believe we are bullet-proof. In our misguided minds there are no obstacles we cannot overcome. Foolishly we believe that, with a little practice and training, we can turn our hand to any task we want, and what's more, produce a respectable, if not high-class performance.

This was my attitude when I accepted the invitation to join Colin Bateman and David Lloyd, two former journalist colleagues, for a couple of days as they cycled around England and Wales. The pair, along with a couple of sons and two friends, including Ian Todd, the former cricket correspondent of The Sun, had decided to raise money for chosen charities by travelling more than 1,000 miles while visiting each of the main grounds of the 18 First Class cricket counties.

Mistakenly - and ever so slightly arrogantly - I felt that if those two bitter and twisted old hacks, gnarled correspondents who had spent most of the previous 20 years sitting on their backsides at the back of a press box while highly-tuned athletes such as myself pushed their body to the limit, could perform such a feat, then so could I.

Okay, I had put on a few pounds since retiring from cricket in 2002, but regular visits to the gym and runs around the streets of Kingston, Adelaide, Lahore, Colombo, Goa, Dunedin and Cape Town when following England had kept me in reasonable nick – well, good enough to keep up with those two old tossers as they rambled across Southern England.

My preparation had gone pretty well, mixing up regular hour-long spin classes with rowing and lengthy cycling sessions for an hour or so while reading the newspaper at my local gym. I was feeling pretty confident; I had even invested in a new set of fairly slick tyres for my cross-country, spring-cushioned bike. My commitment levels were reasonably high too - the night before I set off to join the group in Romsey for the fourth day of their trip, I even abstained from alcohol at the annual Cricket Writers' Dinner in central London, which is quite a feat. Well, all right, I had two glasses of wine with my meal, but not enough to affect my performance the following day or to prevent me from driving home for a good night's sleep.

With my bike strapped reasonably securely to the back of my Volvo convertible - not the ideal car to attach a bike to - I set off around the M25, down the M3 and then on to the M27 looking forward to the challenges that lay ahead. Not once did I envisage the pain and physical state I would be in when I made the return journey some 30 or so hours later.

On my journey from Pinner, I had informed Col and the gang where I was and how long I would be, and when I arrived at Pauncefoot House Bed and Breakfast on the side of the A3090, my colleagues were slowly getting ready for another day in the saddle. A couple weren't moving too well, complaining about a tough previous day. "Wimps", I thought. "Just get on with it."

A couple of the group seemed very interested in my bike as I removed it from my car, giving each other a little knowing nod as I placed a nice silicon cushion on my saddle and leaned my vehicle against a fence. In comparison to my bike, theirs looked old and rickety, as though they should have had a basket on the front and had been used in Mary Poppins. There were no flash handlebars, colourful stripes on the frame or springy suspensions on their cycles. "Bloody fools", I thought.

So off we went, down a little hill to begin with and then left along the A27, a pleasant meandering country lane. I was keen to chat about this and that, what had been happening in the cricket world and how they were going, but for a change Colin and David did not seem too interested in idle gossip. They preferred to concentrate on their cycling. Interesting. Full of energy and enthusiasm, I even went out in front for a while, admiring the scenery and believing there could be few better ways of spending a day.

As the miles racked up, I soon became aware that spin classes and gym bikes are all well and good, but they are not quite like the real thing. There are no bumps or pot-holes in a gym, and no wind. There are very few gradual hills with bends in them that seem to go on forever either. I also realised that my bike, with all its nice little gadgets, was not really suitable for this type of cycling.

While the other members of the group seemed to be effortlessly drifting along, I was chugging. Their gear changes made a nice, smooth slick sound while mine crunched. I quickly realised that the bloody suspension on my bike was absorbing and wasting an ever-growing proportion of the energy I was attempting to put into the wheels through my legs. Christ, I wish I had one of their bikes – they were making it look so damned easy.

After a couple of hours we stopped in a village for a breather. I rushed into a newsagents to replenish a tiring body. I bought a couple of energy drinks and then, after reading all the good they were supposed to do me, I purchased a couple of Boost chocolate bars too. It then hit me: 'Jelly Beans and Wine Gums'. That's what England's cricketers now scoff to revitalise themselves. So I returned to the shop and bought a couple of packets of them too. As we set off my rucksack was about half-a-stone heavier than when I stopped.

For the next hour or so, the cycling was still fun, and I was able to look up and enjoy the countryside. But my legs were beginning to feel a little fatigued. Rather than setting the pace, I was now at the back of the *peloton*, somewhat hanging on to the tail of my colleagues.

Then, as we serenely made our way through Wilton, a pleasant town on the A30, disaster struck. As I was moving along, I heard a loud crack below me and something began to move. "Shit! What's that?" I muttered, as the saddle fell from between my legs and on to the road, leaving my backside rather precariously placed above the metal tube that it had been attached to. I hit the brakes and dismounted. Despite the silicon cushion, that area of my anatomy was already sore, and the thought of what could have happened sent shivers through my body.

Since I was the last bike and was some distance behind the next rider, shouting for someone to stop would have been futile. As I looked around the road for bits of my saddle, I thought: "Bollocks, I'm in trouble here." It quickly became apparent that the bolt that held the saddle to the bike had completely sheared off. Forlornly I looked around for help, but there was none available. I asked someone whether there was a bike shop in the town, to which the answer was "No". I started to believe that that was me done, which, in all honesty, wouldn't have been the end of the world. The taxi back to Romsey might cost me a few quid, but it would be money well spent.

Noticing the drifter had fallen further back, Colin returned to check on my welfare, and on seeing my predicament we put our minds together to see what we could come up with. We then noticed that opposite where we were standing there was a small industrial unit where local farmers could buy machinery – and get it repaired. So off I hobbled rather pathetically in search of a new bolt, and, depending on how one viewed the day, I was either lucky or unlucky.

I explained my request to a slightly bemused gentleman and within a couple of minutes I had what I wanted. Just in case there was a repeat, I bought a couple more bolts and gave him a fiver for his effort. With saddle safely back in place, off we went on our merry way.

The next stop was for lunch, which symbolised that we were about half way. My fellow bikers sat relaxed, laughing, joking and enjoying a pint on the side of the A30 as I deliberated what to order from the menu. With my professional sportsman's head on, I ordered pasta. I joined them for a pint but, wary of what a second might do to me, I left it at that. Even though I had little to say over lunch, other than I was knackered and ask how much further did we have to travel, I would quite happily have stayed in the pub for the rest of the afternoon. But with nobody quite sure how far we still had to cycle to our destination, I had to drag my tired, sweaty and now stiff body back on to the bike.

Semi- revitalised by the food and beer I decided to attack the challenge, and set off strongly, taking on the role of leader again. It did not last long as the rolling hills of Wiltshire took their toll. With my body getting ever wearier, I began to feel a little concerned for my safety as one juggernaut after another swept past me. The challenge had now become a battle of mind over matter, like bowling a fifth or sixth spell on the second afternoon of a Test at a hot and debilitating venue when the opposition are 420-3.

Yeovil was reached and, as is always the case, it is that final bit further, that little bit extra you hadn't expected, which really tests you. Montacute, our destination was only five or six miles away but it felt like 25. Finally, after almost five-and-a-half-hours in the saddle and more than 65 miles covered, with my legs dead, my backside sore and my body hanging off the side of my bike, we arrived at the Kings Arms Inn in Montacute. Rarely, if ever, has a hotel looked as enticing.

My colleagues were staying at the Montacute Toy Museum just up the road and they came back to my billet for dinner in the evening. After a soothing bath and an hour lying on my bed, life did not seem quite so bad and I joined them downstairs for dinner and a couple of well deserved pints. By then I had even regained enough energy to join in the conversation. The evening was made more enjoyable as Liverpool won in the Champions League.

I thought I would be okay in the morning, and did not feel too bad when we met at 9am. Yes, my body was feeling stiff and a little sore from the previous very tough day, but it had been through this before and come through shining. Bristol was the destination today, via Taunton. Rather sooner than I'd hoped, fatigue set in and, having driven from Taunton to Bristol many times before, the image of the hill on the M5 where the motorway separates south of Bristol, set in. I knew that we would not be cycling on the M5, but the journey was extremely tough and I seriously started to doubt whether I could make it.

There was also a sense of guilt. Colin, David and Co. had been brilliant with me on the previous day, but they had a schedule and I was delaying them. Long before we reached Taunton, a 25-mile journey from Montacute, they had had to wait for me far more often than I expected or wanted.

After another tough morning, the County Ground in Taunton was reached. On a good day the entrance to the ground is far from inspiring, but with rain falling and my body knackered, it was something of an oasis, although it did not feel like it.

Taunton, with its batsman-friendly pitch and short boundaries, is not a place I had enjoyed playing at. Indeed, it was at this County Ground where my England career all but finished. In 1999, while Middlesex were playing Somerset at Taunton, I was asked to drive to London on the morning of the Lord's Test against New Zealand as a member of the squad had picked up an injury. I got as far as the Fullers Brewery at the Hogarth roundabout in Chiswick when David Graveney, the chairman of selectors at the time, phoned me to say I would not be needed after all. I turned around and rushed back to Taunton, took one wicket for 100 runs, and never featured for England again.

Now the visit to Taunton on my bike was also the end of the road, so to speak. After a few photographs in front of an empty County Ground to prove we had made it, we headed to a bakery for refreshment. I then announced my intentions to end my ride then and there and said my goodbyes to my colleagues. I cycled to Taunton Station and bought a ticket to Romsey via Bristol. Sitting on a comfortable seat as the train pulled out of Taunton, I realised I had made the correct decision. The only problem was that I had a couple of miles to cycle from Romsey station back to Pauncefoot House, where my car was parked.

I attached my bike to the back of my car again (although by now I couldn't care less if I ever saw it again) and slowly and thoughtfully made my way home. On the journey back to London, I began to appreciate fully the size of the task undertaken by the six blokes cycling to the 18 counties. Cycling around Great Britain may sound a nice idea, and it is, but it is effing hard work, and my full respect goes out to each of them for completing the challenge.

A long, hot, hard, fruitless day in the field is bloody tough, but rarely have I been physically pushed as hard as I had been while cycling between Romsey and Taunton. Even so, I would love to do it again, only this time I would like to be better prepared and, if possible, do the whole lot.

Joining in for a day or two was, in hindsight, enjoyable but it was not the real thing.

Angus Fraser played 46 Tests and 42 ODIs for England.

CHAPTER ONE

The Challenge And The Peloton....

...or how long is a piece of string?

"Bugger the sheep. Bugger the bike."

The bike in question is dumped unceremoniously on the stony edge of the lay-by and slithers down a short grassy slope towards a tiny stream. "Bugger the scenery too," storms Jack as he squats on a boulder. His cycle helmet is thrown to the ground and follows the bike rolling towards the stream. His left and then his right cycling gloves are hurled in hot pursuit.

The said-sheep look up from their chewing, glance at the said-scenery, glance at the said-bike and look at Jack in a rather alarmed fashion. His suggestion has quite put them off their supper.

It is that time of day, which is why Jack is getting rather irascible. We are in the middle of Blea Moor, one of the most remote parts of England, the evening gloom and chill is closing in and we really should be somewhere else by now. The six of us have stopped at the Ribblehead Viaduct road junction, a frequently photographed spot in the Yorkshire Dales National Park. The sun is setting between the arches of the magnificent viaduct that carries the railway line from Settle to Carlisle. The moorland is bathed in soft evening light. There cannot be many more serene views in the British Isles, but just at this precise moment, all that is lost on Jack.

The problem for Jack is that the road junction has a signpost that, for him, quite obliterates the idyllic setting.

It reads: 'Hawes 11'.

Eleven more hard, painful, miles into a north-easterly wind that makes cycling feel as though your tyres are stuck in melting tar. Hawes Youth Hostel is our destination and we have already done 61 miles today and spent six hours in the saddle. It is getting dark. We are cold and hungry, only two of us have lights and one of us has lost the will to live.

As they say: it seemed like a good idea at the time.

Quite where that idea came from I am not sure but I always suspected I would be regretting it on a wind-swept hill somewhere in central England. This was the moment on Blea Moor when it seemed as though our quest could crumble. There would be other moments too: tempers lost on the less than scenic Stoke-on-Trent ring road, tooth extractions, lost saddles, road and nasal congestion all threatened this cycling Odyssey.

Our motley group had done a few long bike rides before, and, as one of the principal organisers, my thoughts often drifted to new trips in idle moments. The End-to-End – John O'Groats to Land's End (or the other way around if you are sensible) – had been the first obvious challenge for four middle-aged men taking up cycling again in 2001. Then we did something similar in France, riding from Dunkirk in the north to Collioure on the Spanish border in the south in 2005, with my eldest son Tom making our

2

peloton five strong. The following year we enjoyed a more gentle circular tour of Ireland, its pubs and rainy hills.

Two years on and the wanderlust had started to itch again. The bike usually stayed in the shed providing the ideal climbing frame for spiders for months on end, but every now and again the cobwebs had to be dusted off and the tyres pumped for another challenge. It was probably something to do with trying to deny the slow creep of middle-aged years.

Usually thoughts about a new venture started to hatch in the most unlikely of places, and so it was again in the winter of 2007-08 somewhere near the Temple of the Lost Tooth in the Sri Lanka hills, or was it while looking at the wondrous scenery viewed from the window of the TranzAlpine Railway from Christchurch to Greymouth in New Zealand's South Island? Wherever it happened, the incubation of a new venture started while I was in some foreign clime working. My job as a sports journalist takes me abroad every winter, as it does one of my cycling companions, David. And, far away from the harsh realities of dual carriageways, cycle lanes strewn with broken glass and raging motorists, the latest plan had taken on romantic, almost poetic, proportions.

I had a desire to see good old central England (and a bit of Wales). On the End-to-End we had skirted the Lake District, the Welsh Border and travelled down the Wessex peninsula. This though was not real England, not the place where people stuck the flag of St George on their car when England played a football match, the place where they believed their local pies were the best in the land, the place outside the M25 that was unified by its loathing of London.

This trip was to take us to parts of England where every town and village appeared to have its own little place in history or interesting tale to tell. The England of ring roads, twinned towns and cricket grounds. Yes, cricket grounds. Now we are getting to the point. Eighteen of them, in fact.

There are 18 First Class cricket counties in England and Wales. Many other counties play the game, of course, but only 18 have fully professional teams that make up Divisions One and Two of the County Championship. My job for more than 20 years has been to write about this blessed sport for the Daily Express, travelling around the 18 counties watching the game, complaining about the weather and the catering, but forming a bond with these often decrepit cricket grounds much like a dog clings on to an old, tatty blanket. David does it too, and Ian used to do it, but more of them later. First to the venture.

The idea was to undertake a unique cycling challenge by riding to the 18 county headquarters that are as diverse in their location and charm as a disused Lancashire cotton mill is to Worcester Cathedral. The start and finish points would be the two grounds the closest together. We would push off from The Oval, the home of Surrey, just south of the Thames in Kennington near London's Waterloo Station and where the first Test match in England was played in 1880. We would, all being well and given a fair wind, finish 16 days later at the world's most famous ground, Lord's – HQ as cricket anoraks call it – in St John's Wood, North London, alongside Regents Park, a ground that is owned by the Marylebone Cricket Club (MCC) and its members, and where Middlesex are the tenants.

The most direct route between the other 16 stops on our

circuit was to take us in a clockwise direction around the country, heading first east to Canterbury (Kent), then back west along the south coast (Sussex and Hampshire) before swinging north-west for Somerset, Gloucestershire and Glamorgan. From there it was north to Worcestershire, Warwickshire and Lancashire followed by a long trek over the Pennines to Durham. Mercifully it was downhill all the way after that through Yorkshire, Derbyshire, Nottinghamshire, Leicestershire, Northamptonshire and Essex, before the last triumphant leg back into the capital and Lord's.

With five Ordnance Survey Travel Maps (scale one inch to four miles or 1cm to 2.5km if you prefer) spread out across the kitchen table and floor, the route was planned using highlighter pen and a piece of string. Now, the piece of string (butcher's best) is my system for calculating distances on maps (patent pending). Initially measured against the map's scale, a length of string the equivalent to 20 miles is cut off with laser precision. This can then be wound around the highways and byways of the route on the map to get an accurate mileage for each leg. At least, that is the theory. String can be a little stretchy and the ends can fray but, heck, what's a few miles here and there between chums?

According to my trusty piece of string, the route around the 18 county destinations amounted to 1011 miles, our longest trip yet. John O'Groats to Land's End had been 899 miles, the French trip a little less than that. In the past we had aimed at 50-60 miles a day. Some of the days on this trip were to be 75-plus. OK, so that's nothing to a Tour de France rider, but to four men the wrong side of 50 and two young bucks not used to cycling, it represented a reasonable challenge. And those Tour riders do not have all their worldly possessions in two panniers weighing a collective 20lbs (9kgs) on the backs of their bikes, either. There were to be no support vehicles for us, no masseurs awaiting us at the end of each day, no mechanic to check the bike over while we relaxed in a five-star hotel. Our digs were to be good, honest bed and breakfasts with a sink in which to wash our cycle gear, in the hope that it would dry on the radiator overnight. David would be doing a quick squeeze of the tyres each morning to check for punctures, he being our mechanically-minded technical and engineering support. As for massages, well that was up to the individual. Every man for himself.

The route planned, it then seemed sensible to perpetuate the cricket theme. Normally we do these rides for fun although there has been an element of fund-raising to a couple of them. This time, we opted to make it a genuine charity ride with two cricket-related causes adopted. One was the Laurie Engel Fund, set up by his parents Matthew and Hilary after the death in 2005 of their 13-year-old son, who was struck down by a rare and aggressive cancer. Matthew, a friend and colleague, has been the cricket correspondent of the Guardian and Editor of Wisden Almanack, the game's famous yellow-covered bible. The fund in Laurie's memory is aimed at building a special unit for teenage cancer sufferers and their families at Birmingham Children's Hospital.

The other charity was Heads Up, a research programme into cancers of the neck and head at the Oxford Ratcliffe Hospital. Hugh Morris, the former England and Glamorgan opening batsman and now Managing Director of the England team, is a patron, having fought throat cancer himself. We knew him well and thought both causes would mean a great deal to friends and colleagues within the cricket world. The appeals were launched and websites set up for both. Now there was no going back.

Ideally we would have liked to have started and finished each day in a cricket town, but that was not to be possible if we were to spread out the distance travelled each day. As it was we had a short day of 45 miles planned in the middle of the trek – Monmouth to Worcester – and several long hauls of 75 miles a day in the north of England, but the trick from past experience was to finish in a town of reasonable size so we could always walk to a pint and a bite at the end of the day and not have to hop on a bus or get a taxi (or, God-forbid, get back on the bike).

The other cunning plan has always been to book each night's stop before the trip began thereby ensuring we had a goal each day. It would be so easy if nothing was booked, to reach a spot for what was intended to be an afternoon cuppa only for the collective will to collapse and for us to decide to call it a day there and then, find somewhere local to stay and intend to make up the lost miles planned on the original itinerary the next day. Do that and we would never make it north of the Thames, particularly if it was raining and the wind was in our faces. Having accommodation booked and a deposit paid was the greatest incentive to keep those pedals turning. And, as the cyclist's mantra goes on the longest of hills: 'you can always turn the pedals just one more time.'

With the route mapped, accommodation had to be found

working on a budget of £25 per person per night. As I was paying for three – myself and my two sons – this was pretty essential. David and I sent out emails to all the counties telling them of our plans hoping to get some publicity and support, and our efforts were rewarded. Kent, Lancashire, Yorkshire and Durham all found us free accommodation in hotels (sheer luxury). Worcestershire helped us get a good deal at their favoured local hostelry. Only Gloucestershire studiously ignored all emails and failed to respond to messages left on answering machines, but when this was mentioned in passing to some of the powers that be at the organisation that runs the game, the England and Wales Cricket Board, they fixed us up with free accommodation at one of Bristol's swishest boutique hotels. For the rest of the way around our route, we found B&Bs ranging from the charming to the charmless, plus a sprinkling of small hotels, several of which cut their normal rack-rate when we told them what we were doing, and one Youth Hostel. All we required of our accommodation were six clean beds, a good shower and a hearty breakfast. Oh yes, and somewhere safe for our bikes overnight. If not, they would be in the bedroom alongside us.

THE PELOTON

Ian Todd. Toddy is the veteran of the pack at 71, although probably the least experienced rider. A man with a vast array of interests and knowledge, he will enliven any evening debate with strident views, whether they are about China's treatment of the monks of Tibet or the attractions of the lass pulling his pint. Those who engage him should not be mis-led by his public school accent or military bearing. He worked for years at the Sun, getting his hands dirty, as we say in the trade, with stories others would not touch. He could be the most aggressive of interviewers at press conferences when players or administrators prevaricated and blustered. He had a particular penchant for getting under the skin of Australia's gritty former captain Allan Border, which took some doing. He also acted as the National Union of Journalists' father of chapel at the Sun for several years in the days when trade unions punched their weight, and he fought many causes against the Rupert Murdoch management. Perhaps he just loved riling Aussies.

He has been retired from journalism for 15 years, but not from life, splitting his time between his garden and bird-watching in Surrey, and yomping up mountains around the world with like-minded adventure tourists. Sadly, Mary, his wife of many years, had died of cancer, but Toddy's charm and striking looks – age had weathered him well – ensured he was never short of female companionship.

If the passing of the years had not diminished his zest for life, it had, however, certainly made him prone to forgetfulness, and the cycling adventures for him started every morning with him scouring bedrooms trying to find his spare pair of glasses, pills and potions, telephone charger, wallet and bus pass – although, with luck, he would not be needing that.

Ian did no training for our rides. None. David, who lives comparatively close to him, tried to coax him out for the odd week-end jaunt before we set off but Toddy's attitude was that years of good fitness – he had been a marathon runner in his pomp and still jogged regularly – would see him through. We had returned from our France expedition in 2005 with our bikes dismantled and packed into bike-bags for the flight home. Toddy's Thorn tourer had remained in the bag since 2005, untouched as he had missed the Ireland tour. Most of us come to regard our bikes as friends, even partners. In Toddy's case his green machine could have sued for divorce on grounds of neglect.

As a rider, Ian was steady and strong. Most mornings would find him easing his ageing joints into action, but come the post-lunch session and he would be beating out a strong rhythm in the middle of the bunch, and by the end of our previous trips he had been as spritely as any of us young 'uns. There was, though, a slight unspoken concern among us this time. It had been three years since Toddy's last ride and he had declared it would be his last. He was also nervous about tackling urban cycling, where you need your wits about you not only because of inconsiderate motorists, but also to take in the road signs and steer clear of the astonishing amount of debris that lingers in the gutters of our towns. David and I both wondered if this might not be a trip too far for Toddy, but he was a determined old bugger and we were delighted to have him along.

Alan Dracey. My nephew – although our birthdays are only a couple of years apart and he would never dream of calling me 'uncle'. A university graduate, and former bus conductor in London, Alan is currently a civil servant in Brighton and lives with his wife Diane in Lewes, Sussex. He has more pedal miles under his belt than any of us, having never owned a car. The closest Alan has ever come to buying a car was the make of his trusty two-wheeled steed, a Peugeot, bought around the time that green shield stamps were still being collected and Lance Armstrong was clambering on to his first mountain bike. Over the years Alan had replaced virtually every part of the Peugeot save the frame and the saddle. Its gearing was wholly inadequate for long laden rides – he had 10 gears while the rest of us had 27 – but the man sitting on it had an indomitable spirit for getting up hills, more slowly than most people would walk them, but getting to the top nonetheless.

Alan had a good 'engine.' He also had a head-down let's-get-on-with-it style that could needle fellow riders who wanted a more gentle approach, certainly at the start of the day. As we eased aching limbs back into action each morning on our previous rides, Alan would be off down the road unaware that the group was trailing behind, chatting about the merits of that morning's fry-up and enjoying riding together. Having a fairly poor sense of direction, he could also get lost easily, failing to spot a direction sign here, a no-entry sign there.

While he had cycled for years, both to get to work and on holidays with Diane, the fact that he had never driven made him unaware of certain aspects of road use...such as bikes not being welcome on motorways and many major roads. He was also disdainful towards bike lanes, particularly those that shared a pavement with pedestrians and mothers with pushchairs. Alan would happily plough on along a teeming dual-carriageway on his bike ignoring the abuse of motorists while the rest of us cycled in safety in the adjacent bike-lane.

On side roads Alan would infuriate car owners by riding two abreast with one of us, blocking the road to anything that wanted to pass, on the assumption that he had as much right there as the person driving the four-by-four behind him, who was growing more puce by the second.

"How much effing room do you want?" angry motorists would shout through a wound down window at Alan when they eventually managed to overtake.

"How much effing room do you need?" Alan would shout back from behind the white beard that added to the impression that here was a member of the Green Party who would quite happily ban the internal combustion engine.

Alan's cycle attire was also somewhat non-conformist and made him stand out from the pack. The rest of us would don modest amounts of lycra, wear functional shorts and cycle tops that:

(a) dried quickly if it had rained
(b) were easy to wash at the end of each day
(c) were sensible and comfortable

Alan wore civvies on his bike and would never expose any bare flesh. He wore his work shoes, tracksuit bottoms and the shirt that he had put on clean the night before. Each day required a new shirt, the stained sweaty ones gathering mould in the bottom of Alan's panniers until we could find a launderette or sympathetic landlady. Alan also wore thick glasses, which made rain a particular hazard for him as they steamed up at the hint of a shower. If it did rain, Alan would have to stop to put waterproof leggings over his trousers and shoes. Beneath all this gear he would also wear elastic knee supports to help his joints, which were trying to remind him that his 50th birthday was a thing of the past.

David Lloyd. He had been a colleague on the newspaper circuit for longer than we both cared to remember. We had done more than 20 years of cricket reporting together, me for the Express, him for a news agency and then for London's one serious evening paper, the Evening Standard, before recently deciding to step off the treadmill and go freelance. He was our strongest, fittest rider. So keen was he that he had a stable of bikes at his home in Hampshire and used cleats, the professional cyclists' alternative to conventional pedals. Instead of a regulation pedal, David's bikes had a small metal pad which clipped into a recess on the bottom of his cycle shoes thus producing maximum performance while cycling whether the foot was coming up or pushing down. Cleats were slightly hazardous in that you had to wiggle your foot to un-clip the shoe whenever you had to stop and put a foot on the ground. Failure to do so would see the rider topple helplessly and embarrassingly to one side when he stopped, feet still firmly attached to bike. For that reason, the other four of us – not Alan, of course, who had nothing so fancy – had toe clips on our pedals into which our feet nestled.

David is known as Toff to his work colleagues, not because he is posh, but because he is one in the old-fashioned sense of being a really good bloke. An Oldham fan, and father of two grown-up daughters, he, like me, had returned to cycling in his 40s having been entranced by the Tour de France, which dominates our interest for three weeks in the middle of every summer when we really should be engrossed in the cricket.

David bought cycle magazines, had a slim enough frame to wear tight-fitting cycle team shirts, and among other machines, he owned a racing, pale green Bianchi, the Ferrari of the cycling world, which he took out on fine summer evenings. He is also hugely competitive, like many men of smaller stature.

The protocol among cyclists is a wave or nod to each other on the road, but some club cyclists get a bit sniffy if they spot a biker on anything less than a racing machine. If one of these types overtakes David without a 'good evening for a spin' acknowledgement, Toff will slip down a ring (gears to a car driver), get out of the saddle to produce more power and tail them in their slip-stream for the next few miles to make his point. Only then will his temper be sated.

As well as being the leader of the *peloton*, David is our lead mechanic with Alan his helper. Both are nifty at changing punctured tyres, and while they may not be quite up to the speed of the Marlboro McLaren pit crew, they can still get a new inner tube on and pumped within 15 minutes beside a busy dual carriageway. David carries a pressure gauge, an industrial sized can of WD40, bits of wire, pliers and Allen keys to suit any emergency. He has been on all of the rides so far, but, to his great frustration, he never completed the first, the End-to-End, having to opt out for a week because of the death of his father-in-law. Cycling from Land's End to John O'Groats remains one of David's ambitions. In the summer before the 18 Counties ride, he had a bespoke touring bike made at the workshops of

Hewitts in Leyland, Lancashire, but just before we set off he opted for his trusty Dawes for this trip.

Tom Bateman. He is my eldest son. Aged 21 and reading history at university, the trip is timed to fit in with the end of his summer vacation from Queen Mary's, London. He did the France ride with no trouble, but wimped out of the Ireland tour half way around because of an aching knee, which he and his sympathetic mother claimed to be the legacy of an old rugby injury. This gives his old Dad no end of ammunition when Tom starts taking the mickey over my slow pace, expanding girth or greying hair. At least the old man keeps going. Bright and interested in the world about him, Tom enjoys the company of older generations and warms to our dinner-time political debates sparked by Toddy. He also loves sport. Given the chance, he would spend 24 hours a day curled up in front of Sky Sports. Like me, he has developed a love of the Tour de France stemming back to 1994 when it went past his primary school in Sissinghurst in Kent. The children had made French flags and lengths of blue, red and white bunting to decorate the school that day, and had been given the morning off lessons to line the road and cheer as the blur of brightly coloured lycra swept past. The children shouted wildly for the UK's Chris Boardman – as if they could spot him in the mass of movement. He was riding for Gan. They were gone.

Tom, like any young man growing up in the English countryside should be, is fit and strong without really trying. On the road he will play Tour de France games with David, bursting out of the pack and attacking on the hills accompanied by his own TV commentary: "And Bateman has broken the hearts of the other riders again, they are going backwards while he makes this *hors categorie* climb look easy, dancing on the pedals like the great Italian Pantani. This is a sublime tactical break and the polkadot jersey will be on his back at the end of today's stage for sure..."

Of course, David does not let him get away with it and matches him to the top of the lung-bursting climb while the rest of us crawl up in the lowest of gears, heads down, praying. Tom also loves his cricket and he and his Dawes will make it around the 18 counties in his Cofidis team shirt providing that knee of his holds up.

Jack Bateman. The second of my three sons, he is two years younger and about to embark on his first ride. He is my greatest concern – after myself. As a teenager with his mates, he had been a keen off-road cyclist in Bedgebury Forest near our home in Kent. He has the perfect wiry frame for cycling, but does he have the resolve? In recent years he has discovered the delights of lager, the occasional fag (although he promises to give up for the ride) and girls.

On school mornings it would take a crowbar and his persistent mother to get him out of bed, so how are we, five other blokes with our own concerns, going to manage to get him moving each morning? He says he wants to do it, though, and has found an old yellow cycle jersey that is too small for me and Tom in the bottom of a drawer. He announces he will wear it from start to finish of the ride. I buy him a Dawes tourer and some panniers and warn that having spent 600 quid on him, he had better see it through.

Jack has become a typical teenager, which, as he is 19, is

16

fair enough, I guess. The phone and the front door are answered with a Neanderthal grunt. His idea of exercise is opening a tin of baked beans rather than let his mother do it. He is in his gap year although what the gap is between has yet to be satisfactorily explained. Having gained some modest A level results, Jack has declared that he has had enough of learning and will be joining the real world of working men after the bike ride. In fact, he has landed a job as a trainee forest worker in the same woods where he used to cycle, and seems to enjoy the outdoor life of Lumber Jack even though it means getting up at 7am. Perhaps that is a good sign for the ride.

With his new bike and determination, Jack set off for a trial ride to get him in the mood a couple of weeks before the start of the '18 Counties'. He decided to drop in on a cricket match at the neighbouring village where brother Tom was playing and which was all of three miles away. Having negotiated the outward leg of his journey and watched the cricket for an hour, with a pint of lager inside him he phoned up his mother to ask if she would mind picking him and his bike up in her car for the trip home. She, of course, obliged. It was not encouraging, but Jack insisted he would cope with the demands of the 16-day trip.

Although Jack did Geography A level at school, he does not have a clue about the topography of the country in which he lives. Give Jack a blank outline of the UK and he could no more put crosses roughly where Glasgow, Leicester, Ipswich and Bristol are located than name the seas around the coast. If he gets lost, heaven help him, even though he will have a detailed route-planner (that's my job) in his panniers. Jack's answer to losing his way will be to find the nearest boozer, order a pint and then ring his mother on his mobile, I suspect. How he will find the company of four middle-aged men is another thing. Perhaps he will surprise me and prove me wrong. I sincerely hope so because we cannot afford to carry a passenger on our trip.

Colin Bateman. I am 54 and can't quite explain the pleasure that cycling gives. Getting togged up and organised to pop out on the bike for a 20-mile ride around our local Kent villages is a chore, and I rarely ride between the big ventures. But with nothing else to think about, with no work or family concerns, I love devoting myself to the long challenges, enjoying the countryside and the sense of achievement at the end of each day. And, sorry to sound like a 21st century parenting guide, it is also a wonderful way of bonding with your teenage children. The every-day cares of life are forgotten when you are coasting downhill or, even better, pedalling wheel-to-wheel in a tight group at close to 20mph along the flat. Even the climbs, once you are in a steady rhythm, the right gear and are confident of reaching the top, become absorbingly good fun.

Newspaper journalism has been my working life and that has taken me all over the country in my car: mile upon mile flogged up and down the motorways or yard upon yard crawled through the traffic jams. There are no jams or motorways on a bike, which is another plus for two wheels. I was also fascinated to discover what I would make of the towns that I had visited so often through work when I saw them from the saddle.

Would I cope though? Overweight and not an

assiduous trainer, I had my concerns. I regularly jog when away every winter in sunny climes reporting on England cricket tours, but cycling demands more of different muscles and puts a real strain on the back. Everyone jokes about saddle sores. "How's your arse?" is the frequently asked question, but most cyclists will tell you it is the back, bent forward over the handle bars, that takes the strain on a long day.

My bike, like Toddy's, is a Thorn, made in Bridgwater, Somerset, by a small company. It is a lovely lightweight machine that is built a bit too much for speed and not comfort for these long tours. It is not as giving as the Dawes for a haul with panniers, and its gearing is not ideal, but I have got used to it and we treat each other kindly on these trips. If my wife Brenda knew of my relationship with my Thorn and its slim gel saddle, she would not be impressed.

My job is *Directeur Sportif,* tour organiser if you like, and I get almost as much pleasure out of this as I do from the ride itself. Scouring the internet for accommodation, finding good places to stop and eat, devising routes that avoid big climbs and trunk roads is strangely satisfying. Then there is the relief when a landlady says she has vacancies and would love to put us up, adding that she will have a hot Radox bath waiting for us on arrival – I kid you not. All of these details get typed onto a masterplan, which is lovingly up-dated as the 'off' approaches and then circulated to the other five riders, who are expected to be duly impressed.

THE CARAVAN

As followers of the Tour de France will know, what precedes the race each day is the Caravan. It is a curious name for something that comes first and does not follow, but there it is. That's the French for you. The Publicity Caravan is the collection of sponsors' vehicles advertising the teams in the race and giving away trinkets and rubbish. We have no such caravan, but we do have plenty of publicity in the cricket world, so much so that our fund-raising nudges £8,000, and several colleagues insist they will be joining us as guest riders for a leg or two.

I am interviewed about the ride on the BBC's Test Match Special by Jonathan Agnew; websites, including that of the ECB and Cricinfo (the world's most read cricket website), carry features about us; the match-day programme for the five one-day internationals against South Africa has a double page spread on 'Six Blokes and Eighteen Counties' with photographs and route planner. There is a momentum building up that I only hope translates into wheels turning on tarmac. The two charities send us tee-shirts to wear and provide more build-up on their websites and in newsletters. This is for real now.

* * *

CHAPTER TWO

The Pilgrims' Way

....London to Canterbury.

Guest Rider: Jasper.

The first day is always a nervy affair.

There are concerns about the bike: is everything still functioning? Will the laden panniers be stable or will they catch anywhere? There are concerns about the body: is everything still functioning? Will the laden cycle shirt be stable or catch anywhere? We are now seven with our guest rider, our biggest *peloton* yet. How will we stay together through the mean streets of south London?

The 'off' in itself is quite a logistical challenge. The meeting point is the Alec Stewart Gates at, to give the ground its full sponsored name, the Brit Oval. Surrey County Cricket Club and Brit have been most supportive of the ride. The county is laying on a departure breakfast for riders and their guests on the concourse underneath the new OCS Stand. Brit, an insurance company, are the only one of English cricket's long list of sponsors to give our fund-raising efforts their support, which was good of them and disappointing of the rest.

Tom, Jack and I travel up from Staplehurst in Kent on the 7.42am train to Waterloo East with our bikes, my wife Brenda and youngest son Rupert (16), who is told by his brothers that he will have to get himself into shape for the next ride. My nephew Alan and his wife Diane arrive by train from Sussex into Victoria, Alan cycling across London to the ground, Diane using public transport. David and his wife Margaret come from Hampshire by car with his and Toddy's bike on board, while Toddy just ensures he gets himself there by train. Various other friends and relatives also turn up to wave us a tearful farewell much like those dockside scenes in old movies in which relatives wave goodbye to loved ones heading off for a fresh start in the New World, uncertain that they will ever see them again. It is much like that for us.

Also there is Jasper Kain, a much-treasured friend of Tom's since they met at playschool, and someone who has become almost part of the Bateman Family over the years. Jasper, also at university in London, has just finished his summer vacation by cycling back from Italy. Not Little Italy in North London, but the bigger one on the bottom of Europe. He has covered 1500 miles including the Col de la Madeleine, a *hors categorie* climb (a climb so steep it cannot be categorised) in the Tour de France. He is lean and keen to say the least in his skimpy lycra, and the more mature among us exchange looks that suggest we are feeling a degree of trepidation.

The egg and bacon rolls provided by Surrey are resting heavily in our stomachs as we pose for a group picture beside the Oval outfield with the splendid Victorian pavilion and landmark gasometer as a backdrop. We kiss everyone goodbye more than once to delay the inevitable and then push off into the Saturday morning traffic and the bus lane around the Oval. Crossing the traffic lights by the Oval tube station, which is always besieged by ticket touts on big match days, we head down Camberwell New Road with Kennington Park on our left. We are heading eastwards for Streatham, Blackheath, Shooters Hill, infinity and beyond.

Our route through New Cross takes us past Pepys Road, where Alan and Diane lived after their University years, and the London Transport depot where Alan worked as a bus conductor. The litter of Friday night is still strewn on south London's pavements and the Saturday morning bustle is building up. We are keen to get the city behind us and hit the open road away from discarded kebabs, broken glass and white vans.

Shooters Hill, which reputedly gets its name from the armed highwaymen who held up stagecoaches and their wealthy occupants as they slowed for the long climb, was our first big ascent. OK, 432ft up to the gothic Victorian water-tower at the summit, may not be the toughest of climbs, but it is enough to get the heart pounding. Any left-over highwaymen could certainly have ambushed us on foot, so slow was our progress.

The tree-lined hill across Greenwich Park has played a major part in the history of transport in England. Part of the Roman road called Watling Street, it has long taken people and goods to Canterbury and the Kent ports. It has been a mail route, and was the place where the inventor Samuel Brown first tested his hydrogen-powered internal combustion engine in 1826, a fore-runner of the car. Now, seven blokes on seven bikes were adding to that rich transport history in their own small way.

Urban cycling does have its good points, one of which is the frequent need to stop. Traffic lights, junctions, pedestrian crossings all give you time to catch your breath – and catch the others.

Of course, the stops can also split the group if some make it across a junction as the lights hit amber and the others have to wait in accordance with the Highway Code (unlike so many other bikers, who give cyclists a bad name, we religiously halt for a red light). Tom and Jasper are chatting at the front as they cycle – where do they get the breath from? – and before long they lose the group, deviate from my meticulously prepared route and are away out of sight somewhere in the south-east London sprawl. It will not be the last time on the first day that the group becomes fragmented. In fact, there is to be a spectacular diverging of the ways before lunch, which is not a good omen given what is to come over the next 15 days.

The route from London to Canterbury looks simple enough on the map: take the A226 to the Medway towns and then the A2 all the way to our first overnight stop and second cricket ground. Straightforward it is not as you weave your way through London's crowded streets. All the places along the way were once small villages with a straight road through the middle dotted with shops, a church, a few pubs and a pond. Now those settlements are part of the Metropolitan conurbation with pedestrianised High Streets and looping one-way systems that, on a busy Saturday morning, become a shoppers' battle ground. Our progress is slow and far from straightforward, but finally we arrive at the bridge over the M25 at Dartford. We had regarded passing over London's infernal motorway ring-road and getting outside the M25 as our first rite of passage. We saw it as marking our progress into the fresh air and countryside of Kent and leaving the urban turmoil behind, but we were to be disappointed. The dense sprawl of suburbia just seems to go on forever through north Kent alongside the Thames Estuary and into what have become known as the Medway Towns. It makes for slow cycling and plenty of stops to check road signs and maps, and ensure no-one is getting lost. As I said, the first day is always a nervy affair.

A steady speed on the flat on these rides is 15mph. In a high gear and given a good wind, that can be maintained without recourse to an oxygen mask. The adrenaline of the first day wants to push us along quicker than that but the inevitable delays of urban cycling put the brakes on our progress.

Along our easterly route is Northfleet, which has a colourful and tragic history. Mentioned in the Domesday Book, Northfleet became the playground for Victorian Londoners looking for a day away from the smoky city. Its chalk pits were turned into wondrous gardens by the Kent Zoological and Botanical Gardens Institution, attracting up to 20,000 visitors a week at the height of their popularity. Tragedy, however, struck one weekend in 1878 when a steamer, the Princess Alice, which was packed with day-trippers from London, collided with a Woolwich coal boat in the Thames with the loss of 640 souls. The gardens have long been closed and Northfleet has lost its charm, particularly to those approaching it on bicycles.

The three youngsters, Tom, Jack and Jasper, are setting a pace that is too hot for us older bikers to maintain. David and Alan are working in tandem, I have dropped about 100 yards off the back with Toddy somewhere in between.

The result is that we have become four distinct groups, the first three all failing to spot the road signs for Chalk, which is specifically mentioned on my itinerary that had been handed out to them before that start. Why do I bother? I, of course, take the correct right turn and find myself in glorious isolation in suburbia. Thank goodness for mobile phones. A ring around establishes roughly where everyone is, and the boys have found Toddy, to everyone's relief. We agree to head for Gillingham to meet there for lunch. Because I alone have followed the direct route, I find myself making up ground and catch the leading group of lads in no time, which I hope will be a lesson to them. As for Alan and David, I have no idea where they are.

Jasper had been a youth footballer with Gillingham, while Tom once had a match of a different kind with a local lass from the town. As a result, both know the area well and Tom recommends a northern approach to the town to avoid Rochester. The five of us follow his route only to find ourselves on a dual carriageway and confronted by the Medway Tunnel and a 'No Cyclists' sign. Doubling back we are lost in a trading estate that has been designed to make every road look identical and without a direction sign in sight. Then, around a corner by a warehouse full of pineapple chunks and other tinned fruits, come our two companions Alan and David, who had also run into hooting horns at the entrance of the Medway Tunnel.

We have lost close to an hour on our schedule for this first day, it is well past lunch time and hunger is gnawing. Rochester is back on the agenda with a pub stop the priority.

What a Carry On, which is quite appropriate as Rochester is the home town of Peter Rogers, the producer of those wonderfully corny old British Carry On comedy films.

As we head towards Rochester, it strikes me that 'Carry on Cycling' would have provided ideal material for the masters of the smutty double entendre:

Sid James: "My, your pair of panniers look fit to burst."

Barbara Windsor: "Oh Sid, they are, and (giggling) the trouble is they bounce around when I go over the cobbles."

Sid: (grinning lasciviously): "I bet they do!"

Kenneth Williams looking pained: "I'm having trouble getting it into the little ring."

Sid: "Have you tried extra lubrication? I find that helps!"

Babs: "I think we should try doing it in tandem, Sid."

Sid: "Wait til we finish the ride, Babs." (More lascivious laughter).

Enter Hattie Jacques wheeling her bike with a puncture.

Sid: "I never thought I'd say this Hattie – but you need a spare tyre."

Hattie: "Kenny had his hands all over them last night."

Kenneth: "Really, Matron!"

The possibilities are endless....

As we roll into Rochester over its ancient bridge, Tom, in his eagerness, disappears along the by-pass while the rest of us dismount and wheel our bikes up the cobbled streets of the Kent town with its bloody history of sieges and sackings. We make for the castle, which was built to protect the river crossing and the Royal Dockyards of Chatham. Realising he is on his own, Tom soon doubles back and finds us, looking slightly hurt that no-one had chased after him. Food, though, was our priority and luckily we discover a pub beside the castle that is still serving lunch. Now, Gary Rhodes, the TV chef (and another local boy) may not have thought much of our jacket potatoes and toasties, but rarely does food taste so good as when you feel you deserve it. And we did on this hot sunny Saturday. I am told that a day of cycling 70 miles burns up 6,000 calories, and that is all the excuse you need for a side order of fries.

The grand plan had been to avoid major roads whenever possible and the A2 – Watling Street – certainly looks pretty major on the maps as it spears straight across northern Kent to Canterbury. I had suggested minor road detours around such delightfully sounding villages such as Tongue and Mockbeggar, but as we are so far behind the clock there is a group decision to stick to the main road, plough on along the most direct route and put up with the heavier traffic.

As we pedal through the afternoon, we settle into what is to become a familiar pattern: Tom, David and Alan leading the way with, for today, Jasper for company. Toddy keeps up a steady pace a little way back while I plod along in the rear with Jack, who is still unsure of how his strength will hold up, on my back wheel, and chatting away about this and that and trying to listen to the latest football scores coming in on Radio Five Live over his headphones. He is desperate to find out about the Arsenal, I am hanging on for news of Bristol City at Cardiff.

Sometimes, particularly on the flat, there is no more than a bike's length between us all. At other times, the gap becomes a chasm and stretches. There are occasions when the distance between the leader and the last man can be as much as a mile. We are all in agreement, though, that you have to ride at your own pace provided the leaders wait at a suitable point for the slow-coaches so we can re-group. It has worked well on our previous rides and it is our unspoken rule again for this trip.

Faversham is the next town on our flat route along the infinitely forgettable A2. It is another of the northern Kent settlements with a rich and, in this case, explosive history. Britain's oldest gunpowder mill was established in Faversham, and the town was once the centre of the UK's explosives industry. In 1916 the town suffered a catastrophe when it was the scene of 'The Great Explosion', the worst in the history of the UK explosives industry, killing 102, many of whom are buried in a mass grave in Faversham's churchyard. Dangers lurk just off the coast here in the Thames Estuary, too. In 1944, a munitions ship from America carrying 1500 tons of explosives for use in the Second World War ran aground and sank. Its cargo remains a danger to local shipping to this day.

A few miles away in the depths of the Thames Estuary lies an altogether murkier tale of maritime mishap. In 1964, an East German freighter carrying 42 new Red London Buses and bound for Cuba, was rammed in the early hours of the morning by an empty Japanese ship. The freighter and its cargo of buses was lost, but no-one was killed, no inquiry was conducted, and no-one was held to account. There remains a theory that the Japanese boat, which was shown to have broken maritime rules for signalling that night, was under the control of the US Central Intelligence Agency (the CIA) and that the ramming of the freighter was a deliberate act of sabotage. This was during the days of America's obsession with Fidel Castro's Cuba being a communist stronghold. The US had placed a trade embargo on Cuba, and the thought of Castro riding around Havana puffing a cigar on the top deck of one of London's 'iconic' red buses appalled the White House, which had urged the British Government not to allow the deal for the double-deckers to go through.

By the time we get to Faversham, the only thing we are thinking of sinking is more nourishment. The sun is getting low and Canterbury is still more than 10 miles away, but sugar levels are dipping again and, almost as if by telepathy, there is a consensus to pull in at a petrol station and raid the confectionery cabinet for Mars Bars and Jelly Babies. Bananas are the other reliable source of nourishment on a long day in the saddle and these emerge bruised and squishy from panniers while we sit on the grass beside the road as the football results come in. Alan's team, Lewes, from the Blue Square Premier, are not playing so he can relax. Arsenal have won 4-0 at Blackburn, so the boys are triumphant. Oldham have beaten the MK Dons 2-0 to keep David content, while Bristol City gain a very creditable goal-less draw at Ninian Park. So everyone is happy as we push off again to Canterbury. The stop has raised morale no end.

I am biased as I live there, but Kent can be a lovely county. However, it can also be an ugly one too. The swathe of countryside and villages across the middle of the county, which includes the Weald of Kent, is charming with its farming communities and oasts built to dry the hops once grown here for the brewing industry. The hop gardens with their long poles have virtually disappeared, but the Weald is still full of the orchards and farms that prompted its sobriquet as the 'Garden of England'. The oasts, with their instantly identifiable tall roundels, are mainly converted into over-priced homes for London commuters these days, and the villages look neat, tidy and prosperous with their greens and communal flower displays.

The top and bottom of Kent, however, is quite a contrast. Its north coast has the sprawl of the Medway towns and farmed prairie fields, open to harsh winds off the Thames Estuary and the North Sea. Its east and south coasts are a mix of run-down seaside resorts and power stations on shingle outcrops. The route across northern Kent to Canterbury may sound lovely, but it is not. It is a grind along a dull main road with little to see.

To make the journey tougher, my estimated distance for the ride from south London to Canterbury using my piece of string is 55 miles – and is clearly well out. It is not a good sign for the coming 15 days. We are approaching 60 miles on this first day and are still counting. I can hear mumbles and grumbles about my piece of string and where it should be inserted.

If the string's accuracy, or lack of it, is repeated for the rest of the ride then I will have some explaining to do, especially to my younger son Jack, who is already beginning to look distinctly fed up as he stares down at my back wheel as the pair of us chug along at the back of the field.

Eventually we hit the outskirts of the cathedral city where the A2 becomes a dual carriageway, and there is nothing for it but to hug the hard-shoulder and withstand the buffeting from the back-draft of the lorries and coaches hurtling by. We crest a hill after a long, draining climb to spot Canterbury ahead and, inspired by thoughts of the journey's end, we start to gather pace when, less than two miles from our destination, Toddy slews off into a lay-by.

PUNCTURE

Would you believe it? On Day One and so close to the end? To make matters worse, the puncture is to his back wheel, which is more tricky to change because of the gears and chain.

We all pull up and David gets to work, reassuring us that "it is always better to get the first puncture out of the way." We are not so sure. Standing there, muscles stiffening and feeling chilly with the traffic whistling by, my team-spirit kicks in: "Tell you what, I can't help much here, I'll go on," I say.

My lame excuse is that we have an appointment with an old mate, Andrew Gidley, who works as a local freelance journalist and wants to interview us on arrival at the ground, where Kent are playing Essex in a vital one-day league match. Gidders has already phoned several times during the day asking for our estimated time of arrival, which we have had to keep putting back. If we do not get to the ground soon, the match will be over and he will be gone. David and Alan, our two mechanics, agree, Toddy munches on another banana sitting on the verge of the lay-by, and I set off with the three lads for the last haul to the St Lawrence Ground, the picturesque headquarters of Kent cricket.

The Canterbury ground has two-tiered white stands at one end and grassy banks at the other, all set off to a backdrop of mature trees. It is often cited as being one of the loveliest in England but looks can de deceptive. The ground also has a reputation among visiting players for being home to the most partisan and unappreciative spectators in the country – and that in a sport in which even the opposition expect polite applause when they score a century.

The Men of Kent – those born east of the River Medway – and Kentish Men – those born to the west of the river – can be a grudging lot. Do not be fooled by the charming ground with its marquees and the quaint tradition of the 200-year-old lime tree that had been part of the playing area until a storm blew it over in the winter of 2005. If a batsman lofted a ball into the tree, no matter how high up in its branches, he was credited with a four, not a six. Now all that is left of the blessed thing are wooden souvenirs made out of its trunk in the county shop behind the stands. Kent County Cricket Club has planted a replacement tree, but sensibly it is well away from the playing area.

When we arrive on our bikes the place is packed, and the rivals from across the Thames, Essex, with their equally vociferous supporters, are closing in on a thrilling victory that would see them promoted ahead of Kent. Our timing is not great for 'Gidders', who is working as the announcer on the ground's public address system and cannot afford to miss a wicket in the frenetic finale to the match. Standing in the car park, he does a hurried interview about our cycling-cricket venture and arranges for photographs to be taken for the local newspapers, before dashing back to his microphone. Tom, Jack and Jasper, meanwhile, are engrossed in the closing overs of the match as they are all Kent supporters.

In my middle-aged confusion of holding my cycle helmet (tip: never wear a cycle helmet for photographs as they make you look daft), cycle gloves and designer dark-glasses, I decide to put my mobile phone down for a moment on a slab of stone that is the tomb of Fuller Pilch, the first groundsman at the St Lawrence Ground who, rather gruesomely, is buried in the car park.

With Essex closing in on victory, we set off to find the hotel, which is less than half a mile away in the New Dover Road. By happy chance, the other three of our group – Toddy, Alan and David – arrive at the same time while a stream of traffic is battling to get out of the exit. A policeman on point duty is doing his best to hold everyone up. Despite the chaos and fading light, and our assurances that we will come back in the morning for our ritual group photograph on the ground to prove we have been there, Alan stubbornly insists on taking some pictures of cars driving out of a gate. We all need a pint by now.

Jasper is staying with his auntie in Canterbury, so as we come out of the ground, he heads off in one direction, the rest of us in another as we seek out our hotel, which has been arranged by the Kent club. It is the Abbots Barton Hotel, one of those mid-market chain hotels that I would be a bit sniffy about if booked into by my company, but which is a veritable haven after a fraught first day on our bikes – and which is being provided free of charge by a friendly manager, who was keen to support our cause when the rooms were booked a few months previous.

Sadly, the generous hotel manager has now moved to another establishment and the staff, in the familiar frosty fashion that is the hallmark of the British tourist industry, are slightly taken aback at having their early Saturday evening interrupted by the arrival of guests, particularly six clad in garish cycle gear and in need of a shower. I had visited the hotel a month earlier just to check up the secure parking arrangements for our bikes and was told that would not be a problem. But, course, the staff on duty tonight are oblivious to this and point to a tree in the car park and suggest we "stick them there".

I have a short fuse when it comes to hotel and restaurant workers – much to the embarrassment of my family – and it is beginning to smoulder when fortunately another member of staff, who does actually appear to have grasped the notion of being in the service industry, arrives to inquire what the problem is. He shows us to an old stone porch normally used for photographs at wedding receptions. It will not be needed this evening and has locking doors. We cram the six bikes vertically into the porch, Jack's milometer computer on his new bike getting yanked off and terminally broken in the process. But they are secure for the night.

Sleeping arrangements are a delicate business and will play a big part in the coming two weeks. As tour organiser, I have to shuffle the pack to keep everyone smiling and ensure tensions do not rise. There is nothing worse for team morale than a grumpy, sleep-deprived cyclist over breakfast contemplating what he will do to his 'roomy' from the previous night.

We have three twins at the Abbots Barton in Canterbury, which is to be our usual configuration. My sons Tom and Jack will be together every night. That suits them and it suits us more mature cyclists, who do not want the bedroom turned into a tip with the TV permanently switched on. And loud.

The other pairings are more flexible. As our old age pensioner, Toddy can, to put it politely, be a little idiosyncratic and often comes to rely on his room-mate. On the France trip, he began referring to David as his *'domestique'*, the name given to riders in a professional cycle team who, quite literally, fetch and carry for the star names. A *domestique* will collect food and drink for the team-leader, shield him in the *peloton*, stay with him if he has a breakdown to pace him back into the pack, even give him his bike in extreme circumstances. David did not do this for Toddy in France but he did look after him, particularly at the end of a day's cycling, making him tea, and ensuring he left nothing behind the next morning. At one stage in France, when Toddy was going down with a nasty chest cold and expecting his *domestique* to also be a nurse, David stormed out of the hotel in frustration and sought refuge in a local bar. It was agreed between us that he and I should share 'Toddy duty' on this trip.

My nephew Alan presented an altogether different sleeping problem: his snoring. While awake, Alan is a considerate room-mate, well organised, keeping his half of the room neat and tidy, never hogging the bathroom, never leaving the shower in a disgusting state. But when the lights go out, sharing with Alan can be like trying to get to sleep beside Runway One at Heathrow. You could nudge him, shout at him, put a pannier over his head, but nothing would stop the sonorous reverberations for long. I, of course, make not a sound when I am asleep.

For the first night I suggest I share with Alan, assuming

I will be so knackered, nothing could keep me awake. Our rooms, unlike our initial experience at reception, are welcoming. Comfy and clean, which is all we ask really. Sadly, I do not stay in ours long enough to check out the array of free toiletries in the bathroom having realised to my horror that my umbilical link with the rest of the world, my mobile phone, must be still sitting on top of the grave of Fuller Pilch, who had no use for it at all.

Still in my cycling gear, I leg it back to the St Lawrence Ground – it would have been too complicated not to mentioning embarrassing to extricate my bike from the porch – and as I arrive the dregs of the supporters are drifting away and the car park attendant is packing up his Thermos.

"Fuller's?" he looks quizzical when I ask him. "The bar is closed now, son." While it is lovely to be referred to as "son" by a septuagenarian, panic is beginning to set in.

"Not Fullers the beer, Fuller Pilch, the groundsman," I say slowly and loudly as if talking to a foreigner.

"The groundsman? He'll still be out in the middle, we've got a second team match tomorrow, you knows."

I take a deep breath. "No. Fuller Pilch, the FORMER groundsman who is buried over THERE, I think I left my phone, a little black Nokia, on top of his tomb."

"Why didn't you say," he says," 'Arry picked that up and took it to the office."

I am so relieved I feel like kissing him, and 'Arry, and the groundsman, come to that, but linger only long enough to pass on my thanks.

The office is locked. Not a soul in sight. You would think someone would still be in there somewhere, counting the takings from a 5,000 crowd, but my hammering on doors and windows does nothing except alert a security guard on patrol around the ground. He gives my cycle shorts a curious look and informs me someone should be in by 9.30 in the morning, and there is nothing for it but to retreat before being arrested.

Walking back to the hotel I take stock of the situation. Here I am having taken the mickey out of Toddy for his forgetfulness, and having nagged my sons about being careful with their possession – and I have lost my phone, a vital piece of equipment. Imagine suffering a puncture and having to find a phone box to call the others, who by then would be five miles ahead of me? I would have to send postcards to my wife instead of the regular text message to tell her I was safe and still loved her. Worst of all, it might cost me money to replace it!

Back at the hotel, the others are showered and spruced up for an evening on the town, so there is nothing for it but to seek solace in a bottle of good red. We have two, in fact, at an Italian restaurant where we toast "the next 15 days" with Chianti. Absolutely shattered, we decide to make it an early night and set off back for our hotel just as the city's night-life is picking up pace. We must have made a curious sight: six blokes of varying ages shambling back through the streets past the nightclubs. But not half as curious as the group of giggling teenage girls queuing up at the door of a dance club with a Shetland Pony wearing a tutu among their number.

Canterbury is stacked full of history and attractive buildings from its dominating cathedral, the headquarters of the Church of England, to its city walls, which have stood since Roman times. It has famous schools and famous forefathers including the playwright Christopher Marlowe and novelist W. Somerset Maugham to more modern 'icons' such as Freddie Laker, Jodie Kidd and Orlando Bloom.

None of them bump into six contented cyclists as they make their way up the New Dover Road, past the Odeon Cinema back to their beds, but even if they had, there would have been no point in asking them for their mobile number.

I still feel wretchedly emasculated because of my forgetfulness.

Day One route: *Brit Oval, A202/A2 to New Cross, Blackheath. A207 Shooters Hill, Crayford. A226 Dartford, Swanscombe, Northfleet, Strood, Rochester. A2 to Gillingham, Sittingbourne, Faversham,Canterbury.*

String Distance: 55 miles.+
Actual Distance: 66 miles.*
Time in Saddle: 5 hrs 32 mins.*
Average speed: 11.9 mph*

+Distance calculated before the ride by my piece of string.
*Miles, time and speed according to David's on-bike computer.

CHAPTER THREE

The Home Run

....Canterbury to Hove

Guest rider: Jasper.

The sun is shining. Again. Just as it was on the first day. Up to now it had been a lousy summer, but I have a theory that September is now the best month of the year for good weather. Once the major cricket matches of the summer are over, the weather always seems to brighten up, which was one of the reasons for planning the ride to start in the middle of the ninth month. Rain is not a big problem when cycling because you soon dry off on the move, but it is so much more pleasant when the sun shines and tarmac is dry.

My strategy for the sleeping arrangements had worked. I was so tired last night I did not even notice if Alan did snore. Refreshed and keen, a full English breakfast is the order of the day at our Canterbury hotel. Even if the closest you normally get to a cooked breakfast at home before dashing off to work is toast, the lure of eggs, sausage, bacon, baked beans and fried bread with lashings of toast and tea when you have a demanding day in the saddle ahead is difficult to resist. Remember, we need that calorie intake to be up around the 6,000 mark, and an hour into the ride the full benefit of that greasy indulgence will start to kick in – or give you galloping indigestion as you crouch over the handlebars.

As the bikes are hauled out of the porch, checked over and the panniers clicked back into place on the racks over the back wheels, Jasper arrives from his auntie's on time shortly after 9am. He has been well fed and is looking alarmingly fresh once again. Perhaps it is because he only has to contemplate doing half this second day with us before bailing out when we reach his home near Cranbrook, which also happens to be where the Batemans live.

In fact, we should have had a real entourage today. So many people had rashly said they would be joining us for this Sunday spin through the Kent countryside in the sun, but when it came down to it, they pulled out. Another cricket-writing colleague and his teenage son were going to come for the day, but a rugby match for the son cropped up; a keen club cyclist who is a colleague on the Daily Express sports desk said he would be here, but he is probably working; a friend, who was a teacher at Tom and Jack's school in Cranbrook, intended to bring his bike out, but he has been laid low by a bug passed on by his baby son.

So we are still seven, but soon to be six and possibly even five. I secretly fear Jack will follow Jasper's lead and opt to abandon the trip a day-and-half into the 16 days, when he gets to taste home comforts again. The lure of his bed and an afternoon of football on TV will be strong. He is finding it tough going and says his saddle is about as comfortable as a rusty razor. He has already adjusted the height and now changes the angle before we set off, saying he will see how it goes.

Since it is Sunday, the roads are quiet and the day is perfect for a cycle across the Weald of Kent, over the North and South Downs to Brighton and finally its posher neighbour Hove, where Sussex County Cricket Club have their homely little seaside ground. Before we can make progress, though, there are two important jobs to be done: the photo session at Kent's ground and, of even greater significance, to re-unite me with my mobile phone.

The St Lawrence is only a few hundred yards away from our hotel and the Kent County Cricket Club office is, unsurprisingly, still locked when we get there. I do, however, find the ground manager, who has a promising bunch of keys jangling from his waistband. After a long explanation from me, he unlocks the door and together we start rooting around in drawers and on shelves and under the counter. Glory be, it's there. He has found it in a desk drawer. Such relief. There are a few missed calls from home showing on the screen, but nothing important on the messaging service. Now for the photos in front of the pavilion to prove to doubting friends that we did actually make it to the ground. Around 9.30, just about on schedule, we set off for a journey I have driven often and know so well.

Cranbrook is my home town and I have devised a relaxing cross-country route to Canterbury for cricket over the years. It is ideal for cycling: reasonably quiet, but on undulating roads with a good surface and varied scenery to make it interesting. There is nothing more boring than long flat straights. We even have an easterly breeze at our backs to give us a helping hand. Of course, other cyclists know about the delights of this route along the A252 too, and somewhere between Chartham, Chilham, Challock and Charing (trying saying that quickly after a few pints) we find ourselves caught up in a club time-trial.

We deliberately slow down so as not to embarrass the men on their racing machines, although a pair do rile David when they whizz by with noses in the air because of our tourers with loaded panniers. David gives them a mouthful of sarcasm, but does not give chase this time accepting his responsibilities to our troupe.

There is a Goose Fair on Challock's broad common, with marquees, animal pens and fairground rides to enhance the impression that this is the most glorious corner of England, untouched by the passing of the 20th century, and we are making good progress, although Toddy has said he is not feeling at his best. Alan, David, Tom and Jasper are ploughing on at the front, but Jack and I are happy to drop off the pace to keep Toddy company and make sure he comes through. We put it down to team-work, but possibly it is simply an excuse to go slowly and conserve some energy.

We are not half way into day two yet and I am beginning to realise the full extent of the challenge ahead over the next fortnight. It is going to be tough. Moving up from the 55 miles-a-day of our previous rides to 65 miles, even 75 at times, on this expedition will be demanding, even gruelling. Pace yourself, Colin.

We are now touching parts of the original Pilgrims' Way, the route taken by pilgrims from Winchester Cathedral to Canterbury Cathedral to visit the shrine of Thomas Becket, the Archbishop of Canterbury who was assassinated in his own church by supporters of Henry II. History seeps out of every part of Kent because of its strategic position beside the Channel and its proximity to Europe, but we have no time to stop and stare, although I do manage to inform my fellow travellers as we pass through Pluckley that the village has earned a place in the Guinness Book of Records as the most haunted village in the country – and we should not linger if we know what is good for us.

Pluckley has a roll-call of at least 12 "official" frightening ghostly apparitions according to local records:

*The spectre of the highwayman Robert Du Bois speared to a tree at Fright Corner.

*A phantom coach and horses seen careering down Maltman's Hill.

*The ghost of a Gypsy woman who burned to death in her sleep.

*The ghost of a miller haunting the ruins of a windmill.

*The hanging body of a schoolmaster in Dicky Buss Lane;

*A colonel who hanged himself in Park Wood.

*The screaming ghost of a man smothered by a fallen wall at the old brickworks.

*The Lady of Rose Court, said to have eaten poisoned berries after being denied her loved one.

*The Phantom Monk of Greystones. There is a suggestion he may have been the unrequited love object of the Lady of Rose Court.

*The White Lady of Dering, a young woman apparently buried inside seven coffins and an oak sarcophagus, who haunts the churchyard of St. Nicholas's Church.

*The Red Lady, reputedly an earlier member of the same ancient Dering family, who also haunts St Nicholas's Church.

*The Screaming Woods, an area of forest outside the village that is haunted by the ghosts of many poor souls lost in the woods.

There are several other "unofficial" poltergeists and phantoms floating around Pluckley adding to its ghostly reputation and making it a Mecca for sightseers on Hallowe'en, much to the frustration of the living residents in the village, who have had quite enough of psychic researchers and ghost-busting coach parties.

As for the *peloton,* our more earthly spirits are still high. We have had a brief stop for chocolate bars from the village stores in Charing and then turn off the A252 for even quieter country lanes that take us over the new high-speed rail line that links London with the Euro Tunnel. Once through the villages of Biddenden and Sissinghurst, we roll into Cranbrook for our pre-planned lunch stop at the Bateman family home and a meal prepared by my wife Brenda with some help from youngest son Rupert. Other friends are in the garden including Jasper's parents, and, as the wine and laughter flows after copious helpings of spaghetti bolognese and cheesecake, the idea of spending the afternoon there lying in the sun becomes increasingly attractive.

The break, however, appears to have had a restorative affect on Jack, who has swapped Jasper's more luxurious saddle onto his bike and is ready to hit the road again. Thankfully, my fears about Jack's staying power seem to be unfounded. Toddy, too, is feeling better after suffering from a few twinges in the nether regions and a complaining calf during the morning ride. We bid farewell to our guest rider Jasper and the family and reluctantly get our legs over again to head south onto the rolling roads of Sussex.

Our hilly route on the A229 takes us through Hawkhurst, once the base of the notorious Hawkhurst Gang, a group of 18th century smugglers, robbers and extortionists who ran amok from Poole in Dorset to the Kent coast, plying their illegal trade and earning their ill-gotten gains. The authorities seemed powerless to stop them so a group of local men of Hawkhurst, fed up with the terror spread around the law-abiding folk, set up their own militia and, in a spectacular hunt, either killed the gang members or brought them to justice.

Hawkhurst is on top of a hill and it is a tough climb up to the traffic lights in the village centre. The sun is now hot on our backs and lunch is laying heavy. We will feel the benefit of the pasta later on, but for now it just seems like extra weight to carry. Once over Hawhurst Moor, there is a long swooping descent before another climb to Hurst Green. The rolling green countryside, now dotted with vineyards, is a feature of the Weald of Kent and is made for cycling and open-top sports cars on a sunny Sunday afternoon. Another twisty downhill takes us over the treacherous (for bikes, at least) level crossing at Etchingham as our route along the A265 follows the River Dudwell into Burwash.

Our next land-mark is, appropriately, Bateman's, a 17th century country house in Burwash that was the home of the author Rudyard Kipling for the last 34 years of his life, and where he wrote among many others things his famous poem "If..."

It was our intention, too, to treat those twin impostors triumph and disaster just the same and keep our heads over the coming fifteen days.

By late afternoon, however, the pleasure of the rolling East Sussex countryside is beginning to wear a wee bit thin. My string estimated 64 miles for today but is going to be hopelessly out again, and although we have a tea stop planned in Lewes, we decide we need a break before then. We collapse on the grass outside another petrol station, this one at Cross in Hand, to take fuel on board. Jack tells me he is delighted with his new comfy saddle and he is looking more at ease as he gets used to his bike and how to get the best out of its gearing.

Making life as easy as possible on these long rides is vital and that includes anticipating inclines, changing down through the gears smoothly before the climb starts to really bite, and keeping your cadence – or pedal-turning speed – at a tempo that suits you. Mis-time a gear change and the leg muscles jar horribly and the bike complains – much like crunching the gears in a car.

When climbing a long hill that has a nasty and

unexpected extra incline just around what you thought would be the last corner before the summit, you and your bike have to work together, and giving her the odd word of encouragement is never out of place: "Come on old girl, let's go all the way, I'll go nice and easy on you if you promise to keep going." It is an old and familiar line in seduction.

We reluctantly re-mount and begin the slow climb out of Cross in Hand on a by-road. We are battling against the clock because of the indulgent 90 minutes spent over lunch and we have another stop to make before we get to the south coast, this time at Alan's home on top of a fearsome hill in Lewes, where his wife Diane has laid on tea and scones, and his in-laws are waiting to provide more family encouragement.

Our country road takes us through Blackboys, so named because the now defunct charcoal works here used to leave a layer of soot on everything, then through Ringmer and past Glyndebourne, a 700-year-old country estate that has its own opera house and is famous for its annual music festival.

From Glyndebourne, it is thankfully just two miles mainly downhill into Lewes, the county town of East Sussex that has a rich and bloody history as a port on a tidal River Ouse. Alan loves his real ale and is blessed in Lewes with the local Harvey's Brewery beside the Ouse, and plenty of good pubs including The Snowdrop, whose name is not as charming as it may sound. Lewes was the scene of the worst avalanche in England's history when, in 1836, a build-up of snow on a cliff rolled down onto a row of cottages claiming eight lives – hence the name of the pub.

Lewes also witnesses the most spectacular bonfire celebrations in the country with seven fiercely competitive local societies staging flaming processions through the town every November 5th to celebrate not only the foiling of the Gunpowder Plot but to commemorate the burning at the stake of 17 Protestant martyrs. Every year an effigy of Pope Paul V as well as Guy Fawkes is burned, 17 flaming crosses, one for each martyr, are borne through the streets and a burning barrel of tar thrown into the River Ouse. It is enough to turn a Health and Safety officer into a quivering wreck.

As for the blazing saddles, they are propped up in Alan's over-grown back garden after the precipitous climb to his home just beyond the narrow streets of the town centre. We are again sprawled out on the grass and devouring too much food instead of getting on with the challenge we have set ourselves.

As pleasant as these stops are, they are making our day too long. We must learn from this and make our food breaks shorter in the coming days. Today, though, we have an excuse as it is Family Day. Having said our farewells again, we have a final eight-mile push into Brighton, which we ride as a group along a cycle path beside the A27 that eventually sweeps us down into the fading splendour of Brighton, taking us past the Royal Pavilion that looks like the set of a Bollywood movie. On to the esplanade, we pass the Grand Hotel, re-built after an IRA bombing during a Conservative Party Conference in the 1980s, as the sun starts to dip towards the English Channel. The Hove cricket ground is another mile westwards, signposted by an imposing statue of Queen Victoria staring sternly out to sea, and we just have enough light for a photo-call outside ground Number Three.

There is nothing much to say about the Sussex County Ground. It is a ramshackle old place, hemmed in by terraced houses and ugly blocks of flats. The pavilion is a non-descript warren, while the Sea End houses possibly the ugliest stand in county cricket, which used to double as an indoor cricket school. Not before time, it is due for demolition as part of the ground redevelopment in 2010. The eastern side of the ground has a scoreboard and some sheds that serve as executive boxes. It is only the top end of the ground that gives the Hove County Ground its character: the grassy banks filled with deckchairs from where the locals and holiday-makers have watched one of the most successful sides in the country in recent years. The county has been bequeathed £12 million by a former president of the club, but the promised redevelopment has been slow to materialise.

Our digs, less than a mile away on the sea-front, are similarly unpretentious, but The Iron Duke is a friendly boozer on the Brighton-Hove boundary and highly recommended by a journalist friend from the Guardian, Paul Weaver, who lives in town and invests much of his hard-earned cash over the bar of this watering hole. Paul has promised to meet us there, having arranged a special B&B rate for us and, true to his word, when we push our bikes up the one-way street to the pub door, he is there with a row of empty pint glasses on the bar in front of him.

It is nearly 7pm and I think Paul has been waiting for about four hours, passing the time in the best way possible in a pub. He has one of those lop-sided grins that only the sober can recognise. Beside him on a bar stool is his lady friend Pat and her little dog, who looks alarmed at the sight of us staggering in with our panniers and helmets. The bikes stowed in the cellar, Paul shouts us a very welcome pint.

As with the Abbots Barton Hotel in Canterbury, I had done a recce of the Iron Duke a few weeks before the ride, mainly to check its location, but also to re-confirm our rooms because the arrangement with the landlord had been very informal. "Mate of Paul's? That's good enough for me," he'd said on the phone. "No, don't bother with a deposit, I'll trust you."

One evening before the ride, Brenda and I had been to the Theatre Royal in Brighton with my nephew Alan and his wife Diane and sought out the Duke for a post-show pint. Brighton does not have the reputation for being 'The Gay Capital of Britain' without reason, and the sight of two middle-aged married heterosexual couples entering the Duke caused quite a stir among the regular clientele that night.

Judging by the tight sleeveless tee-shirts, Freddie Mercury moustaches and body-piercings, this was not a regular haunt of members of the Brighton and Hove Rotary Club. Paul, though, clearly thought the world of the place and he is as straight as they come, so that was a good enough for us. Sure enough, the reservation for three doubles was in the book and they did not seem surprised at all that we would be six blokes sharing.

Arriving hungry and tired after the ride, our mood sank a little when we were told that the kitchen staff did not work on a Sunday evening despite the blackboard menu promising 'Tonight's Special – Chicken Curry and a Pint £9.' We are further dismayed to be told the cook also has Monday mornings off, so there will be no cooked breakfast the next day.

The rooms, up four flights of creaky stairs, are functional, and tonight I am sharing with Toddy. He has the rather disconcerting habit of wandering around the bedroom as naked as the day he was born. Not that he has anything to be ashamed of, mind you. Quite the opposite. It is only that it is difficult to know where to look when handing him his early evening cup of tea as he sits on his bed rummaging through his panniers for his clean undies.

Directly opposite our room is a chapel that looks as if it has not seen any Sunday business for a few years, which is something of a relief. At least there is no congregation gathering outside to see a naked Ian strolling distractedly around the room and past the high sash windows that let in plenty of evening light. All the same, I remind Ian about Brighton's gay reputation, and point out the clear view into our room from further up the Wellington Road, which is filling with Sunday evening strollers.

"They won't see anything they haven't seen before," he informs me.

True enough. Particularly in Brighton.

The post-ride ritual each day is an important one and after a few days on tour, we four senior riders can slip into an unspoken routine as well co-ordinated as anything seen on Strictly Come Dancing. Judging by the chaotic jumble of laundry and cycle gear I see in the boys' room when I pop my head around their door, the young 'uns still have some fine tuning to do on this score.

For Alan, David, Ian and me, the routine involves one person heading into the bathroom to clean up, while the other unpacks his panniers (which does not take long), puts the kettle on and relaxes on the bed. The cleansing routine includes washing cycle shorts and top, which are wrung out in a towel and draped over a radiator or out of the window, whichever looks the most promising. Bathroom clear, the roles are reversed.

On a good evening two sharing can be shaved, washed and ready to hit the town in 42 minutes flat. It gets a little more complicated when three have to share a room.

There is a hitch in the routine this evening in that, while rooms No. 3 and No. 5 have torrents of hot water, No. 4, occupied by Ian and me, has barely a trickle. England's cricketers have ice baths after a tough day to ensure their muscles do not tighten up, but I would not recommend it. We are ready inside 25 minutes flat this evening.

Paul and Pat have gone home by the time we are back downstairs for another pint while we plan our assault on Brighton's nightlife, but as it is now approaching 9pm, we know getting somewhere to serve food on a Sunday evening is the priority. A fish and chip shop with a sit-down section recommended by Pat is the answer, and we just make it in time before last orders. They even have a licence and serve wine, which is a bonus.

As for the famed clubs of Brighton, we are too weary to even think about that by the time supper is over. Even the lads Tom and Jack agree that the only places they want to hit are their pillows. On the walk back to the Iron Duke, thoughts turn to the next meal and the absence of breakfast at our accommodation. We scour the streets looking for likely cafés that might open early the next day and serve a 'Big Sizzler', but there is nothing more promising than a burger van.

The only thing to do is to fall into bed, hope the walls are thick enough to shut out the low rumbling of Alan's snoring and look forward to the next day, which promises to be a flat jaunt along the south coast accompanied by two new guest riders.

Day Two route: Canterbury A28 to Chartham, Chilham, A252 to Challock and Charing. Minor roads to Pluckley, Smarden. A262 to Sissinghurst. A229 to Cranbrook, Hawkhurst, Hurst Green. A21/A265 Burwash, Heathfield, Cross in Hand. Minor roads to Blackboys, Halland, Ringmer, Lewes. A27 cycle route to Brighton and Hove.

String Distance: 64 miles.
Actual Distance: 76 miles.
Time in saddle: 6hrs 7mins
Average Speed: 12.4 mph

Overall string estimate:119 miles.
Actual mileage to-date: 142.
Total cycling time: 11hrs 39 mins.
Average speed 12.2mph.

CHAPTER FOUR

The Coastal Jaunt

....Hove to Romsey

Guest riders: David and Martin.

Alan, the most punctual of risers, sets his alarm even earlier today, the thought of no breakfast at our pub in Hove nagging away at him like the car alarm set off in the nearby multi-storey car park in the middle of the night.

Alan likes his food. I have never seen so much distress on a man's face than on one day of our Ireland bike ride when we stayed in rooms above a restaurant of the highest quality on the west coast. The seafood dinner the night before had been a wonderful experience and we could not wait for to see what was on offer for breakfast. The proprietor-cum-chef had promised us the house speciality of locally caught home-smoked salmon and scrambled free range eggs. To Alan's horror, a mutinous mollusc from the night before had left him feeling queasy, and as David, Tom and I tucked into our breakfasts, he could only watch dolefully as he pecked on some dry toast.

There is nothing wrong with Alan's appetite this

morning in Brighton, and the sea breeze had made him even more ravenous, so he is not going to be denied his cooked breakfast before we leave, cook or no cook at the Iron Duke. Up and dressed before the rest of us had stirred, Alan makes it his mission to scour the town he knows pretty well – he works here in the benefits office – for a greasy spoon café. He marches the deserted streets without spotting anything more encouraging than a newsagents selling sandwiches. The only option might be to splash out on a full English at one of the posh sea-front hotels, but when he returns to the Duke his downcast mood is transformed.

A young man is laying a large table in the dining room, placing out bottles of brown and red sauce, salt and pepper and cutlery. There is also a large jug of orange juice and six glasses. Alan's new best friend is from somewhere in Eastern Europe (aren't all hotel workers, these days?) but his broken English is clear enough to Alan when he asks if he would like tea or coffee for breakfast. Unknown to the bar staff the night before, the landlord has made special arrangements for the breakfast cook to come in this Monday morning for the six cyclists staying upstairs. The fry-up is on its way.

We have two guest riders joining us today, both friends of Alan. The first is David Townsend, who meets us at the Duke. He did contemplate doing the whole 16-day ride but decided it was unfair on his family – a notion I have trouble getting to grips with. It takes all sorts, I guess. Unlike Jasper, David is similar in age and shape to most of us, which is a relief. Martin is due to link up with us a few miles along the South Coast in Worthing.

It is glorious again. We are blessed with full stomachs,

sea, sun and a tarmac coastal cycle path for the start of our journey as we head west to Shoreham and Worthing, weaving in and out of the mums with pushchairs, and holiday-makers making the most of being beside the seaside and with the English weather on its best behaviour. Shoreham is a pretty little place with a fishing harbour. It was once regarded as the Hollywood of the British film industry, but its most recent claim to fame is being the home town of the pop singer Leo Sayer. There is no truth in the rumour that his album 'Endless Journey' was the inspiration for our ride.

The going is flat and we make good time to Worthing, which, beneath its veneer of retirement homes and holiday hotels, has quite a subversive culture that stretches back over many years. In Victorian times, a local liquor-shop owner, fed up with the Salvation Army and their anti-alcohol marches, set up the 'Skeleton Army.' This nefarious group attracted around 4,000 recruits and they waved banners bearing the skull and cross bones with the legend: "Beef, Beer and Bacca." Quite why 'Beef' joined Beer and Tobacco on the banners is difficult to pin down. Perhaps the Skeleton Army recruits were just fond of an alliteration. To disrupt the Salvation Army marches they would throw eggs, paint and rats (or food, fluid and fur to maintain the alliteration theme) at the no-booze brigade, and daub sticky black tar on walls near the Sally Army meeting rooms to spoil their uniforms.

Worthing was in rebellious mood in the 19th Century and it has never really changed despite the proliferation of Zimmer frames and bandstands. In the Swinging Sixties some of England's earliest 'Cannabis Cafés' were set up here (one gloriously called The Quantum Leaf) before being raided and closed by the police. Even the local football team is nicknamed The Rebels.

Its famous residents have included Oscar Wilde and Harold Pinter, both considered subversive in their way, and the Worthing theatre was the place where the Peter Cushing and Christopher Lee, those two blood-curdling stars of the Hammer Horror film genre, cut their fangs as actors.

Not a place, then, to linger without easy access to a wooden stake and crucifix and so, having met our second guest rider, Martin Spring, at the beach-front bus halt as arranged and more or less on time, we plough on to Littlehampton (no jokes, please) and towards Bognor Regis, whose local historians will tell you that the town's most famous royal visitor, King George V, never uttered the words "Bugger Bognor" as he was widely reputed to have done. Pity, really. It is another nice alliteration and on a rainy summer's day, no phrase sums up the place quite so succinctly.

We have sun, however, and the warmth on our backs coupled with the twinkling sea beside us is too much to resist, so we decide to take a mid-morning break in Bognor at a little café on the prom with its outdoor chairs and tables beside the stony beach. It is a good opportunity to get to know our two guest riders a little better.

David is a long-term cyclist who introduced Alan to the delights of the annual 100-mile Bristol to London ride every August. He works for the Foreign Office, but like all people who work at the 'FO', David is very vague about exactly what he does. This confirms to me that he is a spy, and below the convivial well-padded exterior is a ruthless killing machine, no doubt. It is obvious he is not to be crossed, and I suspect his bicycle pump is really a mini-rocket launcher. That pannier probably drains oil and tin tacks on to the road behind him when he rings the bell on his handlebars twice.

Alan also informs me: "David takes his bike with him on foreign postings and has been seen cycling the red light districts of such places as Prague, Vienna, and Berlin." Dirty business, this espionage. No wonder he works under cover.

Martin, like Alan, is employed in an altogether less sinister branch of the civil service, the Department of Works and Pensions. Like all civil servants, he gets loads of time off and is able to indulge in his love of off-road cycling. To the uninitiated, this is exactly what it says on the can: he cycles off roads. Forest tracks, footpaths, hill-sides, even mountain-sides are the haunt of these helter-skelter saddle-bums. It is, in fact, how Lance Armstrong started his cycling career, and Martin is closer to Armstrong's level of fitness and bike-riding ability than ours.

His machine is a state of the art road bike – he has others for the 'off-road' stuff – and he has a suitably lean frame in his all-over lycra, but despite all this he mixes quickly into our motley group, filtering backwards and forwards through the peloton on the road to chat and encourage us as we finally leave the lovely sea behind and head inland towards Chichester, but still keeping to minor roads with the occasional excitement of a level-crossing.

There is always a frisson of anticipation approaching a level crossing in case the bells start to sound, the lights flash and the barriers come down. That is exactly what happens on our route as we allow the 11.40 to Portsmouth Harbour to rattle by. Level-crossing stops are a quaint feature of the Tour de France and they can split the field, although race etiquette says that those already across the railway line before the barriers descend do not take advantage and speed away from those held up until the train passes.

Level crossings also pose a sinister threat: cyclists must cross the rails at more or less a 90 deg. angle or risk getting their front wheel caught in the gap between rail and road, as once happened to Alan's startled wife Diane, who found herself heading for Clapham Junction the quick way.

It is just outside Chichester where we have to cross the thundering A27 and here we encounter one of the more curious incidents of our first three days. As Alan negotiates a roundabout underneath the trunk road, a car with the roof down and full of laughing young people passes by. In their wake, a handful of coins are lobbed in Alan's direction. They do not appear to have been thrown with any malicious intent, simply tossed as you might drop a coin into a busker's hat. The coins bounce and roll all over the road, but it is far too busy for us to stop and attempt to retrieve them. But why were they thrown? We are not cycling with shirts or placards announcing this is a sponsored ride, so they could not have been a donation to our causes. Perhaps coin-throwing is a local sport, or the folk of Sussex are too well off and do not want to be weighed down with small change. Alan, however, regards it as a good opportunity to give another tiresome motorist a piece of his mind, something that is to become a regular feature of the coming fortnight.

This is perhaps a good stage to explain a few things to

those motorists who consider all cyclists as a lower life-form, placed somewhere between the flies and moths splattered on their windscreens. Cyclists do have rights. In fact they have just as much right to a space on the highway as the lorry, the caravan, the Mondeo and, yes, even the four-wheel drive monstrosities used by mothers to take their little darlings to and from school.

Many people behind the wheel of a car live under a series of misapprehensions:

1. They pay Road Tax and therefore own the road.
Wrong. They pay a Vehicle Excise Licence, which is not used to build and maintain roads. The VEL was introduced in 1888. Those driving 'locomotives' paid £5 a year, those pushing or riding on trade carts were charge five shillings (25p) per wheel. It was, indeed, originally intended to pay for the upkeep of the highways but the money was never directly used for that purpose and in 1937 the 'road fund' was officially scrapped and the revenue went into the treasury coffers.

2. Cyclists should ride in the gutter.
Wrong. The 2010 Highway Code states under Section 213: *'Motorcyclists and cyclists may suddenly need to avoid uneven road surfaces and obstacles such as drain covers or oily, wet or icy patches on the road. Give them plenty of room and pay particular attention to any sudden change of direction they may have to make.'*

3. Cyclists should ride on pavements.
Wrong. It is illegal for cyclists to ride on pavements unless in a designated cycle lane.

4. Cyclists should always ride in cycle lanes when they are there.
Wrong. Again, take time out to read the Highway Code, section 63 under rules for cyclists: *'Use of cycle lanes is not compulsory and will depend on your experience and skills, but they can make your journey safer.'*

5. Cyclists should follow the same route as vehicles around roundabouts.
Wrong. Cyclists are advised to cycle around roundabouts in the left hand lane even if they are eventually turning right.

6, 7 and 8. Cyclists are idiots, bloody idiots and f***ing menaces.
Wrong. Cyclists are road users, most of whom know how to drive a car, unlike a lot of car drivers who do not know how to ride a bike.

The city of Chichester is believed to have been the bridgehead for the Roman invasion of Britain, but all we get to see of it is an inner ring-road. We are lost. Gathered at another level crossing, Alan, who is again relying on his notorious sense of direction, sets off with our guest riders Martin and David. Rather non-plussed by this unilateral decision, the rest of us stay put, consulting maps and asking locals passing by on the pavement. To us, it appears we should be heading in exactly the opposite direction to the other group, and so off we set without waiting for them to return. Just to make a point.

As we are leaving the centre of the cathedral city, miraculously we all meet up on the A259, with neither group prepared to concede they had taken a wrong turn. We head towards Havant and then cut inland again for a long climb up the tail end of the South Downs to Southwick with its fabulous views across Portsmouth, the Solent and to the Isle of Wight. Southwick is a most unusual village in that it is owned by the Southwick Estate and no private house ownership is permitted. All the houses have doors painted a rich red as part of the tenancy agreement.

There are forts and military establishments evident all along this coast, and our armed forces police force is trained at the Defence Police College at Southwick Park. Every now and then along our route on the B2177 that skirts the Forest of Bere and crosses the Meon Valley, a sinister window-less building with a tall mast appears in a clearing, the stout fences and barbed wire around its perimeter ensuring it is not mistaken for a public convenience. David, our chum from the Foreign Office, no doubt knows exactly what is going on behind these closed doors, but he is not letting on.

Lunch in a packed hill-top pub with spectacular views across The Solent is followed by a wonderful swooping ride downhill with speeds topping 30 mph – scary stuff with two over-laden panniers pushing you on – towards Wickham, Botley and West End, the home of Hampshire County Cricket Club since 2001.

The county used to play at Northlands Road in the Southampton suburbs, a cosy ramshackle place hemmed in by homes, and with no room for the expansion needed for professional cricket in the 21st century. In the 1990s Hampshire took the bold – and so far unique decision in modern county cricket – to move from their traditional headquarters and invest in a purpose-built ground on a new site out of town.

The scheme to up sticks and move to land leased from Queens College, Oxford in the village of West End, north of Southampton and beside the M27, started in the mid-90s, but faltered when the value of house prices – and therefore the value of the Northlands Road site – dipped. The plan would have hit the buffers but for the intervention of a wealthy supporter named Rod Bransgrove, who injected several millions from his own fortune and made Hampshire the first county cricket club to become a PLC (public limited company) of which he was chairman. The first turf at the new site, a natural amphitheatre on the side of a hill, was cut in 1997, cricket was being played there by the second team three years later, and in 2001 Hampshire made the official move to their new home, which now stages international cricket every summer.

Hampshire has become a fashionable county again, attracting the likes of Australia's Shane Warne and England's Kevin Pietersen to their playing staff in recent years, but as we bowled into the complex, which includes a golf course, a nursery cricket ground, a sports centre and an hotel, there is a match of slightly less significance taking place at the Rose Bowl between the Hampshire ground staff and office staff. No matter what the quality of the cricket, however, the fact that men in white flannels are on the field makes the perfect backdrop for our latest group photographs before we push on for the last 10 miles to our overnight stop in Romsey.

I had struggled to find accommodation in the Romsey area owing to the fact that there was a regatta in the Solent that week. Most places had been booked up a year in advance. In desperation, I emailed Hampshire's wealthy chairman. Rod Bransgrove had always been friendly with the media and on several previous tours of the Caribbean had invited us on to his luxury yacht for an evening party. Well, millionaires tend to do that sort of thing. This time, though, Rod could not help with my request for recommendations for any "cheap and cheerful bed and breakfasts in the Romsey area."

His reply came back: "I'd love to help Colin, but I don't often frequent cheap and cheerful B and Bs. Sorry." Silly me, I should have guessed. I had, however, finally found one just outside Romsey that looked extremely promising and came with the promise of a "Hot Radox Bath" from the landlady.

It is late afternoon and the evening rush-hour is gaining momentum as we set off on the A27 through the conurbation of villages around Southampton and its airport. The road, though, is not too demanding and we have been refreshed by a 'tea-and-cake' break in Hampshire's club bar. David is looking strong and so are our guest riders, but since I am the one who knows the way through Swaythling to Romsey, having driven it a few weeks earlier, I take the lead for much of the time as we leave suburbia and hit the countryside again.

Our B&B is on Pauncefoot Hill just outside Romsey, so we stop at the bottom of the incline and bid farewell to our two guest riders, who head off for the railway station and an easy ride back towards Worthing and Brighton. I look at Jack and wonder how much he wishes he were joining them but he has kept up a good pace today. Toddy has flagged a bit though, which is a worrying sign. He should, however, get a good night's sleep – in fact, we all should. Our accommodation comprises a triple, a double and a single room. Alan is in the single, which means a peaceful night for all.

Just to ensure there is no trouble sleeping, we walk the half-a-mile back into Romsey to what is jarringly called a "gastro-pub". It is a curious choice of phrase to describe a pub that believes it serves good food. The word "gastro" normally proceeds something rather unpleasant to do with the digestive system: gastroenteritis, gastro reflux, gastro bug, gastro bypass. Let's hope none of those follow tonight's rather excellent meal diluted with suitable amounts of ale and wine.

Another look at the bike computers reveals a mileage in the mid-70s. Even given the variations of a mile here and there on our different computers, which are never as accurate as a car milometer, there is a clear pattern emerging – and my piece of string is losing credibility. So far it has been around 10 miles out – approaching 20 per cent – on each of the first three days. If the discrepancy had been in our favour (i.e. fewer miles than estimated) it might have been all right, but as we are undertaking a lot more than I had promised the lads, I sense there are a few mutterings in the dark as we trudge back up the busy hill to our beds.

I hope my string is more dependable tomorrow. Day Four is a challenging one with a star guest rider and a surprise one as we push west across Salisbury Plain.

Day Three route: *Brighton coastal cycle path through Shoreham to Worthing. A259 Littlehampton and Bognor Regis. B2166 to*

Donnington and Chichester. A259 Southbourne and Havant. B2177 Southwick and Wickham. A334 to Botley and West End. A27 to Swaythling and Romsey.

String Distance: 66 miles.
Actual Distance: 75 miles.
Time in saddle: 6hrs 9mins
Average Speed: 12.1 mph

Overall string estimate: 185 miles.
Actual mileage to-date: 217.
Total cycling time: 17hrs 48 mins.
Average speed 12.2mph.

PIER PRESSURE...
by Martin Spring

Some of my recollections on the day I joined the ride to the Rose Bowl:

When the Peloton visited on that sunny day in Worthing, it happened to coincide with the annual arrival of the S.S. Waverley. There were crowds lining the pier reminiscent of a scene from HG Wells' "War of the Worlds".

The Waverley attempted to dock several times for a steam trip to the Isle of Wight. I found out later that it failed due to choppy waters and all the passengers were left stranded. The ship kept hitting the jetty causing some damage, too, but no Martians were blamed!

On a roundabout near Chichester some "generous" motorists threw some coins at us. Sadly I was unable to collect the gift aid on that one.

At lunch we stopped at that pub overlooking the Solent from which there were some truly great views over Portsmouth and the Isle of Wight, which was clearly visible.

I was really impressed by the Rose Bowl cricket ground, and the cup of tea in the bar overlooking the pitch tasted all the better after 70 miles of cycling. I remember feeling really lucky to have joined you all that day from Worthing and wished I could have been on the next day's ride as well with Gus Fraser.

****

CHAPTER FIVE

High Plain Drifters

... Romsey to Montacute

Guest Riders: Angus and Larry

We have a star guest rider today, and it is quite a thrill for all of us. Angus Fraser, MBE, who played with great distinction for many years as a fast bowler for England and Middlesex before hanging up his well scuffed boots and turning to journalism, both as a newspaper correspondent, with The Independent, and broadcaster, is joining the *peloton*. On the cricket field, Gus could appear a real old curmudgeon. He had the look of a hard-done-by foot soldier. He was a grumpy old man before his time, kicking lumps out of the ground in frustration when things did not go his way or giving the poor unsuspecting batsman a mouthful of invective just because he had failed to nick a catch to slip. Gus would bad-mouth his team-mates if their fielding was anything less than impeccable, and he was more than capable of telling an umpire where he had gone wrong. Off the field, though, you could not wish to meet a nicer bloke, although he could still be a bit of a grouch if he disagreed with the tone of the conversation over the dinner table.

Gus was taken with our idea of cycling around the 18 first class cricket grounds he knew so well from his days as a player, and had promised to join us for two legs to show his support. As good as his word, he drove from his north London home to Romsey on this bright Tuesday morning with his bike on a rack on the back of his car. We knew nothing of his cycling ability, but we had little doubt about his stamina. He was, as they say in the trade, 'a big unit,' but he had plenty of strength and stamina, plus that determination not to be beaten that is inherent in almost everyone who has reached the top of their chosen sport. The bike on the back of his car, however, had a more dubious pedigree.

It was clearly built for riding around London parks or forest lanes. It had thick tyres and a giant coiled spring on the frame beneath the saddle, making it look more like a pogo-stick on wheels than a machine that would smoothly transport its rider 120 miles in comfort on the highways and by-ways of southern England. The spring may have provided some cushioning when cycling across a ploughed field, but on tarmac Gus 'pogo-ed' along like a man clinging grimly to a bucking bronco. To make his task more arduous, he has his overnight gear in a backpack. Now, backpacks might be fine for hikers, but for long-distance cycling they are a non-starter. As well as making the rider very hot and sweaty, they can make balancing precarious, especially on a speedy descent. Gus, though, was fiercely determined, just as he had always been as a cricketer who took more than 200 Test wickets.

Like virtually every fast bowler, Gus had had to cope

with his fair share of injuries, such is the nature of the job and the stresses put on the body. His most debilitating injury had been hip trouble, which started in 1990 and caused him to miss 24 Tests, which, in the scale of a cricketer's lifetime, is a hefty chunk. One of the things Gus tried during this time was electrothermal treatment wired into his underclothing around his hips. It worked much the same way as TENS (Transcutaneous Electrical Nerve Stimulation) treatment is used for women in labour. 'Gus and his Amazing Electrical Underpants' became a source of huge amusement on the cricket circuit, spawning all sorts of gags about putting the spark back into his love life. Gus took it all in good humour. Most of the time.

Gus turned up at our guest house at breakfast time, our landlady having kindly agreed to let him leave his car there overnight. The plan was for him and his pogo-bike to get the train back to Romsey from Bristol the following day. By now we were beginning to feel more confident about the challenge ahead, although Toddy was developing a worrying ache in a molar that was to become a major drama over the coming 48 hours.

Our other guest rider was an unexpected one. As we wheeled our bikes down the steep gravel drive of our guest house to the dual carriageway that we had to nip across to make the return journey towards Romsey, Jack spotted something colourful in the stones. It was a rubber lizard, a couple of inches long, and which fitted snugly on Jack's handlebars under a brake cable. 'Larry the Lizard' became Jack's good luck charm for the task ahead.

Romsey had been our choice of stop because of its location near the start of our ride across Salisbury Plain, but unfortunately we do not have time to linger in what is a pretty little market town in the Test Valley. Dominating the centre is its Norman Abbey, part of Romsey's religious history. The inhabitants of the town's nunnery are said to have enjoyed standing naked in the River Test chanting Psalms. Sadly, we did not have time to ascertain whether this devotional act is still carried on today.

Still on the watery religious theme, the Rev. Edward Berthon of Romsey invented collapsable boats, and the boatyard that bears his name is famous for making lifeboats – including those used on the Titanic. Celebrated Romsey residents have included Lord Mountbatten of Burma, Michelin star-spangled chef Gordon Ramsey and your favourite green-tipped gardener Charlie Dimmock, but for me the most cherished of them all must be the Rev. W. Awdry, author of 'The Railway Series', those wonderful children's books that tell of the adventures of Thomas the Tank Engine.

As we point our bicycles up the misty hills around Romsey on the A27, the fat controller is left lagging behind once again. But I soon pick up the pace and we are a group as we hit the busy A36 and push on to Salisbury.

We skirt the south of the city, but wherever you are around Salisbury, you cannot miss its wonderfully elegant cathedral with soaring spire which, at 400ft, is the tallest spire in the UK. The cathedral dates back to the 13th century but is not the first built in Salisbury, or Sarum to give it his old name. When it was decided to build a new cathedral because of disputes between the clergy and the military, legend has it that the site was to be decided by the firing of an arrow, the new church to be built wherever it landed.

The arrow was fired and stuck in a deer, which ran for almost two miles before falling and dying in what became known as New Sarum. And that, the story goes, is where the current cathedral was built. The cathedral contains one of only four volumes of the Magna Carta, the charter that gave us commoners of England our rights – including the ruling that all motorised vehicles must give way to bicycles at all times.

Just outside Salisbury, the A36 becomes a dual carriageway but we are able to escape on minor roads into Whaddon and Alderbury, working our way around Salisbury until we find our major route west, the A30.

Heading into the famous carpet-making town of Wilton, David and Tom are setting a hot pace, which is too tough for the rest of us, including Gus, whose face is contorting with effort as his large frame pounds up and down on his spring-loaded saddle. Finally, the strain on man and machine reaches breaking point and there is an alarming snapping sound behind me as the Fraser posterior comes down on his saddle once too often. The saddle clatters into the gutter and Gus is fortunate not to be impaled on the ragged end of his saddle post like some victim of a mediaeval torture technique.

The others have disappeared up the A30 eager to reach our first pre-arranged coffee-stop of the day, but fortunately I have not had the energy to keep up with them. I stop to help Gus and, once I have wiped away the tears of laughter, we start to wander through Wilton pushing our two bikes and carrying one dismembered saddle looking for a solution. I phone David (how did we cope without mobile phones?) and tell them to take their time and wait for us at the pub. If we both make it. Then Gus spots a battered old sign on the other side of the road that says: *'C&O Tractors. Any make of vehicle undertaken.'* Even bicycles, it seems.

Gus sheepishly wheels his machine into the workshop with one hand, clasping the saddle in the other to the enormous amusement of the mechanics. Their laughter subsided, they fix the saddle in a few minutes, replacing a sheared bolt with a more sturdy one. Thank goodness the disposable culture in which we live has not spread everywhere. In places like Wilton, they still fix things that go wrong. If the Gus saddle incident had happened in London, no doubt the local bike shop owner would have shaken his head gravely and told him he needed to buy a new £500 machine. But not here in the shires. The country is not going to the dogs, after all.

Gus and I set off to catch the pack, pacing each other well along the A30 through glorious undulating farmland with the sun shining once again. This feels like the heart of England with its well ordered fields, trimmed hedges and healthy-looking livestock grazing contentedly, unaware that their future lies on a dinner plate. High on the left we see the Fovant Badges: giant regimental crests carved into the chalky hillside by soldiers garrisoned on Salisbury Plain for the First World War.

Originally 20 badges, some were the size of almost half a football pitch, and were made with painstaking precision, standing out stark white on the green landscape. Ironically, during the Second World War, it was decided to allow the tussocky grass to grow over them so they could not be used as a navigational aid for enemy aircraft. In recent years, however, the Fovant Badge Society has restored eight of the originals to their former glory, and quite a sight they are too for those who make time to stop and pause for a while on the A30 near the village of Fovant, which is where our cycling troops have decamped to wait for us on the patio of The Pembroke Arms.

We still have a long haul and plenty of hills ahead of us and set off with good intent, but the Fraser Saddle Malfunction has put us back, and within 30 minutes we are pulling into another pub car park just the other side of Shaftsbury in search of lunch. Food is most important on these rides. Are we really burning up 6,000 calories a day? It certainly feels like it. Whether that figure is accurate, I have no way of telling, but we definitely eat a lot of stuff we would not normally consider consuming without putting on weight. Mars bars, muesli bars, jelly babies, mints, bananas, biscuits are all devoured on the move. Meals on wheels, if you like. Drinks we would never dream of consuming such as Coca-Cola and Lucozade are guzzled as we top up sugar levels to keep the wheels turning. It is little wonder that cyclists are notorious for having bad teeth.

Our lunch time stop is the usual affair with Alan salivating over the menu in anticipation. The Soup-of-the-Day (leek and potato) and a baguette will do for David, Toddy and me but Alan has his eye on 'Today's Special' of steak'n'ale pie with chips and gravy. Tom and Jack are no slouches when it comes to meal time either, but tend to head down the pasta route as they have heard that is the choice of Tour de France riders. As for Gus, brought up on the bountiful cooking of Nancy, the cook at Lord's who used to provide the players' meals, he orders a large plate of steaming spaghetti to replenish energy levels.

The problem with these stops for a full-blown meal is that they take too long. Muscles start to stiffen, chills set in as the sweat dries and the prospect of getting back on the bike grows less attractive as we sit in the cosy surroundings and grow full. It is becoming a bone of contention between us riders. Our most serious rider, David hints that a 15-minute break with a sandwich and crisps from a petrol station is sufficient. I agree and so does Tom. Alan pales at the thought and shakes his head gravely when we broach the subject, but it is an issue that will not go away, especially as the distances being covered are longer than estimated. We cannot afford to be cycling in the dark as most of us do not have any lights, not to mention the fact that valuable drinking time in the evening will be lost. It seems an age at our stop in East Stour before Alan is brushing the last crumb of flaky pastry off his white beard and declaring himself contentedly full.

Back on the A30, which, to our delight, is surprisingly traffic-free, the group stays more or less intact as we head west towards Sherborne and Yeovil, with the sun getting ever lower ahead of us. Jack, having overcome his apprehension of the first few days of the ride, is growing increasingly confident about his ability to stay the pace, and has started to get mischievous. He sprays Larry with water from his bottle informing us that lizards dry out in the sun. He then decides water is too good for Larry and sprays Tom's bare legs before sprinting ahead, his raging brother in hot pursuit. Why are pursuits always hot? Why are affairs always steamy, troops always crack, brunettes always sultry and infernos always raging? These are the sort of idle thoughts that occupy your mind as you turn the pedals up yet another hill drifting across Salisbury Plain.

The next landmark as we head towards Yeovil is Milborne Port, a curiously named little place as it is miles from the sea or even a canal capable of carrying a decent-sized barge. The denizens of Milborne Port may not agree, but the name of the place is the only interesting thing about it. Yeovil, in comparison, has much to commend it, particularly its nightlife, which had become so boisterous in recent years that the local media re-named it 'Yobville.'

Yeovil has a reputation for being 'The Wild West Town' at weekends as the younger folk from the surrounding villages mix with the townies and the personnel from the nearby Royal Navy air station to let their hair down and sink a few cider-pops. The town has recently introduced the UK's first biometric finger-printing scheme for nightclubs, which involves revellers sticking their finger in a scanning device before entry into a bar. If someone causes trouble, their 'scan' is relayed around all the other nightclubs using the scheme and the boisterous customers are refused entry. The 'InTouch Scheme' is not favoured by human rights groups such as Liberty, but police forces and other town councils are watching the Yeovil experiment with increasing interest.

Yeovil is the home of Westland Helicopters and used to have a thriving glove-making industry – Yeovil's football team is known as 'The Glovers' – and it also used to be the home of one of Britain's most famous cricketers, Sir Ian Botham, who grew up here before joining Somerset and becoming the world's best all-rounder for a few years.

There is a lovely swooping descent towards Yeovil and on the outskirts of town we gather in the wide entrance to an industrial estate, Gus being the last to puff into our retreat as the local rush-hour gathers momentum. Gus is being delayed not only by his machine, but by the frequent wailing of his mobile phone, which he has to stop to answer. Although currently cricket correspondent for The Independent newspaper, he is wanted back by his old county Middlesex as their Director of Cricket. The county, once one of the powerhouses of the English game, have slipped into the second tier of the Championship and are in a bit of a mess. Gus is one of the leading candidates for the newly-created job of Director of Cricket and is getting calls from those close to the county who are urging his return. With the sales of the Independent heading in the wrong direction and a family who would like to see more of him in the winter, Gus is tempted to give up the nomadic life of a cricket correspondent.

Tonight we are staying at one of our more unusual resting places: The Montacute Toy Museum. The prospect of spending the night with Muffin the Mule and Lady Penelope was too much to resist when I spotted it on the internet while looking for accommodation in the area. The museum has two bedrooms on its top floor to supplement its income, but, being late in the season, the curator has gone home for the day and it is arranged that I should ring her 30 minutes before our arrival so she can return to open up.

The battle over the last few miles through the rush-hour traffic is not fun and it is a relief when we swing off the A37 onto a side road to the village of Montacute, with its pretty film-set of a High Street and grand country mansion. As we face one final fairly gentle incline into the village, Jack lets out an agonised groan and several expletives. It is a hill too far for him and he gets off and sits on a bench by a bus stop. I fear he is going no further, but after a few minutes and a Kit-Kat, he re-mounts and we make our way to the museum, which does not disappoint.

It is full of comic book characters that I envisage come to life when human backs are turned, much as they do in the wonderful film *Toy Story*. Can you imagine Batman trying to get to grips with Dennis the Menace? Barbie brawling with Cat Woman over the attentions of Desperate Dan? When we fall asleep upstairs, who knows what fun is going on in Cabinet Two. Falling asleep upstairs, however, is to present a major problem for one of our group.

Toddy's tooth is playing up to such an extent that he feels he needs expert advice. Our destination the next day is Bristol, so he rings a journalist colleague who lives near the city to see if he can fix him up with a dentist. The friend knows someone and the appointment is made. Toddy is now in need of some anaesthetic from the local hostelry where Gus has found a room for the night and where they are showing live Champions League Football on TV.

The pub is doing a thriving business because of the football, which is a shame as the lone barman seems totally incapable of dealing with more than one order at a time. He is perfectly charming, but was never cut out to be on the business side of a bar. An order for three pints of bitter, a Guinness, a lager-shandy and a pint of coke reduces him to a quivering wreck and he has to write it all down before he can start pouring and pulling. We go in search of another member of staff to place our food order – and suggest to Gus that he ought to get his breakfast order in as soon as possible if he wants it ready in the morning.

A quick check around our recorded mileages over supper suggests we have done 65 miles today, just two more than the estimated 63. Faith in my piece of string is restored, for the time being at least, and there is growing enthusiasm that we can conquer the world. So tomorrow's trip to Taunton and Bristol should not be a problem!

There is an added cause for a celebratory nightcap before we depart the pub. David has hurried outside to take a call on his mobile phone during the meal and he returns with a look on his face that is a mixture of pleasure, shock and squeamish uncertainty. "The waters have broken!" he informs us. Six males look at one another as the goals are being re-played on the television. "Is that good?" asks David seeking reassurance.

David is the father of two lovely girls but his involvement in his wife Margaret's pregnancies subsided somewhat after his initial contribution. Medical matters and David do not mix. The sight of a Band-Aid makes him go weak at the knees. As for anything to do with the mysterious workings of the female body, he does not really want to know, so his shock at being told "the waters have broken" was understandable – and not helped by Gus and me humming the theme tune from *The Dam Busters*.

Krissy, his elder daughter, had been pregnant for some time (about nine months to be more precise) and we pat David on the back and assure him this dramatic sounding event is quite normal and nothing to panic about. Still, it is a good enough reason to calm our nerves with a round or two of whisky. His first grandchild is on the way and David needs a good night's sleep. Both he and Krissy have a tough few days ahead.

Back in our museum, the toys, no doubt having heard the key in the door, have halted their revelry, returned to their normal places and adopted their frozen poses again. We are billeted at the top of a three-storey house in two attic rooms containing three beds each. The Bateman family are in one cramped room, the rest in the other.

The effects of the red wine are beginning to wear off and Toddy's tooth is in rebellion. Sleep is not coming easily to our most senior rider but something else is causing him grief: Alan's snoring, fuelled by two pints of best, a hearty lasagne and a bucketful of red wine.

Come a rainy dawn over Montacute, only five of the six beds in those attic rooms will be occupied.

Day Four route: *Romsey, A27 to Whiteparish. A36 to Whaddon, minor roads to Salisbury. A338/A3094 past Salisbury Golf Club to A30 for Wilton, Ansty, Ludwell, Shaftsbury, East Stour, Milborne Port, Sherborne, Yeovil. A37/A3088 then minor roads to Montacute.*

String Distance: 63 miles.
Actual Distance: 65 miles.
Time in saddle: 5hrs 21mins
Average Speed: 12.1 mph

Overall string estimate: 248 miles.
Actual mileage to-date: 282.
Total cycling time: 23hrs 09 mins.
Average speed 12.2mph.

CHAPTER SIX

The Cider Classic

....Montacute to Bristol

Guest Rider: Angus

FEW of us look our best when we first wake up, but nothing could have prepared me for the sight of Toddy this morning in the Montacute Toy Museum. It was relatively early and my sons, Tom and Jack, were still deep in slumber, which was something of a blessing. They are too young and innocent for such a shock at such an hour.

The rain was pattering on the Velux window in the sloping roof over my bed when I awoke. Perhaps that was what had stirred me. The disappointment I felt at the first sight of rain on our venture was soon to be replaced with alarm as I crept out on to the landing between our two bedrooms to retrieve my mobile phone and charger, which had been plugged in just outside the bedroom door. There, sprawled on a long wooden ledge was a prostrate Toddy. His naked body was half covered in a quilt as he snored gently, his head swathed in his paisley boxer shorts, the material going in, out...in, out, with his breathing. A tuft of unruly hair stuck out of one of the boxer's leg holes. An arm dangled loosely towards the floor.

The shocking sight made me drop my phone, and I may have uttered a small squeal too. Certainly something disturbed those in the other bedroom and David opened the door with a look of concern on his face. Alan, peering over his shoulder and blinking as he put on his glasses, said: "Toddy's gone! His bed is empty!" He sounded alarmed, aware that Ian had taken a couple of pain-killers for his toothache on top of the whisky nightcaps just before settling down. I nodded in Ian's direction. David and Alan's gaze followed the direction of my nod and settled, transfixed on the unworldly sight.

We gently roused Toddy, who proceeded to explain the reason for his change in sleeping arrangements during the night – much to Alan's growing consternation. Alan's snoring in such a confined area had bounced off the walls and sloping ceiling of the converted loft, causing a deep throbbing in Toddy's head far worse than the offending molar. His nudges and requests had failed to disturb Alan's blissful, sonorous sleep, and, in desperation, Toddy had retreated to the landing clutching his quilt and a pillow, the bedroom door clicking locked behind him. Alan's snores, however, managed to reverberate through the door, so Toddy had removed his boxer shorts and wrapped them around his head in a bid to muffle the decibels. The story is related over breakfast downstairs among the exhibits, and I swear Paddington Bear and My Little Pony are weeping tears of laughter by the time Ian had finished his toast.

Breakfast over and the rain has stopped. Someone is smiling upon us again. The bikes, parked in the back yard, are wet, as are the roads, of course, but the sun is beginning to break through again as we amble the few hundred yards to meet Angus Fraser outside his hotel, where the 'Tale of the Empty Bed' has to be recounted again before we head off for the long ride to Taunton and Bristol. This is home turf for me, it being the area where I grew up and cut my teeth as a cub reporter on local newspapers. It is also where Alan, my nephew, spent his latter school years, so we are both looking forward to something of a trip down memory lane. There is still no news on the baby front, David getting regular and reassuring up-dates from his wife Margaret, who is with their daughter in the maternity unit.

The first part of our day takes us along single track lanes meandering through farmland, where the only danger is presented by the occasional cow-pat and farm dog running alongside us yelping with excitement at this unexpected activity on his patch. Road signs are in short supply, but we make it to Ilminster in good time before joining the main A358, which will take us to Taunton, the home of Somerset County Cricket Club, the team I supported as a lad with their array of exciting players such as Viv Richards, Ian Botham, Joel Garner, Vic Marks and Pete 'Dasher' Denning.

Richards, 'Sir Vivian' as he now is, was a fabulously gifted batsman. The Master Blaster became his sobriquet. In his pomp, he was without doubt the best batsman in the world, capable of destroying any bowling attack. He was also an immensely proud West Indian who expected respect. The most frequently told anecdote about Sir Viv involves a Glamorgan bowler named Greg Thomas, who could bowl very quickly and, for a short while, represented England.

This story, however, relates to a county match at Taunton, a small ground in the town centre hemmed in by churches, the farmers' market and the River Tone. Thomas was out to get the prized scalp of Richards and was bowling extremely quickly and well. The first ball of an over beat Richards' bat and went through to the wicketkeeper. "It's round and red and you are meant to hit it, boyo," said Welshman Thomas to Richards in the age-old fashion of a bowler trying to wind-up an opposing batsman. Richards the Antiguan remained silent.

The same thing happened with the next delivery, and Thomas repeated his baiting of Richards, who glared back, but said nothing. The next delivery was even quicker, but Richards swung his mighty bat and sent the ball back over Thomas' head, over the stand and into the river. Richards took a step down the pitch, tapped the ground, looked up at Thomas and growled: "You know what it looks like, man, you go and find it."

The Taunton County Ground has undergone vast changes since Richards' day. Somerset has also become the home of the England women's team, and, to keep abreast of the requirements of international cricket, new stands and pavilion have been built, and the size of the playing area increased. To do this, the club had to purchase part of the adjoining St James' Churchyard and exhume human remains buried there hundreds of years previously as part of what must be one of the most macabre sporting developments in the country.

The roads are wet so we are clearly following the rain, but so far only a few drops have fallen on us as we make the long steady haul along the main road that links Ilminster and Taunton. Our progress is sedate, perhaps because we are aware that Gus, our guest rider, is struggling to get his muscles moving again today. There is little chatter this morning. We are concentrating on getting a good first leg of about 25 miles behind us before we make our first stop, and as we pass under the M5 and into Taunton, we are grateful to see the familiar brown road signs showing three stumps and a ball that point the direction to the cricket ground. We dutifully line up with our bikes outside the wrought iron 'Sir Vivian Richards Gates' which grace the main entrance to the Somerset County Ground for our group photographs. Gus is looking as weary as if he had just bowled a 10-over spell into the wind against the Master Blaster in full cry. "Sorry guys, I am going to have to bail out here," he tells us looking a little rueful. "I don't think I can make it to Bristol. Total respect for what you are doing."

Instead of leaving us at Bristol, about another 30 miles away, Gus plans to get the train from Taunton back to Romsey, an idea that had clearly become increasingly appealing during the morning's hard slog. But first he insists on farewell coffee-and-cakes in a town centre café. We consider the Castle Hotel, made famous by the award-winning chef Gary Rhodes, but instead find a bakery and snack bar that is much more appropriate for seven cyclists in need of sausage rolls and jam doughnuts.

The route to Bristol is a simple one, following the A38 all the way. Being the main route to Birmingham and the north, this was once a busy trunk road, but the arrival of the M5 has left it to the use of local traffic. A few miles outside Taunton we start to cross the Somerset Levels, a wonderfully evocative area of low-lying pasture-land drained by a criss-cross of ditches known locally as rhines. This area with its curiously named villages – Middlezoy, Chedzoy, Westonzoyland, Bawdrip, Burtle, Moorlinch – can take on a sinister feel when the mists settle over the watery flats. Walk into a quiet village shop out here and you might feel like an extra from the League of Gentlemen.

The roads have no kerbs, white lines, cats eyes or lighting, and at night the rhines, with their still, dark water and reeds, await any careless driver who is trying to find a back way home after a cider too many. I know because I travelled these hazardous lanes many times in my youth, driving my three-wheel red Isetta bubble-car slipping home from a late-night rendezvous with sixth-form colleagues from Sexey's Grammar School near Wedmore. The school's name, by the way, came from its founder Hugh Sexey and had nothing to do with what went on in the changing rooms after mixed swimming lessons.

The area is known as King's Sedge Moor and it was here that the last pitched battle was fought on British soil in 1685. This was the final skirmish of the Monmouth Rebellion, and the rhines are said to have run red with the blood of the rebel army of James Scott, the 1st Duke of Monmouth. He wanted the throne from James II, who had succeeded his brother Charles II. James Scott was the illegitimate son of Charles II and believed the crown should be on his head. For his troubles, that head was to be separated from the rest of his body in the Tower of London.

Monmouth's 'pitchfork army' of farm-hands, artisans and general rebel-rousers, was under-manned and ill-equipped, and no match for the forces of the crown. They were put to flight in a battle at Westonzoyland, and those who did not perish on the Somerset Levels ended up in front of Judge

Jeffreys (aka 'The Hanging Judge') at the 'Bloody Assizes' at Taunton Castle. There was no community service and suspended sentences in those days. Back then, justice was more unsympathetic. Most of the 1,300 brought up in front of the Judge were either hung, drawn and quartered or, if he was in a good mood, transported to Australia.

One rebel who did escape lightly was Daniel Defoe, who had joined the up-rising. Defoe lost much of his land and wealth, but was given a pardon and survived to write one of the world's most enduring tales, Robinson Crusoe.

The Battle of Sedgemoor is an important part of England's history, but one that most holiday-makers on their way to and from the West Country pass in oblivion as they hurry by on the M5. Only if they stop at the Sedgemoor Motorway Services might they give it a moment's thought, as there on the wall is a mural commemorating the bloodshed on the nearby fields.

The Somerset Levels, while not good for rebellions, are fine for cycling apart from the terrible pot-holed surface of the A38, which appears to have been totally neglected by the local municipal authorities.

We make steady progress through North Petherton to Bridgwater, headquarters of the spectacular Guy Fawkes Carnival Processions that take over the towns of Somerset every winter. The floats, pulled behind lorries or tractors, are prepared by dozens of carnival clubs that plan in secret all year for the night-time parades. They produce tableaux that depict scenes from history or modern culture, usually accompanied by pulsating music and flashing lights. It is the highlight of the year for many and huge news for the local media.

As a young reporter on the Mid-Somerset Series of Newspapers based in Wells, I covered dozens of these events, which were often surrounded by stories of sabotage and subterfuge. The carnival clubs would go to great lengths to keep their plans for the forthcoming parade secret. The floats would be devised and built behind locked barn doors months in advance. Spying raids were made on these barns by other clubs. On the afternoon before the night of the parades, the floats would be lined up on a side road ready for the procession, and they were heavily guarded. It had been known for the generators, towed behind the floats to provide the electricity required, to be vandalised or have sugar poured into fuel tanks so they would not work. Tyres were punctured, fists even thrown in the battle for carnival honours.

Being my patch, I inform my fellow travellers that my instincts say that we should get as far as Churchill, just the other side of the Mendip Hills, before stopping for lunch. So much for local knowledge. As we approach Brent Knoll, a pimple on the Somerset Levels a few miles north of Bridgwater, we decide we badly needed another stop, and pull into a pub for more copious quantities of food and drink.

Back on the long, flat straight stretches of the A38 heading north, we pass Cross, a hamlet that had always held intrigue for me when I was a keen young journalist on the local weekly newspaper after a scoop. The most famous resident of Cross at the time was Frankie Howerd OBE, a gifted, but very secretive, comedy actor, who had appeared in the 'Carry On' films, a long-running TV hit 'Up Pompeii' and an impressive catalogue of other film and show appearances. Howerd's secrecy was born out of his homosexuality (illegal in the UK until 1967), which most people in 'the business' knew about, but which was not public knowledge. In Howerd's heyday in the 1960s, 70s and 80s, such a revelation could have ruined his career. Titter ye not, but today camping it up is almost a plus.

We also cycle within a few miles of Cheddar, where I spent most of my childhood and where my nephew Alan lived for the last few years of his schooldays. The A38 here, being the main link to Bristol, is very familiar to both of us and we are aware that the relative comfort of the Somerset Levels is about to end. Ahead of us are some tough climbs. The first long ascent is up Axbridge Hill and across the western end of the Mendip Hills. This, I inform the others, once again using my intimate local knowledge, will be the toughest ascent of the day. Wrong again.

At the top of the climb is a turn off for Shipham, where I used to grace the village football field playing in goal for the Butcher's Arms, who were members of the prestigious Cheddar Valley Sunday League Division Three (our worst defeat was 16-0). From the top of every climb there is a rewarding descent for the cyclist, and we swoop down into Churchill, our group now strung out along the A38, Axbridge Hill having found some of us out. Jack and I are seriously lagging behind, with Toddy, nursing his throbbing abscess, not far ahead. The other three are not to be seen, but as the route is straightforward all the way to Bristol, this is not a problem.

What is a problem is Redhill, a relentless climb up to Bristol International Airport. I had passed up this hill hundreds of times before in my younger days en-route to

Bristol, but not until I attempted it on two wheels did I realise just how tough an ascent it was. The road tilts up, climbs steadily and then grows steeper near its summit. It is too much for Jack and me in one haul. We have to pull into a petrol station for a breather, water and jelly babies before setting off again. Talking of babies, David has checked in again and there is still no news on the grandchild front.

There are different methods for climbing hills, but most of us have a preferred one. Counting is favoured by David, our cycling enthusiast. He will look at the climb ahead and, depending on how far it stretches, will give himself a number to count to, usually 100, 200 or 300. Then he will put his head down, look at the road just ahead of the front wheel and count each turn of the pedals. The theory is that you concentrate on the counting and not the pain. I prefer little chants in rhythm with each turn of the pedal in stanzas of four: 'I-will-not-stop, I-must-not-stop, I will-not-stop'. Jack tells me his chosen method is to visualise the glistening glass of lager on the bar at the end of a hard day's graft. Alan, no doubt, visualises duck confit served with orange jus and steamed seasonal vegetables. My eldest son Tom sees himself breasting the line in the polka-dot jersey of the King of the Mountains in the Tour de France, while, at present, Toddy has his mind's eye on that dentist's chair and imminent relief. Each to their own, as long as it gets you to the top and the lovely sight of the road ahead tilting downwards again.

As usual, the others are waiting on the grassy verge at the brow of the hill, chatting and refreshed by their stop as Jack and I gasp up the last few yards. We are back together as a group of six and push on past the airport at Lulsgate

Bottom. Perched 600ft up on a plateau, it is a curious place for an airport, being shrouded, as it so often is, in low cloud which can make landing impossible. Even the military, during the Second World War, found it hazardous to use, but a new runway was laid in 1941 because of the strategic position close to Bristol and Atlantic Ocean. Curiously, the first plane to use the military runway belonged to the Luftwaffe, the German navigator being thrown off course by the RAF's radio signalling counter-measures sent out to confuse the enemy. He thought he was bringing the plane down at Brest on the German-occupied French west coast. Instead Fritz was in farmer-occupied Somerset, where the cider apples grow.

Bristol is now under 10 miles away and bringing the end of the day's ride down to single figures in terms of mileage is always a great boost to the spirit, particularly on tough days like this. The rolling hills of north Somerset are not to be underestimated. Each climb is, of course, followed by a descent but then, instead of some respite on the flat, we soon find ourselves climbing again. After freewheeling down from the airport, we face another struggle up the side of Dundry Hill and again Jack and I are losing touch with David and Tom at the front. We manage to make up ground on the long, sweeping downhill section to Barrow Gurney, where the A38 separates two reservoirs, whose banks rise high above the road that takes us on the Bedminster Down with its vista across Bristol.

It has been a hard day on poor cycling roads and over demanding terrain. Toddy has done exceptionally well to battle through despite the pain he is in and his lack of sleep last night. Normally so chatty, he has kept his thoughts to himself for most of the day. Pain-killers may have helped, but the prospect of the visit to the dentist this evening must have been hanging over him. Tom has had a few problems of his own, but his have been of a mechanical kind. The right hand pedal on his bike keeps working lose and instead of simply rotating as he cycles, comes off the shaft every now and then. With David's help, he manages temporary running repairs, but it is something we are going to have to keep an eye on. Losing a pedal at 30mph on a descent is not to be advised.

David has again been our strongest rider. The miles he puts in every week riding for pleasure near his home in Hampshire are paying dividends as he copes relatively easily with the climbs, passing us all on the way up the long hills even if he has dropped to the back of the field on the flat to give the slow ones among us some encouragement. Carrying less middle-aged weight than the rest of us helps David, but he is also the best rider of the *peloton*. Alan, to his credit on his faithful old Peugeot with its lack of gears, is usually not far behind, pounding out his steady rhythm. Tom is strong and growing stronger, while Jack and I keep going at our own sweet pace gaining in confidence daily that we will finish.

It seems ages ago that we said goodbye to Gus. It was ages ago. The lucky so-and-so has probably been re-united with his car in Romsey by now. Still, we have the delights of Bristol to look forward too. It is, for me, the best city in Britain.

It is the place where I spread my wings as a fully indentured journalist in the late 1970s. Armed with my National Council for the Training of Journalists certificate after four years on the weekly papers based in Wells, I headed for the big time in Bristol and the much-respected regional daily newspaper, The Western Daily Press. At the time, the WDP was flourishing under the editorship of Eric Price, who had become something of a legend in the world of provincial newspapers.

He had arrived in Bristol from the Daily Express, which had been the best selling newspaper in the land. He re-modelled the ailing WDP on Beaverbrook's Express, and sales rose steadily to 60,000-plus. Eric ruled the editorial floor like a tyrannical newspaperman from a Hollywood film, wearing trademark braces and arm-bands to hold up his shirt-sleeves. He had a mischievous smile and an unpredictable volcanic temper.

He was reputed to have hurled typewriters out of second storey windows of the WDP's old offices in the city centre if unhappy with the copy of an unfortunate hack. It was said he once tore up the story offered by one journalist, throwing the bits of paper to the wind out of the same windows. A few minutes later, the Telex machine clattered into action, the news agencies confirming the tale Eric had just rubbished. Unabashed, he despatched the junior staff to the streets below to collect the pieces of paper so they could be Sellotaped back together.

By the time I joined the staff, the paper had moved to its new premises on Temple Way where, fortunately, air-conditioning was installed and the windows did not open. The building was hailed as the most modern newspaper office and print-works in Europe and, as such, attracted escorted tours, with the guide being a former Miss Bristol.

One evening, with the production in full flow on the

editorial floor, we had a VIP visitor: Margaret Thatcher, the leader of the Conservative Party, who was widely tipped to win the next General Election and become the UK's first female Prime Minister. Eric, a true-blue Tory, was an admirer, and determined to put on a show. When Mrs Thatcher and her entourage appeared around a far corner of the open-plan office, Eric launched into a theatrical rage, throwing copy back at startled sub-editors, tearing up the efforts of the page-design man and shouting abuse at any reporter who dared to lift his head above his desk-top.

Thatcher was no doubt duly impressed, and came over for what appeared a jovial chat with Eric, whom she could count on to back her to the hilt in his editorials come election time. As soon as she disappeared for the next stage of her tour, Eric subsided into smiles and kind words for everyone.

He was a joy to work for, to be honest, although the few female members of staff may not have agreed. Eric was of the old school, believing that the only place for females on a newspaper was the women's page or as a copy-typist, writing down what the reporters dictated over the telephone. Few women made it as far as Eric's sub-editing team that sat around the big wooden table, with him in the central position on one side, but one who did was the tenacious and buxom Barbara. When Eric grew bored, he would aim paper-clips across the desk hoping to land them in her ample cleavage to spark an indignant reaction. In those days PC stood for Police Constable or Public Convenience. Political Correctness was not in Eric's dictionary.

The Bristol based papers produced a string of journalists

and broadcasters who went on to work in the national media but perhaps the most famous old boy of the WDP is playwright Tom Stoppard.

Bristol's chequered history is centred around the docks, which have these days either been turned into tourist attractions or swish waterfront homes and eateries. Bristol was at the heart of the slave trade in the 18th century with manufactured goods being taken from Bristol to Africa, where the empty ships were loaded with captured slaves who were taken in appalling conditions to the Americas to work. When they were unloaded, they were replaced by sugar, tobacco, rum, rice and cotton to be brought back to Britain. And so the trade went on, bringing great wealth to Britain – and Bristol. It is estimated that during this triangle of trade, 500,000 slaves were taken from Africa by ships from Bristol. No-one is proud of this part of the city's history but equally no-one wants to air-brush it from its heritage. The names of two of the major roads in Bristol still bear testimony to those days: White Ladies Road and Black Boys Hill.

When I was in my last year at school and before I had decided to venture into a career in journalism, I wrote to Bristol's famous Old Vic Theatre School asking for careers advice. I had never shone in my few forays into school drama but there was something about the stage that I found entrancing. I thought there must be plenty of jobs back stage that I could do. The Bristol Old Vic had helped many fine actors learn their craft including Peter O'Toole, Gene Wilder, Patrick Stewart, Daniel Day-Lewis, Jeremy Irons and Pete Postlethwaite. Why not me? I never received a reply and that career path exited stage left.

Bristol's most celebrated thespian must be Cary Grant, whose statue adorns the city centre near our hotel tonight. Born Archibald Leach, at the age of 16 in 1920 he ran away, not quite with a circus, but with a stage troupe, as a stilt walker. The troupe went on a tour of America, and Archie liked the place so much he stayed, changing his name and finding fame in Hollywood as a debonair leading man with a unique easy-going charm that led to him being named the second 'Greatest Male Star of All Time' by the American Film Institute. Humphrey Bogart pipped him for first place in the list.

Long before my time, fellow-cyclist Toddy had also worked on the Bristol papers and claims to have given a young Tom Stoppard a helping hand. Whether he also knew Cary Grant, he would not confirm. He does, though, know Bristol, and as we head into Bedminster, he decides to take his own route to our hotel via a place very close to my heart: Ashton Gate, the home of Bristol City Football Club. The rest follow me through Bedminster's pedestrianised area and past the old WD & HO Wills tobacco factory to the quayside and then on to our plush overnight accommodation, the Hotel du Vin. We just pip Toddy to it.

We are dead beat and as the Gloucestershire County Ground is another couple of up-hill miles away on the route we will have to take in the morning, we abandon plans to go there this evening, deciding to start a little earlier tomorrow and call in on our way to Cardiff.

The staff and other clientele in the chic reception area of the 'du Vin' are somewhat taken aback as the six of us stagger in, weary and sweaty in gear that has not seen a washing machine for five days. This is a place where the cheapest room is £175 per night and they are not used to guests turning up on bikes with their luggage in an assortment of plastic bags. The rooms are all purples and browns, with sumptuous quilts and flat screen televisions, and the bathrooms are kitted out with complimentary organic toiletries and a 'monsoon' shower that is worth the £175 alone.

The hotel website reads: 'Located close to the rejuvenated waterfront in Bristol, this unique luxury boutique hotel has 40 bedrooms, including several stunning double-height loft suites.'

Valet parking is available too, but oddly, there is no mention of a bike-rack.

To the surprise of the staff, a check on the screen at reception does, indeed, confirm we have three rooms booked and paid for in advance by the England and Wales Cricket Board (Note to diary: no more knocking pieces about the 'buffoons in blazers' running the English game').

The rooms have unfathomable names rather than numbers, which makes finding them in this converted 17th century warehouse with its maze of corridors impossible. When we do finally stumble into our twin-bedded boudoir, Alan, my room companion tonight, explains that the bedrooms are named after famous vintners or the such-like. As pleasant as a glass of Chateauneuf-du-Pape, Chateau Rayas (the 1995, of course) might be, a pint of lager-shandy is more the order of the day.

We are in and our bikes are safely parked in what will no doubt be their best accommodation of the whole trip: a vast garage with heavy oak doors, exposed timber beams and a vaulted ceiling. But no monsoon shower, alas.

Toddy is soon picked up by Scyld, (pronounced shield) our newspaper colleague who has fixed up his dental appointment. When he returns, minus tooth and abscess, we pile into a nearby bar at the bottom of Christmas Steps to meet Alan's sister (my niece, if you are paying attention) and her husband.

The debate soon gets around to Bristol's most famous citizen. Having gone through the entire Bristol City squad, we move on to Isambard Kingdom Brunel, Cary Grant, Tony Benn, John Wesley (of Methodist Chapel fame) Johnny Morris (Animal Magic), William Wordsworth and the Green Cross code man David Prowse. Without doubt, though, we settle upon John Cleese of Monty Python and Fawlty Towers fame, who was born in Weston-super-Mare and went to Clifton College in the fashionable part of Bristol.

Cleese is Brisol's most celebrated citizen.

No he's not.

Yes, he must be.

No, 'fraid not.

Yes, yes, yes.

No, never.

Is this a five-minute argument or a ten-minute argument?

We are also in disagreement about dinner. Toddy understandably does not feel like eating anything that cannot be sucked through a straw, David fancies a Chinese, the boys and I want Indian. As there is more European football on television tonight, we opt for takeaways, which must have been another first in the Hotel du Vin, where the restaurant 'offers a menu rooted in classic European cuisine with a contemporary edge.' The thought of a takeaway quite appals Alan so he decides to stay in the pub having spotted 'Goat Curry' on the 'Today's Specials' blackboard.

While Toddy was losing a tooth, news came through that David was gaining a grandson. Jacob had come into this world a healthy, bouncing, Oldham supporter. Mum and baby were doing fine, and so was Grandad. Never one to be slow to stand his round, David had even more cause to get them in tonight.

Quite why, I was not so sure, but we were all feeling rather pleased with ourselves by the time we got to bed. But one of our number was not going to make it on to his bike in the morning.

Day Five Route: *Montacute, minor roads through Stoke-sub-Hamdon, Seavington St Michael and Whitelackington to Ilminster. A358 to Taunton. A38 to Bridgwater, Highbridge, Churchill, Lulsgate Bottom, Barrow Gurney, Bedminster and Bristol.*

String Distance: 62 miles
Actual Distance: 68 miles
Time in Saddle: 5hrs 44mins
Average Speed: 11.8 mph.

Overall string estimate: 310 miles.
Actual mileage to-date: 350.
Total cycling time: 28hrs 53mins.
Average Speed: 12.1 mph.

STRINGING PEOPLE ALONG...
By Ian Todd

Whatever the answer to the question: "How long is a piece of string?" I know only that if it's Colin's piece of string it's as long as you like – plus 10 per cent at the very least. I mean, of course, the piece of string he gets out of his pocket before these epic rides we've undertaken and, with the help of his Ordnance Survey maps, claims to measure the distance of each leg of our rides with, in his own words, "a fair degree of accuracy."

Now, you can fool your fellow riders some of the time, but not all of the time, and I knew all about Colin's measuring from what bikers call the End-to-End ride from John O' Groats to Land's End a few years earlier. Thus, when we gathered at The Oval that first sunny September morn for a gentle opening run down the Old Kent Road to Canterbury, I mused: "I wonder exactly where we will be when Colin's guesstimate of 55 miles to the St Lawrence ground are up."

To be fair, I don't remember exactly. It could have been when we were lost in the middle of an industrial estate on a bit of deviation from our navigator's plotted route. Or it could have been the point a few miles outside Canterbury where Toff (David) and Alan were on hands and knees and generally grubbing around mending my first puncture. I don't do punctures or even pumping tyres. A septuagenarian has to have his perks, and Toff's my man. Anyway, what I do remember is that after 55 miles, the sight of Canterbury Cathedral and the gentle sound of leather on willow at the county ground were still a good hour away.

Every rider has his little crises on these rides, most of which the others never know about. On a previous trip through France, a heavy cold went to my chest and I was almost forced to give up half way through. On this ride, Colin's middle son Jack didn't realise what he'd let himself in for until he got his cycling legs and went from strength to strength. Alan had a dodgy couple of days with a troublesome knee, and Colin had a low when we were in the Midlands.

My problem this time was a tooth that had been nothing but trouble for years. Infuriatingly, the pain flared up on only our fourth day soon after we left Romsey as I tucked into the slipstream of the ample Gus Fraser, who was joining us for a couple of days on what looked like a 12-year-old's mountain bike. The sight of a truly big man like Gus pedalling away furiously on a machine that was never made to measure would have been funnier if it hadn't been for the pain in my mouth and the worry of what to do about it.

It was no surprise that Gus's saddle collapsed after a few miles only to be repaired in next to no time by a friendly agricultural engineer. But the aching tooth was not so easy to resolve, and it wasn't the only problem as I tried to sleep that night at the pretty village of Montacute in a room for three with Alan and Toff.

I realised I was lucky that on two previous rides I had never before roomed with Alan because he could snore for Britain. I had to leave around midnight, but even as I lay on the landing with my underpants around my head to try to keep out the glare of a light I couldn't turn off, the throbbing in my head was matched by the throbbing from the bedroom. Toff swore he slept through it. Little liar!

What to do after a night without sleep and toothache still raging? The answer was to ring Scyld Berry, amiable Editor of the Wisden Cricket Almanack and cricket correspondent of the

Sunday Telegraph, who is based near Bristol, our next port of call. "Do all I can, old man," said Scyld. And he did.

We bade farewell to Gus at Taunton and pedalled furiously up the A38 to Bristol, where our man Berry had accomplished Mission Impossible – a 7pm appointment with a local dentist operating out of a trading estate. By 7.30 I was minus a molar and 80 quid, and by 8pm I was eating a pappy Chinese takeaway. Who says you can't get things done in a hurry these days?

The dentist's advice was for me to take things easily the next day. I did exactly that, while the others suffered. As they took in the Nevil Road ground at Bristol and then cycled over the Severn Bridge to Cardiff before completing one of the longest days at Monmouth, I did a little cheat: I took the train to Newport, then cycled leisurely a mere 35 miles on a glorious late summer's day compared to their 84. I even had time to chat to a farmer taking a break in his harvest field, and I was greeted in late afternoon by Matthew Engel, his wife and daughter. Then, as I sipped a cool shandy, I did a cheeky interview with the local paper, giving the reporter unashamed tosh about what a slog it all was for a guy in his seventies but happy to do it for a worthwhile cause. When the others arrived in the gloaming a couple of hours later and well and truly knackered I didn't even feel guilty.

They say these things are a test of character – and that's mine.

CHAPTER SEVEN

Border Patrol

...Bristol to Monmouth

Guest Rider: Jamo

Today is one I am not looking forward to. It threatens to be the longest of the entire ride for one thing. For another, it involves a lot of urban cycling. It is also principally in the Principality of Wales – and all of the problems that entails, more of which, later. It will also be hilly. But above all, it involves us doubling back on ourselves as we have to cycle from Newport to Cardiff and back to Newport again before heading northwards up into the hills and towards the Midlands. Cycling along roads you know you are going to see again in a couple of hours is psychologically draining so we will have to fall back on that often recited phrase: "When the going gets Taff, the tough get going."

We are also without Toddy, whose dentist has advised him not get back on the bike this morning fearing he would feel weak and groggy after the previous evening's treatment. Ian sensibly decides to catch the train from Bristol Temple Meads to Newport (lucky blighter) and take his time during the afternoon to cycle a gentle 20-30 miles to Monmouth and our overnight stop.

Breakfast in the Hotel du Vin lives up to its reputation and is spectacularly good, particularly the Scottish smoked salmon and scrambled eggs on a toasted English muffin. Unfortunately, it is downhill from there for the rest of the day, metaphorically speaking, of course. From the very start, our bikes are pointing upwards as we climb from the ever-changing city centre of Bristol along the Gloucester Road, which is a bustling narrow thoroughfare crammed on each side with small shops that attract swarms of vans and shoppers. It leads us to the Nevil Ground, home of Gloucestershire County Cricket Club and our first stop on a misty morning.

Gloucestershire are hardly one of the power-houses of English cricket. In fact, they have never won the domestic game's major title, the County Championship, but they have produced the country's most famous cricketer: Dr. William Gilbert Grace, aka W.G. Grace. The good doctor was born little more than a six-hit away from Nevil Road in Downend in 1848 and bestrode the game like no-one before him or since.

In his book 'The Top 100 Cricketers of All Time,' Christopher Martin-Jenkins, one of the most respected commentators on the game, writes: 'Whether WG was the greatest cricketer ever to buckle a pair of pads I have taken impertinent leave to doubt. That he was the most famous there has ever been is not, of course, in question. He remains the embodiment of cricket.' Martin-Jenkins placed Grace second in his top 100 of world greats behind only Sir Don Bradman, the legendary Australian batsman.

WG was a large man with an even larger beard. He was an all-round athlete and an all-round cricketer in every sense, particularly in his latter years as his girth spread. He broke all sorts of batting records and was, after Queen Victoria, the most recognisable face in the Kingdom for many years. His deeds are commemorated with a plaque at the entrance to Gloucestershire's ground, by which we dutifully pose for photographs before setting off to leave the country.

Passports and visas checked, we are bound for Wales via the Old Severn Bridge which, despite carrying a motorway, also allows cyclists and pedestrians to cross the mile-wide expanse of the muddy River Severn, avoiding a 60-mile detour to the next bridgehead at Gloucester. A vehicle ferry used to cross the Severn here from Aust to Beachley but the strong tides and treacherous mud-banks made it an unreliable service and a real bottle-neck for motorists. The ferry closed the day before the first Severn Bridge opened in 1966, and the wreck of the old ferry now rests nearby in the mud of the River Wye under a railway bridge near Chepstow. The ferry has been granted immortality, however, by the folk singer Bob Dylan, who is pictured standing in front of it with the Severn Bridge under construction in the background, on the album cover of the soundtrack for the Martin Scorsese film 'No Direction Home'. Not a lot of people know that.

Bristol is still very busy even though the rush-hour has passed and we stick closely together as we pass Filton Airport, where the super-sonic white elephant Concorde was developed, and then pass under the M5 on the A38 where a sharp left takes us down a steep escarpment on minor roads through Lower Almondsbury and across the flat fields that were once the flood plain of the River Severn, the longest river in the UK, rising as it does 220 miles away in the Cambrian Mountains of mid-Wales. Quiet roads, the sun on our backs, synchronised cycling through lovely countryside: this is what the trip is all about. The blue direction signs for the cycle route across this great river soon appear and take us through several back-gardens and on to the cycle and pedestrian track that clings on to the side of the bridge for dear life. We are running late for our agreed meeting time with today's guest rider, but we still have to stop for some rather spectacular photographs of us on the bridge.

The first Severn Bridge carried the M4 that stretched from London to Cardiff, but the volume of traffic and weight of lorries became a problem that its designers had not envisaged. Ever increasing repairs resulted in the bridge often being closed, causing major delays. The only solution was another bridge, and in 1996, the New Severn Crossing three miles downstream was opened. We, though, were quite content with the original, which still sways and bounces disconcertingly as you cross.

As we cycle over, we are on the look-out for our latest – and last – guest rider Steve James, who was rather vague about whether he would meet us on the English side or on the Welsh side. Steve is another former cricketer turned journalist, who has become a good colleague. Known to his new Press mates and former cricketing pals as Jamo (pronounced Jay-mo), he was born a few miles from the Severn Bridge in Lydney, which is in that curious bit of Gloucestershire that sneaks around the Welsh side of the

River Severn. Despite his Englishness, Jamo is an adopted Welshman having spent all his playing career with Glamorgan, the only Welsh county in the Championship. He was a doughty opening batsman who was hard to shift. He played twice for England in an era when England was blessed with good openers. He was also a fine rugby player, but dodgy knees eventually took their toll on his sporting life and he has swapped his bat for a pen, which he uses trenchantly on the Sunday Telegraph.

Jamo still remains fiercely fit but because his damaged knees prevent him running, he has taken up cycling and, unlike Angus Fraser, has the perfect machine for flying over the tarmac, which he does regularly every Sunday with his local cycle club.

We meet up after our cycle path has taken us across both the Severn and the Wye and on to *terra-firma* beside the main road to Chepstow. Jamo has already cycled about 20 miles from his parents' home without barely breaking sweat on his suitably fast-sounding 'Specialized Allez', and the six of us set off on the A48 towards Newport. Our guest is soon setting a hot pace and my eldest son Tom, much to my annoyance, is in racing mode today, with the competitive David hanging on to their coat-tails, unable to resist the pursuit. The inevitable happens and the tear-away trio miss the left turn for my meticulously planned route on a quieter B-road, which, as I may have mentioned before, they have in clear detail on the 'itinerary notes' handed out to each rider. If they cared to even look at it, that is. My directions, for all the good they were, might just as well have been written in Welsh, like most of the road signs we were now encountering.

Why does Wales insist on bi-lingual road signs? Can anyone explain? In the rest of the United Kingdom, even on the Isle of Wight, we get along fine with a standard set of signs that we are all expected to learn to pass our driving test. But in Wales, those bi-lingual signs become a road hazard in themselves as you approach them and frantically try to work out what is being said in the mass of English and Welsh instructions.

It has clearly even bemused the sign makers in Wales (many of whom do not understand Welsh themselves). One sign near Cardiff telling cyclists to dismount read: *"llid y bledren dymchwelyd"*. Translated into English, I am told that said: "bladder inflammation upset." Someone is taking the piss, surely?

Collecting madly, badly translated Welsh road signs has now become a hobby much like collecting Toby jugs and train-spotting, and there are dozens of internet sites dedicated to Welsh gobbledegook.

The most absurd has to be the bilingual sign that told drivers in English: 'No entry for heavy goods vehicles. Residential site only.'

Perfectly clear. But how about the Welsh?

'Nid wfy yn y swyddfa ar hyn o bryd. Anfonwch unrhyw waith i'w gyfieithu'

That may look like an anagram from The Times crossword but in fact it apparently translates into: 'I am not in the office at the moment. Send any works to be translated'.

The sign writers, not understanding a word of Welsh, had simply repeated the out-of-office email reply they had received from the council translation department and printed it on to the road sign.

There was no such excuse, though, for the racers up ahead to ignore the perfectly signposted – and shorter – route towards Newport through the villages of Caldicot, Magor and Langstone that Alan, Jack and I take. After a while, aware that we are not with them, the other three think they had better ring through. I tetchily inform them we might see them for coffee when our roads converge again, which they do just outside Newport, where we arrange to meet at a garden centre café for our first stop of the day.

The sensible three arrive at the garden centre and there is no sign of the other trio. Tetchiness starts to turn to anger, especially as Jack is getting a little panicky (a) about the safety of the others, (b) his hunger pangs, which are gnawing away and (c) his father stomping around blaming Tom, a theme that is to build up over the coming few days.

"We're here, where are you?" I say down the phone at Tom.

"We're here, where are YOU?" he replies.

"You are not here and neither is the bloody café. There is no café, just a tatty garden centre offering cut price horse manure and a new stock of gnomes," I say. "And anyway, none of this would have happened if you had stuck to the planned route instead of playing silly racing games. This is not a bloody Audax* event!"

"We ARE here," implores Tom, "And we are standing outside on the pavement so you can see us."

I look up and 200 yards or so along the road are three small figures by a big sign for 'PLANTS' plus the words

---

*An Audax is a cycle event in which the competitors have to finish between two set times.

'CAFÉ OPEN' blazing out in 10ft high red letters. I wonder if the café serves humble pie (*darostwng bastai*)?

Sustenance always revives the spirits, and as Jamo has offered to pay, the rock cakes and coffee at the garden centre café taste even better. It is time to check maps because although our A48 route to Newport looks simple enough, we know that getting around the town will not be easy and that the road signs will not be much help.

Newport (*Casnewydd*) thrived during the industrial revolution of the 19th century because of the coal dug out of the South Wales valleys, and for a while its docks were bigger than those at nearby Cardiff, or *Caerdydd*, if you prefer. Like all the towns and cities in the area, it has had to diversify in recent years with the demise of the coal industry. It has a neglected down-at-heel feel to it now, although the City Council, which works tirelessly to attract new business, would doubtless disagree.

Not my favourite place, Newport. I was first sent there in 1974 as part of my journalists' training course based at Cardiff College for Food, Technology and Commerce (now, inevitably, called a university) to cover a football match involving Newport County, then a League team. When I returned to my Austin mini parked nearby, the window had been smashed and radio stolen.

The good folk of Newport, being so close to the English border, are clearly troubled with their bi-lingual identity, too. It was here during one of those moral outrages that sweeps through the British public every now and then that a confused mob attacked the home of a doctor, having not come to grips with the difference between a paediatrician and a paedophile. They daubed the word "Paedo" across her front door.

Once we find it, the Newport Ring Road – *cana cerrynt* – is not a barrel of laughs either, and is even tougher when ridden in the knowledge that you will be back here again pretty soon battling with its roundabouts and traffic lights. But it has to be done so we get our heads down and churn out the miles towards Cardiff. It is flat, but that is all this part of the world has going for it despite Jamo continually extolling the virtues of Wales. Sorry, *Cymru*.

Jamo is so fast that I swear he is in danger of being caught on the speed cameras that are posted on every road in and out of Cardiff city centre. Tom is not far behind with David on Tom's back wheel catching the benefits of the slip-stream (an old pro's trick, that one). The result is that by the time we approach Cardiff Castle – *Castell Caerdydd* – we are hopelessly strung out again.

The Castle dominates the centre of the Welsh capital with its towering exterior wall. It is thought there have been various defensive forts, ramparts and keeps on the site for close to 2,000 years but the transformation into what visitors see today began in 1868 when the 3rd Marquess of Bute decided to construct a gothic fantasy-land that should go down as the first theme-park in the country. He commissioned the building of the Winter and Summer Smoking Rooms, the Chaucer Room, the Arab Room, Lord Bute's Bedroom, a wondrous clock tower and a Roof Garden. It was a sumptuous extravagance – which the Bute family sold to the City of Cardiff for £1 in 1947. Even given that £1 was worth considerably more in those days, it was still quite a bargain.

A few steps away beside the River Taff is the Millennium Stadium, an eye-catching monument to modern architecture where today's equivalent to the jousting knights from the castle do battle, kicking and throwing a ball about instead of ramming each other with long sticks. We are now almost at the home of Glamorgan Cricket (*Criced Morgannwg*) that was once charmingly called Sophia Gardens but now has the unprepossessing title of the Swalec Stadium (*Stadiwm Swalec*). Swalec might sound like an ancient Gaelic word for a battlefield but it is merely a humdrum acronym for the South Wales Electricity Company that has bought the naming rights to the redeveloped ground.

Cardiff's original wealth was produced by the coal industry. The port area at Tiger Bay became the busiest docks in the world and at the Coal Exchange in 1907, the first ever £1million deal was struck for the purchase of goods. Tiger Bay's other – and more enduring – export is the voluptuous Dame Shirley Bassey, one of the world's great cabaret performers and the only singer asked to sing two theme songs for James Bond films: Diamonds are Forever and Moonraker, neither of which were translated into Welsh.

The Welsh are renowned for their musical talents and Cardiff has produced a choir of famous entertainers from Ivor Novello to Shakin' Stevens, Charlotte Church to Catatonia and the Super Furry Animals, many of which still roam the streets at night down by the old docks.

Cardiff also witnessed one of the most unusual contests involving an England cricket captain or, to be more concise, a recently deposed England cricket captain. The dashing Ted Dexter goes down as one of the game's most colourful players. A delightful man with an aristocratic air (he was always known as Lord Ted although he was never elevated to the peerage), he once flew himself to France in the middle of a Test on a rest day to go to the races.

In 1964 he captained England to defeat in the Ashes series against Australia, lost the captaincy but was still selected for the winter cricket tour that followed. He did, however, have to delay his departure to contest a seat in the October General Election standing as the Conservative Party candidate in Cardiff South-East against James Callaghan, one of the leading politicians of the Labour party, who was about to become Chancellor of the Exchequer, and who later became Prime Minister. Dexter's campaign today would be the equivalent of Andrew Flintoff running for Parliament against David Miliband. Dexter lost but by a surprisingly small margin collecting 22,288 votes to Callaghan's 30,129.

There is cricket being played as we arrive at the Swalec stadium, Glamorgan are doing battle with Leicestershire, a basement battle in division two of the County Championsip. It is hardly a match to make the pulse race, but it is nice to find a ground being used rather than being deserted. With Steve James in our group, we immediately demand attention at the main gates, as he is still something of a legend in these parts. His appearance has barely changed since his playing days and he is well known to fans and gatemen alike.

He has alerted the doyen of the Welsh Press, Ed Bevan, too. Ed, up in his Radio Wales (*Cymru*) box at the back of the stand wants to interview David and me about our cycle venture, live on air too, which is scary. While we are ushered into the studio, an announcement is made over the Tannoy about our arrival and our charity fund-raising. Fame at last. All this, of course, adds to the delays and time is ticking by. My piece of string is skulking at the bottom of the pannier in the knowledge that he has got today's estimated distance well out again. We have a long way to go and no time for one of our indulgent lunches.

Standing in the sun on the tarmac just inside the main gates, we spot a sandwich wagon, and even Alan agrees this is the best option. Ten minutes later, we are back in the saddle and heading for Newport again. This is a tough hour-long haul through the traffic before we can feel we are making progress again by heading north towards Monmouth and, hopefully, a reunion with Toddy. He has phoned to say he will not wait for us in Newport but instead take his time and make his own way to our overnight stop. We have also arranged to meet Matthew Engel and his wife Hilary in Monmouth. They live not far away and Matthew wants to provide us with some moral encouragement and join us for dinner by way of thanks for the support we are showing for the Laurie Engel Trust. Matthew's work for the charity has made him well versed in generating publicity and he has alerted local radio and TV stations that are dispatching reporters to our overnight stop at The Prego, a restaurant with bedrooms in the heart of Monmouth's crowded lanes.

Getting out of Newport a second time takes some doing and involves asking lots of locals for advice, but once clear of the town and just north of the M4, we are pleasantly surprised to find South Wales is transformed into a landscape of little lanes, charming cottages and the elegant River Usk, whose valley we plan to follow on quiet by-roads from Caerleon (*Caerllion*) to the town of Usk. This is what cycle-touring is all about, particularly when the sun is shining. It is now late-afternoon and Toddy has rung again to inform us that he has arrived and handled the first wave of media interviews. The suspicion is he may not have come clean with the local reporters and told them that, despite being a Septuagenarian, he had simply left the rest of us behind and arrived first in Monmouth.

Caerleon, along with York and Chester, was one of the Roman Empire's three permanent legionary fortifications in Britain once the fractious Welsh tribes had been put in their place. Many romantics believe it is also the location of King Arthur's Camelot, round table and all, but all that concerns us is burning the calories, not the cakes.

My mood is not improved on the road out of Caerleon at seeing Tom up ahead watering someone's front garden. He has pulled in by what he thinks is an innocent country hedge, but we are still in a residential area and this is clearly a well-maintained border of someone's home. In the Tour de France, the more agile riders manage to relieve themselves while still on the move, (quite how with cycle shorts on I have never worked out), and while I am not suggesting this method to Tom, I do think he should find a more suitable place to pee. I give him a fatherly piece of my mind as I speed by into what is clearly well-watered countryside.

My nephew Alan is the lead rider in this glorious part of the world and, perhaps because of the pleasure of getting out onto the open road, he misses the sign for Raglan – and, like Welsh sheep, we follow him along a twisty lane over the thundering dual carriageway that is the A449 and head for a place called Gwernesney, which, just so happens to be on my original, meticulously schemed itinerary before it was changed on advice from Jamo.

Going to Raglan had been Jamo's suggested route and,

because of his local knowledge, we settled on that, but now we were back on the Bateman Way – and boy, do we suffer. The hills on the twisting country lanes through Llansoy and Llanishen are llong and llaborious but the mellow early evening views across drowsy fields and valleys are stunning. Even Jack is moved to take a long look at the countryside of this fair island of ours and instructs me to prop the bike up against a rusty five-bar gate and pose for a photograph. It is one of those magical moments on the ride and the distance between the two of us, the other four in our group and our destination barely seems to matter.

By the time we get to Mitchell Troy, a few miles out of Monmouth, the light is failing and those with lights – David, Alan and Steve – rather smugly turn them on as we hurtle down our road on smooth tarmac into Monmouth, where Toddy has, apparently, became quite a media whore, seeing to the every need of any rapt reporter and eager cameraman around and giving his graphic account of the tough ride around the country and his struggling chums, who are "still some distance away and really not worth bothering with."

On the outskirts of Monmouth, we re-group at a junction. The milometers are already reading 80-plus and poor Jamo still has approaching another 20 miles to do back to his parents' home in Lydney. The original estimate of 71 miles is well out. My piece of string is in disgrace and everything about our aching legs, sore backs and numb behinds tell us this has been the longest day so far. It has been seven hours since we pushed our bikes out of the cobbled courtyard of the Hotel du Vin in Bristol this morning. The saving grace is that tomorrow is planned as the shortest day of our trip and we can indulge ourselves with a little lie-in.

I have been looking forward to tonight's stop since I booked it. The Prego looks a rather swish sort of eatery, and all we have to do is stumble downstairs to our tucker – once we have found the restaurant with rooms. Monmouth is charming, but charm is not what you need at the end of a long hard day. As the town is clustered around two rivers, the Wye and the Monmow, we know we have to cross the 13th century gated-bridge into the old part of town. Situated on the Welsh-English border, Monmouth has been the scene of many disputes, most notably the Battle of Monmouth in 1233 at which the rebels defeated the Royalists. Monmouth Castle was the birth-place of Henry V, he of Agincourt fame, and it is through Agincourt Square that we make our way up the final incline into town.

In Agincourt Square stands a splendid monument to Charles Rolls, whose ancestral family home was nearby. Rolls was to become most famous as half of the car-making duo, Rolls-Royce, but he was also a passionate aviator and his statue in Monmouth depicts him holding a bi-plane, a rather sad tribute to his premature death at 32. Rolls was the first man to fly a non-stop double crossing of the English Channel (there and back) in June 1910, but just a month later he recorded another first when the tail of his Wright Flyer broke off and he became the first man in Britain to perish in a plane crash.

Our destination is tucked away in a row of shops and we wheel our bikes down an alley to the rear car park where waiting is Matthew Engel and wife Hilary, whose late son Laurie, and the Trust set up in his memory, is part of the reason for us being here. Their delightful daughter

Vika is also among the welcoming party that includes the family dog, who is quite overcome by the sight of so many hairy legs and lycra shorts. There is also Toddy, who is showered, dressed for the evening and regaling us with how he kept the media hordes happy.

A member of staff from the restaurant emerges bearing a silver tray, bottle of Champagne and glasses, which is a magnificent gesture by Matthew and Hilary. We toast our achievement so far and the miles to come. Hilary has to get Vika home to bed but Matthew stays with us for a long, sumptuous and rather liquid dinner that he attempts to pay for. I think, in the end, we go 50-50 with him, though judging by the rows of empty bottles on the table, any testimony to what happened that evening has to be regarded as a bit hazy. Suffice to say, the next day will start with throbbing heads and raised voices.

Day six route: *Bristol A38 to Gloucestershire County Ground, minor roads to Lower Almondsbury, Tockington and Aust. Cycle path across old Severn Bridge joining A48 towards Caerwent. B4245 to Caldicot, Magor rejoining A48 to Newport and Cardiff for Glamorgan Cricket Club in Sophia Gardens. A48 back to Newport, B4236 to Caerleon. Minor roads to Usk, B4235 to Gwernesney, minor roads to Llansoy, Llanishen B4293 to Trellech, Mitchell Troy and Monmouth.*

String distance: 71 miles
Actual distance: 84 miles.
Time in saddle: 7 hrs 5 mins.
Average speed: 11.8mph

Overall string distance: 381 miles.
Actual mileage to-date: 434.
Time in saddle: 35 hrs 58 mins.
Average speed 12.1mph

A BRIDGE TOO FAR
By Steve James

I only did one day. It was enough, believe me. At the time it was the hardest day of my life. Fielding for six hours on a cricket ground? A piece of cake.

Granted, I did make things a little difficult for myself by cycling some distance to meet the boys and then some distance again afterwards to get to my parents' house, but, still, what a day. At the end of it my speedometer (or wireless cycle computer as they like to be called these days) read 93 miles. It felt like 193.

I like cycling, and these days I do a lot of it. With dodgy knees like mine it is an ideal substitute for running. Every Sunday morning a group of us pedal around the hills of suburban Cardiff for a couple of hours. But before the day on the '18 counties' ride, I'd only ever done a 40-mile stint. And the first time I did that, I got off my bike and, much to the amusement of those around me, promptly fell in a heap on the floor. It did not occur to me that legs full of cramp and fatigue are no good for standing on.

There is no easy way of joining and leaving one of these rides. By their very nature they are not meant for slothful day-trippers like me. You can't just leave your car and then go back to it that night: the ride will have moved on about 80 miles.

But I had a plan of sorts. My parents live in Lydney, Gloucestershire. That's not far from Bristol, location of night-stop five on the tour. I could meet the boys at the old Severn Bridge, cycle to Sophia Gardens (bugger calling it the Swalec Stadium as they want you to nowadays – I played there for 20 years and it was and always will be Sophia Gardens to me) with them, then up to Monmouth, where they were resting for the night, and finally back across the Forest of Dean on my own to Lydney.

But there were problems. Firstly I was not particularly well on the day. A pathetic excuse, yes, but I could feel some sort of cold-flu coming on the day before. I was never going to miss the day – I'd been talking with Col and Toff (David) about it every day I'd seen them that summer- but being a sickly child I knew I might be out of action for a while afterwards. I was. About two weeks. But please don't feel guilty, guys.

Second was the Severn Bridge. Col wanted me to meet them on the English side, which would mean, after my half-an-hour jaunt from Lydney to Chepstow, going over the Bridge twice, there and back. Problem? I've been petrified of that Bridge ever since I was a kid. A gang of us used to go down there sometimes. Never once did I manage to cycle across it like my mates.

I wanted to meet Col on the English side. And to this day I've never told him that I tried three times to get across. The furthest I got was about 30m. Underneath me felt like a surface that was swaying wildly in the wind (it was actually a sunny, windless day). After the third attempt I was in a bit of state and had to grab the side railing. Two random cyclists came past and were concerned about my welfare. "I'm OK," I lied. I managed to crawl – almost literally – back to terra firma. And there I waited for the group. It was a bit of wait thankfully. By the time they arrived I was fine. I never said a word. Just met everyone (apart from Toddy who was feigning a poorly tooth) and got on with the business of pedalling. I tried to make small talk and as we moved along the outskirts of Chepstow asked a little trivia question: "Which recent Glamorgan cricketer hailed from Chepstow?" The answers were rather half-hearted. Cycling heads were on. I told them it was Adrian Dale and decided to get my head down, and on.

A little too much apparently. Moving out of Chepstow towards Newport is a quite a steep hill. Full of energy and not having already cycled for days on end like the others, I attacked it aggressively, to be followed impressively by Tom and Toff. "Which way?" they asked at the top.

"Straight on," I replied without thinking, as this was a route I took regularly. And on we went. After about 10 minutes we realised no-one was behind us. Col's route was down some B-road around Caldicot rather than the main A48 I preferred. Nightmare. Poor Tom had to make some awkward phone calls. Col was not happy. We arranged to meet further down the A48. It was a rather strained re-union. "This is not a bloody Audax," said Col, with some feeling. I felt sorry for Tom. It was my fault. I'd only been on the ride a few minutes and already I was causing trouble! I thought it best I paid for coffees and cakes at the garden centre we stopped at soon afterwards. It was the least I could do.

Thankfully the ride to Sophia Gardens went smoothly. Once there Col and Toff even did a radio interview with the cricketing voice of Wales (not an oxymoron, honestly!), Edward Bevan. Food was taken. The mood was jolly. I even saw my wife, who at the time was doing some part-time physio at the club. Everything felt good.

It didn't last. The afternoon was hell. This was supposed to be my patch, but we got lost at least twice. Clueless. Asking for directions in Newport – at least five miles from my home – was especially embarrassing.

Never have I been so glad to see the town of Monmouth. As a schoolboy there I used to quite like seeing it disappear in the distance of a night. Now it brought joy. I never realised the hills around it were so steep. Poor old Jack was really struggling. He was not the only one who was mightily pissed off when we came across a sign saying 'Monmouth 8 miles'. Nothing wrong with that in itself, except that about 10 minutes earlier we'd seen one saying 'Monmouth 6 miles'! Country miles and all that.

Toddy was there in Monmouth, not exactly looking like a man who'd had seven teeth, or whatever it was, removed, and the delightful Engels too, a reminder of the worthy cause we were contributing to. The conversation was wonderful, but it was time to go. A quick half-hour and I'd be back in Lydney, devouring a hot meal.

If only. It took more than an hour. And it seemed a lot longer. Darkness descended and the temperature dropped. I was freezing. Absolutely knackered, too. Never again, I vowed.

Until...in 2009 I managed to complete the Wessex 100 miler. For anyone who knows about the Brassknocker Hill – cruelly scheduled as the last mile of the ride – they will know why that day now ranks as my hardest. But, just like after Sept 18 2008, I didn't have to go again the next day. Col and the boys did. They did that for 15 days. Serious respect

CHAPTER EIGHT

The Ferryman Cometh

...Monmouth to Worcester

"Where's Jack?"

It is a refrain that is becoming tiresomely familiar. We are standing outside the back door of Prego on the tarmac car park. Our bikes have spent the night in an ancient, leaning wooden shed that the owners use to store all sorts of paraphernalia you might need in a restaurant and they have been retrieved. Jack's has been wheeled out for him. David has done the rounds with his tyre pressure gauge and can of WD40, giving the cogs and chains a rewarding spray after all their hard work yesterday. He has even had time to put a little extra air into Toddy's rear tyre and checked Tom's rogue pedal, which is still working loose on occasions. The panniers have been clipped into place on the racks over the rear wheels. We have donned helmets and cycle gloves. But no Jack and it is nearing 9.30, well after our normal departure time. I am seriously considering leaving him behind.

My question is directed at Tom, whom I hold responsible for his younger brother. "Well? What's he doing?" I ask, having seen Jack about an hour ago devouring a massive breakfast.

"I don't know, I told him to hurry up but I'm not responsible for him, don't blame me."

I did.

"You're his roomy, you have to hurry him along in the mornings. You know what he is like and everyone is waiting for him. Again."

David, as ever, tries to placate me, saying it is a short day anyway and there is no rush, but my bad mood will not subside, which probably has something to do with the little man tapping away with a hammer inside my skull. Who ordered that round of whisky nightcaps? Tom retreats back upstairs to chivvy his brother but half-way up the stairs meets Jack descending with his belongings falling out of two plastic carrier bags.

"Where have you been Jack? We're all waiting. It's very inconsiderate of you," I tell him.

Jack has the sort of endearing smile that gets him out of all sorts of scrapes and he is forgiven by the others while poor Tom is still bearing the brunt of my displeasure. It is very unfair on the eldest, but then life is unfair and I console myself that this is a good lesson for him. We get on very well most of the time, but Tom does always like to have the final word and never backs down in an argument. I have never known anyone more sure he is in the right. Except, of course, me. My wife says we are very alike. Cannot see it myself.

And that's the end of the matter.

In a huff, I push off first and do not look back. It is up to the others to keep up and if they don't, they have their detailed route guides if, that is, they care to check them. Today is short – fewer than 50 miles – but potentially tricky as we discover instantly. It appears the only way across a large main road is through a pedestrian and cycle underpass that doubles up as a public convenience judging by the stench.

No sooner are we on the road out of Monmouth than we veer sharp left into a 'No Through Road' that becomes The Peregrine Path, alternatively called the *Llwybr yr Hebog* as we are still just about in Wales. The Peregrine is part of the National Cycle Network, an ever-expanding route-way that covers more than 12,000 miles. This one, running through delightful woodlands beside the river Wye, is one of the shorter routes covering just three miles from Monmouth to Symonds Yat, and our river crossing in the Forest of Dean between Gloucestershire and Herefordshire.

For the first time we leave tarmac, which could create a problem for our narrow high-pressure smooth tyres, which are perfect for roads, cutting resistance to a minimum as they do, but not ideal for muddy forest tracks where a bit more grip and give is needed. Fortunately it is dry and the surface underneath is mainly compact mud and small chippings. It is flat, dry and the morning sun twinkles through the forest canopy. There is even time to catch a glimpse of the peregrine falcons that inhabit these parts. This is glorious and the angst of the morning subsides with the hangover as we glide through the woodland towards the curious settlement of Symonds Yat, that is split East (Gloucestershire) and West (Herefordshire) by the somnolent Wye, which runs through a deep gorge here with no bridge to link the two communities on either bank.

A little cluster of cottages and a pub gather around the only route across the 50-yard stretch of brown water. It is a rope slung over the river that the ferryman uses to haul a short, flat-bottomed barge across from one bank to the other. He stands at one end of his barge much like a gondolier in Venice and flicks what can best be described as a lasso along the overhead rope, pulling himself and the little vessel across in stages. It is so simple, it is delightful. Surely there cannot be a more contented man on a sunny September day than the Symonds Yat Ferryman? Wanna bet?

But first, before the crossing, we pose for photographs and decide a settling coffee is the order of the day before our voyage. The sign by the crossing says to check in the public house for the ferryman if he is not by his boat and, sure enough, the ferryman is sitting in the pub, chatting to the landlord over a cuppa. Alan tells him cheerily that he will soon have some business, but he does not seem enthused. Alan, refusing to allow his mood to be deflated, enthusiastically tells the landlord that he would like to order four coffees and two cokes. Please. Both men look at the clock which shows 10.47.

"No coffee 'til 11, we're not open yet," says the Landlord gruffly.

"And no ferry 'til 11, either," says the ferryman with an equal lack of charm.

And the pair continue their conversation as if we are invisible.

Doesn't the service industry in this country just make your heart swell with pride, and this at a beauty spot that attracts visitors from all over the world as well as the United

Kingdom? It has often seemed to me that the ethos of the service industry in Britain is to not provide the service when the paying customer actually wants it: like shops that close for lunch just at the time when factory and office workers can get out to do their shopping; like car parks that are locked for the night just before you get out of the cinema; like theatres that close on Sundays and like publicans who have a deep-seated loathing of the public.

Welcome to Symonds Yat West. Alan tells mine host that we will skip the coffees and informs the ferryman we will be waiting for him when he is ready. When we get back outside, David is eyeing the little green barge with trepidation. David cannot swim. Having been a colleague of his on the cricket-writing circuit for more than 20 years, I have known that for a long time, but I never suspected that he had a fear of small craft too.

When the monosyllabic ferryman emerges, he climbs on board and holds his craft as steady as he can while we manoeuvre ourselves and our six bikes down the stone steps and onto the boat that bobs alarmingly in the murky water. Shifting the bikes is not easy with heavy panniers that make balancing them difficult. The six bikes will just about squeeze into the bottom of the barge but we have to sit precariously on the metal ledge around the edge holding on to our steeds with one hand and onto the rim of the boat with the other. There is certainly no danger of David rocking the boat as he is paralysed with fear, staring ahead at the far bank as a ship-wrecked sailor clinging to a plank of flotsam might stare longingly at a remote desert island.

The ferryman flicks his lasso along the overhead rope like a fly-fisherman casting a line and pulls it taut, heaving the boat with him. It takes us probably no more than 10 minutes to make the crossing, during which time, despite our attempts at convivial conversation, the ferryman utters not a word to inquire where we are headed, to pass comment on the weather or to offer a solution to the deprivations of the disenfranchised peoples of Robert Mugabe's Zimbabwe. As we dock on the little wooden jetty on the Gloucestershire side, we pay him our £1.50 each (£1 per person, 50p per bike) opting not to tip, and push our bikes up the steep 100-yard path to the narrow road which runs through Symonds Yat East.

This may be our shortest day in terms of distance but we are making slow progress having covered no more than six miles in two hours. We are also lost, so Toddy starts knocking on the doors of a row of cottages that are holiday lets, and empty at this time of year. Eventually we find a local walking her dog, who points us in the direction of Goodrich, Kerne Bridge and Ross on Wye. We set off again but unfortunately, within a mile, our intended route along a B road is blocked by a police car parked from kerb to kerb, blue lights flashing, and a 'Road Closed' sign in the middle of the tarmac. We have to divert on to the busy A40 dual carriageway, not a place for cyclists. Riding on the hard shoulder, we can see over the wooden fencing to our left just why our route is blocked. A gruesome looking mangle of two cars fills the road and the shape of a person lies hanging out of the door of one of them. Our chatter fades and we pedal in silence each with our thoughts. It is not a nice way to be reminded just how vulnerable you can be on the road, especially on a flimsy bike.

We are relieved to get off the A40 at the first available

exit and slip on to the quiet B road through Kerne Bridge towards Ross-on-Wye. This is picture-book England with undulating green pastures, neat hedges and the sun glinting off the river as we cross it heading north thinking about the coffee-stop we did not have in Symonds Yat West. On the outskirts of Ross, David and Alan, the two front riders, stop beside a modest-looking pub waiting for the back-markers to catch up and are accosted by the landlord and his wife, who are pottering around the garden with its wooden tables and bright advertising parasols. They are new to the pub business and clearly still have a lot to learn. They actually engage David and Alan in cheerful chatter and encourage us in to stop for coffee in the garden. If, one day, they hope to progress in the business and take over an idyllic watering hole in a beauty spot such as Symonds Yat, they really do need to stop encouraging trade like this and giving the impression of actually being pleased to serve customers.

Ross-on-Wye is an apt place to rest for 20 minutes and ponder what Britain has to offer the tourist as the town claims to be 'The birthplace of the British Tourist Industry.' Apparently, it all began in 1745 when the Rector, Dr. John Egerton, started organising boat trips along the Wye Valley with its cliffs, castles and abbeys. Almost 40 years later, William Gilpin produced a book called 'Observations on the River Wye', which, it is claimed, was the forerunner of the current tour guides.

I am not so sure Dr Egerton does not have some explaining to do, because holidays are a curious thing. You spend half the year planning and saving for them, complaining that you badly need a break, but you return from holiday more frazzled than when you started, at loggerheads with the family and desperate to see home again to get back to decent food and a comfortable bed. Work the next week comes as a blessed relief, but we still insist to our work-mates that we had a wonderful time.

As my job involves travelling to the cricket-playing regions of the world – Australia, New Zealand, South Africa, the Caribbean and the countries that make up the Indian subcontinent – I do not see any attraction in getting on an aeroplane and flying somewhere where the sun shines relentlessly almost every day. There is surely nothing more boring than throwing open your curtains every morning knowing you are going to see blue skies and a piercing sun? Where's the uncertainty, the tingle of anticipation that you get when you peek out from behind your curtains in the UK? Our weather is never boring, and without the rain we would not have such a green and pleasant land. I have seen too many parched, barren landscapes around the world ever to moan about the rain in our country. Anyway, it rarely rains in September, which is why we plan our bike rides for this month. Take my word for it: the ninth month of the year is the best for weather and the school holidays are over. It is the perfect month for a holiday.

After a week on the road, we are feeling strong and confident. Our machines are behaving (apart from Tom's pedal) and we are deep into our itinerary. The daily routine is established and the 12 miles from Ross-on-Wye to Ledbury on the peaceful A449 through the village of Much Marcle is a doddle. Apparently, around this time, the world was heading into a ruinous financial crash. An American company called Lehman Brothers had filed for bankruptcy four days earlier and the world's stock markets and banks were on the critical list. Gloriously oblivious, the only financial concerns we have on our journey through England are whose turn is it to get the coffees in?

Ledbury is a fine old English market town. The sort of place where everyone should live, the type of community that guide books would call 'thriving'. In keeping with being in Herefordshire, jam and cider were made here (the cider still is) with produce from local farms. It has nice shops and a bustling High Street that is not too busy so as to give you a headache. Ordinary, pleasant people going about their ordinary, pleasant lives appear to throng the pavements. If Ledbury has a subversive underbelly, it is not obvious to the six cyclists free-wheeling down its main road on the look-out for a promising café for lunch.

The middle of the town is dominated by the 17th century timber-framed Market House, an extraordinary structure that is a building on stilts made of chestnut. It was originally designed as a grain store and was elevated about 10ft above ground level presumably to keep vermin and thieves at bay. Underneath the building is a paved area that has become something of a meeting place with its stone seats and railings. It makes a perfect place to secure the bikes while we investigate an interesting place to eat that, according to the sign in the window, specialises in local produce. The café does not disappoint, and Alan in particular is delighted to discover they serve a local ale to wash down his mountainous ploughman's lunch.

Back on the move, the main A449 road to Great Malvern is straightforward enough, but I have devised a minor detour on a B road through West Malvern, which in theory cuts off a couple of miles and should be more picturesque.

The turn-off to Colwall Stone is clearly marked, but once through the village we are in for a rude surprise. This is how Alan describes it in his tour diary:

'We swing left and almost immediately find ourselves climbing. The road goes up and up, in places savagely so, and I am reduced to grovelling in my lowest gear just hoping it won't get any steeper. This seems to go on for about five miles although I suspect it is nearer to two.'

Told you, you should not have had that beer, Alan.

To be fair, it is quite a climb, and while my OS Map has the words 'Malvern Hills' written across the road, there is no mention of mountains. The climb is of the hairpin variety, which are tough on cyclists. If the hairpin goes to the right, we are on the outside of it and the gradient is easier, but the very nature of hairpin bends is that they double back on themselves, and the left turning bends can be excruciatingly steep and often sprinkled with loose chippings that makes the going tougher. The temptation is to swing out wide on these bends across the road to reduce the gradient, but motorists do not seem to understand if a wavering cyclist gets in their way. All you can do on these tough climbs is to settle into a low gear and establish a rhythm, and not look up until you feel your straining chain start to ease a little.

Psychologically, it is important for me not to be in the lowest gear on a climb. It is always nice to know there is one final gear-change to go to ease the pain if need be. Being in bottom gear can be a crushing feeling if your thighs and knees start screaming at you that they can go no further. Only once in our four long rides have I failed to make it up a hill and had to walk, and that was on the first day of our first ride from John O'Groats to Land's End. Coming down the Caithness coast we had a swooping 13 per cent hairpin descent into the Berridale Braes, and my lack of experience was exposed on the climb from the bottom. Mistiming my gear-changes, I clunked down the cogs, lost momentum and ground to a halt, unable to get going again on such a steep ascent. Reassuringly, David was also forced to walk up the incline. It was a humbling experience although, even though we were pushing our bikes, we passed Alan, who was pedalling his Peugeot at a tortoise pace. Cyclists (serious ones, at least) are scornful of those who have to push their bikes up a hill and thankfully it has never happened to me since. One day, too, I intend to return to beautiful Berriedale* and conquer that damned hill.

The Malvern Mountain feels steeper than Berridale Braes but there is no way any of us are stopping. We are now tour veterans (apart from Jack, who is complaining loudly about the person who devised the route and his piece of string) and we crest the top, breaking out of tree-cover onto a glorious hill-top road with wonderful views, grassy banks and bench seats, which we fall onto to catch our breath and contemplate the long down-hill finish ahead of us into Worcester.

With the weight of the panniers on the back of our bikes and a growing confidence about our road-craft, we dive down the narrow descent through houses and parked cars

---

*While Berriedale has a middle 'e', curiously Berridale Braes has lost it, presumably stuck in one of the gravel escape roads near the foot of the hill.

back on to the A449 in Malvern and pass the little industrial estates at Malvern Link, where one of the gems of British industry is produced: the Morgan car. I first came to this factory in the late 1980s when rain washed out play one day in a cricket match that I was reporting on at Worcester. I have always loved sports cars, not so much for their speed, but for the driving sensation of being in a low-slung, hard-sprung two-seater that responds to the driver unlike the modern, massed produced vehicles. I had never been able to afford a new sports car but had owned an MG sprite, an MGB GT, two Lotus Elans (Oh, they were wonderful when they were not up on the ramp at the local garage) and a Triumph TR7 at various times before the family started to come along and make two-seaters redundant.

On that rainy day at Worcester almost 20 years ago, my thoughts on visiting Henry Morgan's old factory, where they turn out 11 hand-built cars in a good week, were simply to window shop like a wishful kid outside Gamleys at Christmas. With two young children and a big mortgage, there was no way I could buy one. Anyway, there was about a three-year waiting list so what was the point? By the time I left the factory after my sight-seeing trip, my name was on that waiting list.

The Morgan Car Company is the oldest privately owned car business in the world. It was started in 1910 by Henry Morgan, a railway draughtsman with a love of cars, and in many ways has resisted the march of progress ever since although the vehicles now have four wheels instead of the original three. The cars still have a frame made of ash (when you buy one you get a wood treatment certificate as well as an anti-rust guarantee), they have running boards, a bonnet that opens from both sides on central hinges, leather and walnut interiors and windows that screw into place rather than wind down. They are soft-top by nature and beautifully idiosyncratic, but are powered by sports engines made by Ford and BMW. The firm is still family run, employing 160 workers and their cars are, I am delighted to say, still in demand both sides of the Atlantic.

In a concession to my family status, I ordered the two-plus-two, which has two small bucket seats in the rear just about suitable for toddlers. The wait for the car started and I had almost forgotten about it when, a little more than two years later on December 22 1989, I took delivery of my British Racing Green little beauty: the 'windy car' as Tom and Jack called it, their caps and homework often blowing away as we swept into the school car park. Malvern may have its spa water, girls' college, hydrotherapy paraphernalia and Edward Elgar devotees, but it has nothing to match the great British treasure that is the Morgan Motor Company.

As we pass Spring Lane, an innocuous road that leads down to the factory, with a heavy heart I cast a glance to my right. These days, when I say I am going for a spin, it is on two wheels not four (the Morgan had to be sold about four years later to finance a new fitted kitchen, such is life). We are now just five miles away from Worcester, where arguably the most picturesque county ground in the country has been turned into a fetid eyesore.

The ground, known as New Road, is beside the River Severn, where the swans glide by under the over-hanging trees growing from the path beside the water. On the opposite bank, Worcester's magnificent cathedral towers over the small city, its school, famous pottery and narrow lanes. It is a quintessential English county town (although officially it is a city) with a cricket ground within walking distance of the shops. That accessibility makes the ground feel an important part of the community, and supporters do wander in for a couple of hours at the cricket to enjoy a pint or the fabulous home-made cakes served in the ladies' pavilion every afternoon. It is little wonder that teams from abroad like to start their tours here to the 11 o'clock chime of the cathedral clock.

The reality, these days, is no idyll. New Road is still a splendid spot to watch cricket, but the county is struggling financially, which is not helped by the winter flooding of the ground by the Severn that appears to be becoming more frequent. This year the flooding has been particularly bad and has come to haunt the county in mid-season, forcing them to move their home matches to a club ground in Kidderminster. As we cycle into the deserted New Road ground, the mayhem caused by the Severn bursting its banks is plain to see. On the white painted wall of the pavilion is a dirty brown line at head-height that indicates the high-water mark of that summer's flood. The outfield is no longer verdant green but a filthy brown, covered in silt that smells like a mixture of sewage and decaying animals. Worcestershire will make good as they always do but with global warming and more extremes of weather seemingly upon us, you wonder how long they and their lovely ground can continue to battle against the odds and the tide. The chief executive from a few years back was a reverend, but even he has moved on, so the chances of help from on high are receding quicker than the floodwaters.

The kindly staff in the cricket club offices, God bless them, have done a deal for us at a smart city centre hotel, the White House, which is no more than a five-minute bike-push away through the pedestrianised shopping area. We are in for a comfy night, as are our bikes, which are propped up on the plush red carpet of a banqueting room that is not being used. The hotel has a swimming pool, sauna and steam room, of which we take full advantage. Having been a short day, there are few aches and pains but it would be churlish not to make use of the facilities all the same.

My roomy tonight is Toddy, who has lost his glasses, telephone charger and bottles of potions as usual, but nothing is going to dent our up-beat mood, not even the very average Chinese set-meal that we are served in a nearby restaurant. Over dinner we check our mileage readings for the day and, lo and behold, my string's reputation is restored. The mileage estimate of '45-ish' is, in fact, almost spot on as we have done 43 today. Tomorrow, though, is going to be altogether more of a challenge as we head into the ominously titled Black Country.

Day Seven Route: *Leave Monmouth A4136 south then left on to Peregrine Way cycle path to Symonds Yat West. Ferry to Symonds Yat East. Minor roads to A40 then B4229 to Goodrich over Kerne Bridge to Ross-on-Wye. A449 to Ledbury and towards Great Malvern. Left on to B4218 to Colwell Stone, join B4232 to West Malvern. Rejoin A449 to Worcester.*

String Distance: 45 miles
Actual Distance: 43 miles

Time in saddle : 4 hrs. 02 mins.
Average speed: 10.7mph

Overall string estimate: 426 miles.
Actual mileage to-date: 477.
Total cycling time: 40 hrs.
Average speed 11.9mph

WHY PEOPLE DO IT...
By Matthew Engel

On April 20, 2004 my son Laurie, a happy, sporty, sparky 11-year-old – whose previous worst ailment had been athlete's foot – went off for what we thought was a routine doctor's appointment. He was diagnosed with a rare and cruel form of cancer.

Seventeen months later, on September 22, 2005, he died, aged 13. And our family's life was shattered for ever.

At the celebration of Laurie's life, we started raising money that we hoped might provide a new Teenage Cancer Trust (TCT) unit at Birmingham Children's Hospital, where he was treated. We thought this would somehow provide a replacement for the slummy existing facilities, though we had not the foggiest idea how it might happen. Not the foggiest.

On February 22, 2010, the new unit opened. The staff and patients and everyone who has seen it are thrilled to bits, and many have been kind enough to give us the credit.

It is true that if Laurie were here, the unit would not be. The hospital management had it down on some wish list, unclear how it might be paid for, or where on their cramped site it might go. The whole truth is that we did a great deal less than many people think.

In those terrible weeks after Laurie died money began to come in from various sources. But the big breakthrough came just before Christmas when I wrote an article* for The Guardian which told Laurie's story and inspired a massive influx of

* http://www.guardian.co.uk/lifeandstyle/2005/dec/03/familyandrelati
onships.health

donations. Perhaps even more significantly, it was read by Paul O'Connor, then the hospital chief executive, and made him realise that the situation was urgent.

And so a series of meetings began, to work out how and where this unit might go, with my wife Hilary and me adding our occasional tuppence worth. Eventually, a plan emerged to take the aerial route: putting the unit on stilts above the ambulance bay. Simultaneously, the Laurie Engel Fund was growing beyond our wildest fantasies. I had told the TCT's chief fundraiser, Richard Shaw, during our first conversation that I was sure we could raise £10,000. Within months, we had hit £250,000.

It actually took us a while to realise that the cash pile was growing without us doing anything much. Sure, we had planted the seed, and done the initial watering. But soon, like a child, it had taken on a life of its own.

All the grand fundraising ideas came from other people. It was Laurie's cousins who suggested a sponsored walk on what should have been his 14th birthday: eighty of us trekked across the mountain ridge that overlooks our Herefordshire home. It was the local youth club that started the football tournament in his honour, now an annual fixture. It was our daughter Vika – just six when Laurie died – who said she would swim 50 lengths of the local pool, and did it.

I assumed the enthusiasm would fade away quickly. But by 2008 half the country seemed to be walking, running, swimming, canoeing, climbing, skydiving, eating, singing, dancing…all to raise money for our fund, and that summer culminated in the boys' cycle ride round the nation's cricket grounds.

There was a quiz night on Majorca and a homemade lemonade stall in Maryland. A friend, terrified of motorways, was sponsored to do four miles down the M54. Many of the people raising money were strangers or, as I prefer to say, friends we hadn't met. The most touching donations came from two people who knocked on the front door.

One was an elderly local farmer who we did not know, shyly clutching a £10 note. The other left an envelope. Hilary, with what was now a practised eye, guessed it might contain 20 quid. It was a cheque for £10,000. That was early in 2010, and it took us over the £900,000 mark. But in my heart, I rank both these donations together.

How did this all happen? I think there were three main reasons. Firstly, I had the advantage of being a journalist, with access to print and the airwaves to achieve publicity.

Secondly, we had a story to tell that everyone grasped at once, and it spoke to every parent's worst fears. It was Laurie who fell victim to this terrible fluke, this lottery-win-in-reverse. But this sweet and loving boy could have been anyone's son.

And thirdly, our objective was understandable and achievable. We were not asking people to find a cure for cancer or an end to world poverty. People knew their money would go to this one cause.

We had built a pioneering relationship with TCT whereby we raised funds only for them while they committed to use our money only for the Birmingham unit. Support us, we said, and it will be built. They did, and it has been.

This is the 14th unit in the UK opened by TCT. And they make a huge difference. Whatever the illness, there is a problem about teenage patients. Do you put them in a ward with the geriatrics or the kiddies? And it is far more crucial for cancer patients – including the majority who, unlike Laurie, will come through – because they may be in and out of hospital for years.

When Laurie was in Birmingham, he was immensely

frustrated because there was nothing for him to do: he could have played with toy cars but it was hard to get access to a computer. There was no fun, but also no peace and no privacy, because the ward was so cramped and inadequate.

The new unit has more than twice the space for each bed plus kitchen facilities, a games console, big-screen satellite TV, a hi-tech jukebox which can link up with MP3 players.... a place, in short, where patients' friends will come because they want to, not out of duty; a place where sick teenagers can be teenagers and not just sick.

Indeed, there is a problem of success. Before, there was a certain equality of suffering; now the younger kids can see that there is a better way. And why shouldn't they have better facilities too? If they don't deserve them, who does? There are battles left to fight. But I think Laurie would be proud of what's been done. Not by us, but by a cast of thousands.

The story of what happened next is at:

http://www.guardian.co.uk/theguardian/2009/dec/05/laurie-engel-fund-teenage-cancer-trust

CHAPTER NINE

The Midland Miles

....Worcester to Stafford.

Toddy is up early, standing naked at the hotel bedroom window talking on his mobile phone. Fortunately our senior cyclist has his back to me as I lie in bed. He is speaking to his son Martin, a Lieutenant Colonel in the British Army based at Catterick, very close to where our route will take us in three days' time. The plan is that we should meet up at our stop in Hawes on the Pennines for an evening meal and laundry service. Martin's wife Gina has very kindly offered to take in our increasingly unpleasant bags of washing and get them cleaned overnight: a rare treat for both the clothes and for us.

Keeping clean is essential on a long bike ride otherwise – without going into too much gruesome detail – sores and chafing can become a major problem. It is important to wash through cycle shorts and shirts every night, but there is only so much you can do in tepid water with a bar of soap in a hotel washbasin. Drying clothes overnight on radiators reluctant to give out more than a hint of heat is not easy either. Our evening wear of jeans and casual shirts is also becoming increasingly crumpled and whiffy, too.

Toddy turns around and announces that all is arranged with Martin, who has been on a recce to Hawes and found the best pub in town for our dinner in a few days' time. Time spent on reconnaissance is never time wasted as they say in the Queen's Royal Lancers, the tank regiment under Martin's command. Ian then flicks on the kettle, oblivious to the dangers of the steaming spout, which, alarmingly, is at the critical height to his naked torso, and makes us both tea before disappearing into the bathroom in good heart. He has clearly fully recovered from the early aches and pains of our trip and the rogue tooth that had to be removed, which is good news for all concerned as we had all privately expressed doubts about Toddy's ability to last the course with us youngsters, David, Alan and me all being in our mid-fifties.

The real youngsters, Tom and Jack, have made early-morning use of the hotel swimming pool while David and I have been out and about in Worcester before breakfast buying newspapers, chocolate bars, biscuits and fruit to keep us going on the road. Clearly everyone is feeling optimistic after yesterday's short ride, and as we enter the second week of our trip. Alan is delighted with the presidential size of his White House breakfast and, while a few of us are beginning to cut down on the 'Full English' and order poached eggs on toast instead, he is maintaining his intake of calories and farm animals. We are packed and paid up and on the road by 9.15 on another sunny day. What could possibly go wrong?

PUNCTURE. That's what.

If clouds have a silver lining, however, this one was

hallmarked. Our second puncture of the trip happened to Jack mid-morning and turned out to be a God-send.

We had left Worcester on the A38 heading towards Bromsgrove and Birmingham for that vaguely-defined area of England known as the Black Country, and our ninth county ground, Edgbaston, the home of Warwickshire County Cricket Club. We would soon be half way through the 18 grounds that dictated our curious route around the country.

Our bikes, reluctant at first to leave the comfort of their carpeted hotel suite, soon slipped into the rhythm of another fine morning on the bustling roads around Worcester as we pushed northwards on the A38. It was a comfortable, flat start to another day. The main road takes us around Droitwich Spa and out into what will be a brief stretch of countryside riding on a day that we know will involve us jostling with heavy traffic for most of the time.

England's second city, as Birmingham likes to be known, is a sprawling conurbation and from my experience, the main arteries are always busy. So, I have devised an ingenious route into town via what look, on my OS maps at least, to be quieter B roads through the splendidly named Catshill and Lickey. The trouble with side roads is that they are rarely well signposted, and after entering the southern suburbs of Birmingham, we become split up and lost by the time Jack's front tyre makes contact with some broken glass, a common hazard for cyclists on our urban roads.

Fortunately Jack is cycling with Tom and the pair of them begin to ring around to bring the group back together. It turns out we are spread over a small area near Lickey End (I have resisted looking up the origin of this name for fear of what I might discover). David and Alan, our two mechanics, were heading out of town in the general direction of Wales when Jack's urgent call for help came through, so the puncture really has done us all a favour.

Ten minutes later, sprawled across the wide pavement outside a row of smart commuter homes, David and Alan make short work of replacing the inner tube – the old one can be repaired later at our next overnight stop – while I study my maps and itinerary, puzzling as to where we have gone wrong. The route looks simple enough, but the turning to our next landmark, Catshill, is proving elusive. Clearly the local population all use sat-navs and have no need for signposts.

I am just beginning to wonder if we might have to retrace our steps when Tom (our Tom-Tom) points out that directly opposite us is the smallest of road signs in a privet hedge that reads 'Catshill Road'. Eureka! We are back on track and re-united thanks to Jack's puncture and Tom's observational qualities. The lads do have their uses after all.

It surprises me that the Politically Correct Brigade has not mounted a campaign to have the name of the West Midlands area known as the Black Country banned. The phrase stems from the days of the coal mines, coke works, iron foundations and steel mills that turned the air into a polluted soup and laid a dark dust on everything. It may be a myth – an urban one in this case – but it is said Queen Victoria instructed her staff to lower the blinds on her train when she passed through these parts, such was the unappealing landscape outside her windows. What is not a myth is that the author J.R.R. Tolkien, who lived in Birmingham for 16 years, based his grim fictional region of Mordor on the Black Country.

Other phrases with the word black in them have been out-lawed by the Political Correct Gestapo, who believe these words have a perjorative over-tone. Nonsense? Perhaps. But several words and phrases have disappeared from our rich lexicon. You would never call a bruise caused by catching your finger in a drawer a 'black man's pinch' these days. Heaven help us, but even 'black marks' and 'blackboards' seem to be no go areas.

Anyway, the Black Country is not very black any longer and certainly has no country. The pollution has been largely eliminated because of the decline in our heavy industries, the passing of open fires in homes and EEC legislation on vehicles and what is pumped out of their exhaust pipes. The country is a better place for it whatever anyone tells you about "the good old days", and most of Birmingham's soot-covered buildings have either been knocked down or cleaned up.

The West Midlands may not be the most attractive area of the country but it does have the virtue of being pretty flat, spread as it is across the Birmingham Plateau, and we make good steady progress through the residential streets and past the huge disused sites of the Longbridge car factories until we reach the posh side of the city and Edgbaston, a suburb that truly deserves the moniker 'leafy'.

The cricket ground, which has been used for Test matches for more than 100 years, is one of the major venues for cricket in England. Like the city around it, Edgbaston is more functional than fabulous, but it has a good homely feel to it and, boy, do England like playing here. With two major football teams close by – Birmingham and Aston Villa – the Edgbaston patrons are known for their partisan and sometimes raucous support of England when they turn up for the summer game. Saturday afternoons at Test matches in Birmingham are boisterous affairs full of very macho men who seem to delight in dressing up in fishnet stockings, wigs and false breasts for the day. England often prosper at Edgbaston and the players are convinced the local support has much to do with that.

With the help of bus and cycle lanes, we slide through the unrelenting traffic and arrive at Edgbaston shortly after mid-day, our first stop at a Test ground since we left the Brit Oval a week earlier (although Glamorgan's Swalec Stadium was to stage Test cricket the following summer).

Warwickshire has produced its fair share of famous players including opening batsman Dennis Amiss, who helped change the face of cricket in the 1970s when, struggling to cope with the hostility of Australia's fast bowlers, he went out to bat in what was fundamentally a motor-bike crash helmet. Until then, the only protection a batsman's head had from bouncers was a cloth cap and an extra layer of Brylcreem (which was produced at a chemical factory in Birmingham). Amiss, not unreasonably, decided that as he had protective padding for his legs, hands, groin, arms and chest, why not protect the most vital part of the body? When he first wore the ungainly helmet, the idea was greeted with derision in cricket circles, but 30 years on, no batsmen would think of leaving the pavilion without his helmet even to face slow bowling. Of course, the nanny state has also made protective headgear compulsory for children playing even the most harmless game of bat and ball.

Another innovation spawned at Edgbaston was the

'Brumbrella', which was literally rolled out in the 1980s as the answer to the British summer weather. Its name stemmed, of course, from the nickname for Birmingham folk – Brummies – and it was simply a giant roll of plastic sheeting. Powered by petrol engines, the 80-metre metal tube was rolled out when the clouds threatened, covering most of the grass in a blue plastic sheet keeping not only the pitch dry, but most of the outfield too. Like most great ideas, it was brilliant in its simplicity, and was so much more effective than the traditional system of protecting against rain, which involved small squares of tarpaulin being dragged onto the field by the groundstaff and held down with tent pegs. When the rain stopped, the tarpaulin then had to be dried with kitchen mops until someone came up with the idea of a giant motorised squeegee mop.

The only trouble with the Brumbrella was that if the engines packed up, there was no way of getting the thing off the field. The steel tube proved heavy and unreliable too, and occasionally cracked under the strain of all that plastic weighed down with rain water. When it was replaced, the new plastic tube also cracked, so the Brumbrella was rolled up for a final time and scrapped.

Full marks, though, to Warwickshire for trying…as they did with one of their playing heroes Ashley Giles, who had a much-deserved benefit year after helping England regain the Ashes from Australia in 2005. Giles was a fine, resourceful cricketer and the best slow bowler in England for a while, although he was never a great spinner of the ball in the Shane Warne category. A cheerful character, Giles always acknowledged his limitations although he knew his worth to England's fine team from that era.

When his benefit year arrived, the club decided, tongue-in-cheek, to commission commemorative mugs to be sold in the club shop bearing Ashley's face and the legend: 'Ashley Giles – King of Spin.' The first batch came back form the pottery with the wording: 'Ashley Giles – King of Spain.' For the rest of his career, which was ended by injury in 2007, Giles, who became Warwickshire's Director of Cricket and an England selector, happily answered to 'Your Majesty.'.

The county's other famous fathers include England captains Bob (RES) Wyatt, Bob Willis and Eric Hollies, the spin bowler who dismissed Sir Donald Bradman for a duck in his last Test innings at The Oval to ensure the legendary Australian ended with a career with a Test average of 99.94 rather than 100-plus, which no cricketer has achieved or is ever likely to achieve.

Edgbaston was also the scene of the highest score ever made in first class cricket, the 501 scored by the West Indies' Brian Lara playing for Warwickshire against Durham in 1994, and while my eldest son Tom, who had played a few matches of youth cricket for Kent, would love to linger and dwell on the history that seeps from every nook and cranny of the ground, there is little time to spare after our obligatory photo-session outside the deserted dressing rooms. It is one of the drawbacks of our demanding schedule.

We head off for lunch at a café in a very pretty park opposite the ground, a place well known to David and me from our days working at Edgbaston. The park is full of parents and young children enjoying the sunshine, the boating pond and the ducks, for whom it is always feeding time. We feel rather incongruous sitting at a table with our cycle gear and panniers, munching on toasted sandwiches and scones while outside toddlers stare at our bikes chained up to the white picket fence. It is the calm before the storm of the Birmingham Inner City Ring Road.

We have to make our way directly north passing those other parts of the Black Country better known for the three Ws. Cricket has its own Three Ws: the famous West Indian triumvirate of (Sir Clyde) Walcott, (Sir Everton) Weekes and (Sir Frank) Worrell, who captivated the cricket world after the Second World War. In the Midlands, however, the three Ws mean Wolves, West Bromwich and Walsall, who have not captivated anyone other than their own die-hard bunch of followers for quite a few years. It is Saturday today, but fortunately only Birmingham of the Midlands' teams are at home to add to the early afternoon traffic, and as we are heading out of town, that is not likely to affect our progress.

Alan admits to some trepidation about this leg of the journey. He is not familiar with this part of the world, which on a map looks a mass of impossibly confused roads and urban sprawl up the M6 corridor. The plan is to join the Inner City Ring Road, which runs very close to the cricket ground, and follow that until we pick up signs for Walsall and the A34. The ring road has been used for motor racing in the past and many of the locals seem to believe this still applies when they use the six-lane dual carriageway. There are, thankfully, clearly defined wide bus-lanes everywhere, which also serve as cycle lanes and provide us with plenty of protection and space once the roundabouts have been negotiated.

Birmingham is an important port of call on our ride for

another reason. It is where the special unit is being built for teenage cancer suffers with the backing of the Laurie Engel Fund, one of our chosen charities on the bike ride. A year later, David and I were to visit the Birmingham Children's Hospital with Matthew Engel, Laurie's father, who set up the fund in memory of his son. Matthew took us there one Sunday lunch-time during a Test at Edgbaston to show us the progress being made. He explained that while he felt the treatment provided for Laurie at the Children's Hospital had been the best available, the surroundings for his teenage son were pretty dire. Teenagers are caught in the middle of a difficult age gap for the National Health Service. They are generally too old to be on a children's wing, but the last thing they really want is to be stuck on an adult ward with the very elderly – and with nowhere for parents to stay overnight.

The state of the art £2.5 million wing being built by the Teenage Cancer Trust alongside the Birmingham Children's Hospital would solve that problem, providing comfortable accommodation for the patients, and rooms, or beds at least, for parents. Seeing the actual object of our fund-raising taking shape was a special moment, even if our modest donation probably paid for only one of the window frames.

We stick closely together on the ring road, making sure everyone safely negotiates each roundabout before moving on to the next. As we join the A34 for Walsall, I tell the others confidently that the traffic will thin out now. But if it does, it is not obvious. The road lumbers through the charmingly-named Bloxwich and on to Walsall, where we have to navigate another far more modest ring road

David (left) and I pose for a pre-ride publicity photo at Sussex's cricket ground.

Ready to go at the Oval beside the famous gasometer.
(l to r): Toddy, me, David, Tom, Jack and Alan with Jasper adopting the curious pose.

Canterbury pilgrims (l to r): Jack, Jasper and Tom.

The pub at Hove (l to r) : Alan, David, Toddy, Tom and Jack.

Oh, we do like to be beside the seaside. Tom and Jack at Worthing.

Highly sprung: Angus Fraser had a good engine but not a good bike.

Spot the ex-player.
(l to r): me, Tom, Jack, Gus, David and Toddy at Taunton.

A moment for Grace. Tom (l) and Jack by W.G's commemorative
plaque at Gloucestershire's Bristol ground.

Severn Up. David (left) and Jack on the cycle path over the old Severn Bridge.

Steve James chats with a friend at Glamorgan's ground in Cardiff wondering when the rest of us will catch up.

Daffs and Taffs. I have made it to the home of Welsh cricket.

The only way from Symonds Yat East to Symonds Yat West is by this rope-hauled ferry across the river Wye.

Ferry Nervous. David (background) clings on for dear life on the Symonds Yat ferry while (l to r) Alan, Toddy and I enjoy the ride.

Knackered. A bench provides a welcome break after a tough climb in the Malvern Hills for (l to r) Jack, Tom and Toddy while Alan takes a photo.

Browned Off. Toddy and David at the stinking, silt-covered
Worcester cricket ground.

A deflated Jack watches David (l) and Alan repair his puncture on
the road to Birmingham.

No Standing Please.
(l to r): David, Alan, Toddy, Jack and Tom at Edgbaston.

What's up Fred? David gets a surprise visitor at Lancashire's Red
Rose Lodge, where cardboard cut-outs of Andrew Flintoff pop up
everywhere.

Wheeler Dealer. Jack finds a new machine at one of our pub stops.

Another long slow slog on the route from Settle to Hawes with Jack taking my back wheel.

He may be in his seventies, but Toddy would let no hill defeat him.

A much-needed stop in the evening sunshine in Ribblesdale (l to r):
David, me, Tom, Alan, Toddy.

Hawes 11. The offending sign that tipped Jack over the edge with Ribblehead Viaduct in the background.

One for the album: me and the last of the evening sunshine at Ribblehead Viaduct.

The pitch at Headingley Carnegie is likely to take some turn today.

Mist stopped play, so the head steward at Trent Bridge is delighted to pose for our group photo (l to r): David, Toddy, me, Tom and Alan.

Where's the Old Man sending us next? Jack (l) and Tom study my meticulously prepared itinerary at Derby.

Pub Stop. Could be anywhere but this is in Furneux Pelham. Toddy takes tea, Alan takes ale and David tunes into to the football results.

Five go wild in Bedfordshire. Jack's idea of a group photograph with (l to r): David, Tom, me, Toddy and Alan.

Just two grounds to go after we arrive at Northampton. (l to r): Alan, Jack, Toddy (hidden) Tom and David.

The delight is obvious….Big Al meets Big Mac for the first time.

We've made it. In fading light we line up opposite the Lord's pavilion. (l to r): David, Jack, Alan, Tom, me and Toddy.

cluttered with road works and cones before we start to run into more rural surroundings and quieter roads. By now most of the north-bound traffic is pounding along the M6, which runs parallel to us a few miles to the west.

There is a sense of relief that we have the Midland mass behind us, and while the scenery is hardly stunning, we can see trees and green fields again. It is only another eight miles to Cannock, which is only 10 miles short of our next overnight stop in Stafford, so we decide to stop for a short break at a petrol station for the final push of what has been a surprisingly easy day.

The A34 is a good fast road of gentle undulations, and on this sunny Saturday afternoon is not too busy. To the east is Cannock Chase, a designated area of outstanding beauty with woodlands, heathlands and rare flora and fauna. It is a beautiful part of middle England, but for those of us of a certain age it has sinister connotations. In 1966, I was in my first year at grammar school in Somerset, the Beatles were in full swing and Sir Alf Ramsey was telling us England would win the World Cup that summer. It was also memorable for the gruesome 'The A34 Murders' or the 'Cannock Chase Murders' as they were also known.

With today's almost frenetic coverage of news stories, when the most tedious of press conferences is turned into a live event by the 24-hour-a-day television and radio channels, shocking events dominate the bulletins and phone-ins on Radio Five Live for days. Everybody, no matter how poorly informed or unqualified to comment, is invited to air their views on what a colleague of mine has dubbed 'bloke radio.' It makes for the most inane listening.

Just what today's news editors would have made of the

A34 Murders is difficult to imagine, but even back in 1966, when memory tells me the daily news coverage in the Bateman household in Cheddar was confined to an early-evening 15-minute bulletin read by Kenneth Baker on the BBC after Children's Hour, the story gripped an appalled nation.

In January that year a massive man-hunt had discovered the body of a seven-year-old who had been abducted. She was found by soldier who was part of the search team. She was naked and had been raped. The search also found two more bodies of girls, a five-year-old and a six-year-old, both from the Birmingham area who had gone missing the previous year. All three victims lived within a 17-mile radius of each other. The shocking find sparked one of the biggest murder hunts ever staged in this country. A grey Austin car had been seen in Cannock Chase around the time of the disappearance of the eldest girl, Christine Darby, and the police set about checking on the ownership of more than one million vehicles of that make. More than 150 detectives were put to work, 35,000 homes visited, 80,000 people interviewed, but no-one was arrested at the time.

In November 1968, almost three years later, a 10-year-old girl escaped from an attempted abduction by a man in a Ford car in Walsall, and a witness noted the registration and informed the police. This was traced to Raymond Leslie Morris who had been interviewed four times as a suspect in the death of Darby, but who had not been charged as his wife had supplied him with an alibi. When the police raided Morris' flat in Walsall they found pornographic photographs of children, and at the subsequent trial for the attempted adduction, his wife retracted her alibi that he had been shopping with her at the time of Darby's disappearance in 1966.

Morris, a Walsall man aged 39, was convicted of the murder of Darby and remained the chief suspect in the murder of the other two girls Margaret Reynolds and Diana Tift. He was also identified as a suspect in the disappearance of a 10-year-old girl in the same area in 1966. Her body has never been found. Cannock Chase will forever be associated with one of the darkest deeds in British criminal history.

Perhaps it was appropriate that one of the last places we passed that day before arriving in Stafford, our overnight stop, was Weeping Cross.

My research on the internet for accommodation in Stafford had not been very promising. There were no attractive looking pubs, while the long list of guest houses appeared to be catering for the commercial traveller rather than the occasional visitor. I had opted for one that looked presentable enough from the photograph on its website, had enough beds for all of us and was on our road into town. It was also not too expensive. There turned out to be a reason for that. It was the worst place we were to stay at on our trip, and that included the Youth Hostel at Hawes.

The large mock-tudor house looked fine from the outside, perched as it was on a raised area of bare ground by a road junction. The door was opened by a man in his mid-to-late 20s who was friendly enough, but appeared to have little idea about being in the guest house business. This was probably because he did have little idea about being in the guest house business. He informed me that he and his partner (whom we were never to see) had recently taken over the property and were new to the trade.

One of the pre-requisites of a guest house is cleanliness but our host's appearance made it feel as though we were stepping into student digs. He was dressed in a scruffy beige tee-shirt and jeans and his straggly hair looked as though it had seen neither shampoo nor comb in the last few days. Before we had been shown to our rooms, he also asked us for payment in full for our stay.

When I questioned this, he told me I would be surprised as to how many guests do an early-morning runner. I pointed out to him that we had just locked up about £5,000-worth of bikes in his shed and he had the key, so we were hardly likely to nip off without paying our £22.50 per-person bill. He appeared to see the logic in this but still asked for the money, so we paid up, eager to get to our rooms, get showered and sample the delights of a Saturday evening in Stafford, especially the real-ale pub that had been recommended to us.

Our host, in fact, was pleasant enough but was clueless as to what guests might expect from an overnight stay. I wondered out loud to my room-mate, who was Alan this evening, whether, in fact, the owner had ever stayed in a guest house himself. There was no soap in the bathroom nor was there a mirror, and it is not until something as basic as a mirror is missing that you realise how much you need one, particularly if you want to shave.

We did have the usual tea making facilities in the bedroom but a closer inspection revealed there was the slight drawback of having no teabags and only powdered milk. On the dressing table was a photocopied piece of paper with a list of breakfast items on it – bacon, sausage, beans, eggs (fried or scrambled), tomato, toast – with a little box beside each. Guests were asked to tick which items they required and leave the list with the proprietor before 10pm that night. Can you tell what you will want for breakfast the next day at 6pm the night before? I can't.

Breakfast was the anticipated huge disappointment. To Alan's utter horror, there were little pats of margarine on the table (no butter), the side plates were greasy, the sausages made of sawdust. There was no fruit available, there was one individual serving of marmalade between four per table, and, heaven help us, only instant coffee. I cannot stand instant coffee. In fact, I cannot see the point in it. Put in charge of the country for a day, instant coffee is one of the things I would ban along with music in restaurants, televisions in pubs, car park charges and dogs. Our host, who was doing the cooking and waiting on table in the same grubby beige tee-shirt at breakfast, will not go far in the accommodation business.

The previous evening in Stafford had turned out to be as disappointing as our digs. It started with me having a row – another one – with Tom, over something quite trivial such as him ignoring my suggestion as to where to cross the busy road to our lodgings. Our disagreement reached a full blown row as we were packing our bikes in the shed.

"Look Tom, I want to enjoy the rest of the ride and I cannot do that with you forever answering me back, being rude, thinking you know it all," I had said to him in measured tones. "I think it would be best if you just went home or off to university, you can get a train from here tomorrow. Either that or perhaps I'll go home and leave you lot to it."

It was, of course, an empty threat and I certainly did not

want him to quit the trip, but, to my shame, I said it all the same, and he was soon on the phone to his mother asking what he should do. She told him to ignore the old man, who would soon forget the conversation had taken place once he had a pint and several glasses of red wine inside him. She knew me too well, and, I guess, was entitled to after more than 30 years of living under the same roof.

There was still a frosty silence between Tom and me as the six of us wandered towards the little pub next to a busy railway line, that had come with a glowing recommendation from the lad at the guest house about the quality of food and beer served. Despite its unprepossessing location in a small housing estate, the pub certainly looked cosy, with candles everywhere giving it a warm glow as dusk closed in. We enthusiastically ordered the local brew and asked to see the menu, but the cheerful landlord had a minor bombshell to drop: "Sorry, lads. Power cut. That's why all the candles are lit. Leccy company reckons it will be about two hours before it's back on so we can't cook and I've given the kitchen staff the evening off. We can do you a bag of peanuts or some scratchings, though."

This was not what we had in mind so we finished our pints in the beer garden and headed back into town anxious to get somewhere to eat. Food is a very important part of our daily routine and none of us felt like a late night. We wanted to be back in our palatial guest house rooms in time to see Match of the Day, so we were keen to find an eatery. We came across a Frankie and Benny's New York Diner, which is one of those chains that offer food that looks enticing but flatters to deceive. There are pictures of the dishes on offer on the menu, which is always a worrying sign.

The staff, though, are wonderfully enthusiastic and what they serve fills a hole. By now, Tom and I were getting on like a house on fire as we compared the respective merits of the ribs 'n' chicken combo with smoke-house sauce and the Special Double Burger with bacon and melted cheese with onion rings on a sesame seeded bun. All with chips. We were also buoyed by the news that both Bristol City and Arsenal had won their respective matches today. It was a contented group that wandered back to our beds knowing that the next day offered something very special at the end of it.

Day Eight Route: *Leave Worcester by the A38 to Droitwich and Upton Warren. B4091 to Bromsgrove. A488 towards Redditch then B4091 to Catshill and Lickey. Through Longbridge joining A441 for Kings Norton and Edgbaston (Warwickshire County Cricket Club). Pershore Road to inner ring road (A4540). Join A34 to Walsall via Perry Barr. A34 to Cannock and Stafford.*

String Distance: 52 miles.
Actual Distance: 59 miles.
Time in saddle: 5hrs 5mins
Average speed: 11.6mph

Overall string distance: 478 miles.
Actual mileage to-date: 536.
Total cycling time: 45 hrs 5 mins.
Average speed: 11.9mph

PRESSURES ON THE PELOTON
By Tom Bateman.

Phew! I have made it through the first week.

This was my immediate emotion when we reached a sodden New Road in the picturesque City of Worcester, not because I find the relentless cycling particularly difficult, to be honest, I don't...shhh! My sense of relief was due to the memories of my last ride, abruptly ended by a persistent knee problem that forced me to sit out the final two days. Frustrating to say the least.

This memory was at the forefront of my mind during that first week of the 18 Counties ride, stressing over every niggle and analysing each shot of pain, which, when cycling, is a regular occurrence. The thought of leaving this ride early was something I didn't even want to contemplate, such was the enjoyable nature of the cycling. Yet by the end of the next day, sitting in a dreary B&B in Stafford, when I was just starting to think my knee was going to hold up, I found myself ringing home to ask about train times back to Kent.

"Mum, could you find out train times from Manchester to London please?"

The pleased tone from my Mum's voice, which she had when she answered the phone, quickly turned to one of concern,

"Why? What's the problem? What happened? Are you ok?"

Perhaps I should have explained why I wanted her to run this errand in advance, to avoid such a panicked response from my normally unflappable mother. Thankfully it wasn't my knee, although at the time I probably wished it had been – thirty minutes earlier my father and I had exchanged angry words following the silliest of disagreements.

In my excitement anticipating a warm shower and dinner, I dashed across the busy main road as soon as I saw the Bed and Breakfast car park. Meanwhile, the others (needlessly!) continued 30 yards up the road to use the pedestrian crossing.

This may sound like a trivial event to disagree over, but at the end of a stressful day navigating through Birmingham (now I know why it's called the second city – it seemed to go on forever) my Dad had, understandably, quite a short fuse. Of course I took the bait being the 'know-it-all son'.

This was never going to be resolved – both father and son as adamant as each other, determined not to back down. On reflection, perhaps I should have admitted my mistake and gone up for that much anticipated shower. Instead of that rather sensible option, a long shouting match proceeded in front of an audience of a bewildered B&B manager and a slightly embarrassed peloton. The climax of the argument was a disheartening declaration from my dad, fuelled by the heat of the moment: "If you are going to carry on like this, perhaps it would be better if you went home or back to university."

Of course I did not go home. My father quickly came to apologise, explaining he hadn't meant what he'd said (which I knew already deep down), I returned the apology and off we all trotted for dinner in good spirits.

It was when we reached Bristol that I came to the conclusion that cycling 50-70 miles a day was not breaching the limits of my fitness. Unfortunately, the physical act of cycling is just one tiny part of the overall challenge. It might sound like a cliché, but 90 per cent of a ride such as this is mental. The 'Stafford Episode' highlights the type of psychological obstacles that can regularly occur.

During the ride, flare-ups between my father and me, if not daily, were at least a regular occurrence. The effect of an argument can, almost literally, drain all the energy from your legs.

One other incident sticks in my mind: on the way out of Newport I had to relieve myself in a roadside bush, which I managed to do without any honking cars. What I hadn't realised was this bush also lined the edge to someone's driveway.

"Tom what are you doing? That's someone's driveway you're pissing in! You're so thoughtless sometimes", said my father in a stern, fed up voice as he whizzed past. Needless to say, an argument ensued. This argument took a degree of enjoyment out of a day I was feeling particularly good about, enjoying the hilly terrain and the challenge of keeping up with a serious guest rider.

When you are mentally not right, the cycling can seem doubly difficult. This was the case even on the very last day. Everyone was in good spirits riding into London, which we seemed to reach in no time having started at Bishop's Stortford that morning. Once again I was finding the cycling relatively easy going and I was enjoying the last day of full cycling that I was likely to have for a while.

While in London, where I go to university, the most cycling I normally get is from my flat in Mile End to my girlfriend's house in Kentish Town. It just so happens this was not far off the route we would be taking to Lord's, so I was nominated to lead.

This may sound easy enough: just cycle a route I had tackled countless times, only with the bonus of being much fitter and not wearing jeans and a hoody...simple! However, it wasn't as easy as this. Much like the mental strains of having an argument with my father can drain the legs, so too did the stress of having to make sure that five other cyclists were on my tail through busy London traffic.

Suddenly the pleasant autumnal afternoon sun became sweltering and jarring, the hill in Angel, which I would normally ascend without a pedal pushed in anger, was like one of the Yorkshire Dales, and the London traffic, which I was accustomed to negotiating, was transformed into a deadly obstacle.

After having thought the day was going to be straightforward, something that was never actually the case on this ride (I often anticipated easy days only to be proved wrong with unnerving consistency), I arrived at Lord's drained and weary.

It is safe to say that the mental strains of a ride can transform the experience for you as a rider. Feel good and, on the whole, everything seems plain sailing; add a bit of stress and suddenly the real difficulty of a ride such as this becomes all too apparent.

Luckily for me, thanks to the good organisation by my father, great morale among the group and most importantly a huge slice of good luck, times of mental stress were few and far between so this made the riding extremely enjoyable and RELATIVELY pain free.

CHAPTER 10

The Second Half

...Stafford to Manchester.

It is another lovely Sunday morning and a significant day in our ride: today we start the second half of the challenge. Although we are still heading north, we are into the last week, a psychological mountain has been climbed. It is strange. You spend months preparing for a venture like this, eagerly looking forward to it and then, once it starts, you are counting down the days for it to end. Perhaps it is the fear of not being able to complete it that makes the first week an anxious one; there is always the worry that some ageing part of your body will pack in and force you to get the train back home crestfallen and without having completed the route. As you get closer to the end, those fears start to fade, and reaching half-way is a significant achievement. It is a pity the breakfast in our Stafford digs cannot match our feelings of well-being.

Sunday roads are quiet, particularly early in the day, so we take advantage and set off at 9.15. There has been nothing much to delay us over the breakfast table and there is no bill to pay. The bikes have had a good night's rest in their shed and we roll out into the deserted streets of Stafford jostling good-naturedly for position in the pack. Harmony has descended upon the *peloton* and we ride as one, taking it in turns to be the lead bike, chatting about last night's Match of the Day and laughing about our lodgings. Tonight we are in for a treat as, courtesy of Lancashire County Cricket Club, we are staying at their own Red Rose Lodge, which is situated in the Old Trafford ground, that is not to be confused with the other Old Trafford where they play football, which is a half-a-mile away. Thanks to Lancashire's very supportive Media Manager, Rebecca, we have been offered free accommodation at the hotel and, for the first time on the trip, we have a room each. While sharing is fine, it is bliss to be able to spread out and do exactly what you like in the privacy of your own room. We cannot wait to get there, which is perhaps why we appear to be making such good progress as we head along our rolling B-road towards Stoke-on-Trent through Burston, Hilderstone and Meir Heath.

Staffordshire is one of England's hidden gems. It is a county most people whizz through on the M6. Sandwiched as it between the Manchester and Birmingham conurbations, it might not appear to have much going for it, but appearances are so often deceptive. The county's history is built on the mining and pottery industries, but it also has some of the most outstanding scenery in Britain, particularly in the north, in the Peak District National Park. Here, just a few miles outside Buxton, on Axe Edge Moor, lies Flash, officially Britain's highest village at 1519 ft (463m). For a while there was an Anglo-Scottish dispute to the claim of being the highest village, Wanlockhead in the Lowther Hills flying the Saltire for those north of the border. So along came The BBC's 'One Show' to settle the dispute with some help from the people at the Ordnance Survey Office, who measured the highest house in Flash to be higher than the highest house in Wanlockhead. By how much, I am not sure, but the prize went to the folk of Staffordshire. By its very nature of being perched so high, Flash was a tough place to live and scrape a living. In the 18th century an enterprising local gang turned to supplementing their income by producing counterfeit money, which has given rise to the expression 'Flash Money'. Fortunately, for the sake of our legs, our route takes us to the west of Flash and well away from the hills of the Peak District.

Staffordshire also boasts the site of the UK's largest explosion when, during the Second World War, a bomb and ammunition store at RAF Fauld near Hanbury went up. Almost 4,000 tons of high explosives being kept in disused underground gypsum workings exploded, the blast being heard as far away as Somerset and the resulting seismic waves being recorded in Casablanca. The Fauld Explosion was the largest non-nuclear explosion of the Second World War. It destroyed a nearby dam and reservoir, a plaster works was flattened, a farm disappeared and a crater almost three-quarters of a mile wide was created. It is estimated that 78 people, both military and civilian, died from the blast and the subsequent flooding caused by the breached dam.

No-one is quite sure what caused the Fauld Explosion although it is thought likely to have been the result of an Italian prisoner-of-war mistakenly using a brass tool to remove a detonator from a bomb rather than a wooden one.

The 300-foot deep crater is still clearly visible from the air although now largely over-grown with trees. It has become a memorial for those who perished and the site is fenced off as it is thought there are still live explosives buried there.

After cruising through the undulating Staffordshire countryside for ten pleasant miles, our Sunday morning bonhomie is shattered by the advent of the Stoke Ring Road in our path. On the map, the route north through the Potteries to Kidsgrove looks straightforward enough, but the road planners of Stoke City Council have other ideas, sign-posting us onto a three-lane roaring dual-carriageway that is definitely not intended for bikes. Unfortunately I am a few hundred yards behind the leading pair of Alan and Tom when they decide to sweep down the slip road onto the race-track that is the ring road. While the signs designed for the motorist point towards the Ring Road for those bound for Kidsgrove and the north, I thought common sense would tell any cyclist to head straight into the city centre on the old main road, which is quieter and more likely to be a direct route through the town. Alan and Tom, however, do not see it that way.

These ring roads are really no place for cyclists, as car drivers are keen to let you know with blaring horns – and in many respects I don't blame them. There is a hard shoulder but it is strewn with gravel and broken glass as usual, forcing us to cycle in the left-hand carriageway. This would be OK but for the filter roads joining us from the left and which we have to cycle across between the traffic joining the ring road race-track. It is hairy stuff cycling through this concrete valley with its high sides. I am growing more and more agitated with every honk of a car horn and as my shouts to those riding ahead are drowned out by the roar of people-carriers taking reluctant children to granny's for Sunday lunch.

I can see us circumnavigating this cycling hell-hole all day, doing lap after lap, never able to escape, but Tom and Alan finally decide to pull off at an exit road and wait for us to re-group. I am pretty fed up by the time I arrive, telling them breathlessly that dual carriageways are no place for cyclists. My temper is fraying. Tom is being head-strong (again!) while Alan cannot appreciate that not all motorists are going to follow the Highway Code to the letter and show fawning respect for cyclists. Toddy is too pre-occupied with his panniers, which are making a worrying rubbing sound against his back wheel, to care, while David and Jack have the maps out and are sharing sweets. As usual. What happened to this glorious Sunday?

I suggest, in slow moderated language as if talking to a group of half-wits, that we head into the town centre, which will be quiet on a Sunday, and pick up the local signs for Kidsgrove, of which there are bound to be several.

Unfortunately, I am wrong. Again.

Like all keen football fans, I know that the only Football League team in England not named after a place is Port Vale, a lower division club that is based in Burslem, one of six towns that make up the Potteries. Port Vale is neither a Port nor in a Vale, by the way, so I should have guessed they like a little mystery in these parts, hence no signposts for Kidsgrove. It is as if the sign-makers decided to have a day off when they got to 'K' and simply moved on to 'L' when they got back to work. The city is also a mass of one-way roads and pot-holes and no fun at all for cyclists. I make a mental note not to come back here unless on four wheels, or preferably two caterpillar tracks and in a bulldozer.

Finally, we crack and do what no self-respecting male wants to do. We have to ask the way. After several blank looks (why is it that people these days seem to have no idea about the geography of their own home town and the whereabouts of the neighbouring towns?), one elderly man carrying home his Sunday papers points confidently back in the direction from which we have just come, tells us to look out for the elaborate red-brick Victorian municipal building and keep going. We are back on track at last but the good time we made in the morning has been lost and we are in need of a break, which we take just on the outskirts of Kidsgrove. Tesco stores are not my choice of a fun day out on a Sunday morning, but they do have handy coffee shops and plenty of metal trolleys to chain a bike to.

Back on the road we make sublime progress on our much more simple route up the A34 past Mow Cop and Scholar Green, whose wonderfully named railway station which once served both villages was immortalised in the song 'Slow Train', a lament to the Beeching rail cuts of 1964 sung by the comedy duo Flanders and Swann. The busy north-west main line still hammers through here as does the more serene local canal, which we follow to Congleton.

High to our right is a rocky outcrop known locally as 'The Cloud', which is perched on the edge of the Peak District, but we are sticking to the relatively flat A34 across the Cheshire Plain. The roads are good, the traffic light and the terrain easy going, so much so that we find ourselves approaching the wealthy commuter belt of Manchester before we have even stopped for lunch.

I recognise many of these roads, as the cricket journalists' fraternity often stay around Wilmslow and Alderley Edge for Test matches and one-day internationals at Old Trafford. There are plenty of good pubs and restaurants too, and a little private cricket ground which used to belong to one of the game's more colourful characters from the 1980s 'Lord' Tim Hudson, and which became a meeting place for players and Press.

The pony-tailed Hudson, a self-styled eccentric, became Ian Botham's agent and staged matches involving some of cricket's greats at his Birtles Bowl ground with its brightly painted pavilion. In the 1960s, Hudson had been a disc jockey in America and claims to have coined the phrase 'flower power' during the early days of the hippie era. He is reputed to have discovered the Moody Blues pop group and travelled with the Beatles on their first US tour.

Back in the UK, as opposed to the USSR, this flamboyant cricket-lover with his striped blazers suggested that he was going to turn Botham into a Hollywood star. It never happened, of course, but Beefy did get to play for 'Hudson's Hollywood XI' at Birtles Bowl alongside some of the sports biggest names such as Imran Khan, Viv Richards, Clive Lloyd and Gary Sobers. He even had the honour of playing against a Fleet Street XI at Birtles in those heady days when Test cricket stopped in the middle of a match for a 'rest' day on a Sunday.

It all went a bit sour for the Hudson-Botham frienship when Tim announced to the world: "I am aware he smokes dope, doesn't everyone?' Botham (now Sir Ian) and the cricket authorities were not amused and that was the end of his partnership with Hudson. A decade later a weed-covered

Birtles Bowl (dandelions and moss – not the other sort of weed) was up for sale, and Lord Tim was back in the U.S. He is still going strong, though, and appears to be as engagingly potty as ever, judging by his web-site.

Wilmslow and Alderley Edge form one of the most ostentatiously wealthy areas of the UK. If they have a bit of cash in these parts, they will have a bit of flash, too. I have been told there are more millionaires per square mile in these two villages than in any other part of Britain. This is where the footballers of Manchester United and Manchester City tend to live, and their agents and solicitors, who do not go short. The Porsche showrooms in the middle of Wilmslow must do a healthy trade. In the posh part of town there are flower baskets in the walkways that lead to bijou cafés where people sit at outside tables and admire their cars parked nearby. It is hardly 't' grim north' in these parts.

The restaurants are plentiful and busy on this sunny Sunday afternoon and the local diners in their elegant finery do not want to rub shoulders with a group of sweaty cyclists in lycra. As we walk along the pavements of Alderley pushing our bikes and looking for somewhere to eat, the head waiters appear to be eyeing us with suspicion, so we re-mount and head on a little further out of town towards Wilmslow to find a more low-brow pub with a large car park and garden tables where we can de-camp. It is early afternoon and we are just 12 miles from our destination! This ride is becoming all too easy. A mood of what-could-possibly-go-wrong has descended upon us as we indulge in a long, liquid lunch, read the Sunday papers and phone home to catch up on family gossip and reassure loved ones that we are all safe and sound.

The remaining few miles into the city of Manchester and to the home of Lancashire County Cricket Club takes us through Wilmslow and past the airport on flat minor roads. It is easy navigating, too, and I am given the honour of leading us home today, not because I have ridden well, but simply because I know the way. The previous summer when I was in Manchester for a one-day international, I spent time on reconnaissance, working out how to get from the south of Manchester into the city centre without using the motorway network that is as manic as the one around Birmingham. We simply follow the signs for Stretford and there before us are the grand wrought-iron entrance gates of Lancashire County Cricket Club with its red rose emblem picked out in bright paint.

Old Trafford is a friendly place but in much need of that bulldozer when I have finished with it in Stoke. Apart from a glorious three-tiered red-brick Victorian Pavilion (built for the amateur players while the professionals had to use a shed at the other end of the ground), it is difficult to imagine an uglier, less user-friendly cricket ground. It was hit by German bombs in 1940 and then repaired by German prisoners of war, but even the Teutonic influence could not alter the fact that the pavilion had been built parallel to the pitch, affording the members the worst view on the ground. Serious cricket watchers like to watch the game from behind the stumps or as close to it as is possible, not sideways on where it is impossible to detect the nuances of the battle between batsman and bowler.

You may have heard that it rains from time to time in Manchester, yet there is no shelter for the spectators on the sprawling concrete terraced seating at the Old Trafford ground apart from those members in the pavilion or the wealthy supporters in the executive boxes. The loos are foul, the chip vans are greasy, the amenities basic. To its credit, the Lancashire club is in the midst of a major redevelopment scheme as I write. Not before time.

The club should have a ground to be proud of, being the biggest in terms of membership in the country. It is also a county steeped in cricket history that once enjoyed great success, and has produced many very fine players. The recent role call includes long-serving England captain Michael Atherton and the country's most adored cricketer Andrew Flintoff, whose life-sized cardboard cut-outs adorn the stairwells and landings of the Red Rose Lodge and scare the life out of any resident who stumbles out of their room bleary-eyed in the morning. 'Freddie' Flintoff is anything but a two-dimensional cricketer. It seems incongruous to see his cardboard image advertising a budget hotel.

Another of Lancashire's favourite sons is fast bowler Jimmy Anderson from Burnley, just "up road" from Manchester. Jimmy is one of life's gentle souls off the cricket field: a genuinely nice guy who does not appear to have been changed by the fame and money that have come his way. He is a trusting sort, some might suggest gullible, who tends to take what people tell him at face value. And that makes him easy prey for David Lloyd, the prankster.

This is not our David Lloyd, of course, but David Lloyd, the former Lancashire and England batsman who has done just about every job in cricket save being masseur for the women's team (although I am told he once applied for this post). He tried his hand at umpiring, coached Lancashire and was England's head coach, too, for a while before joining the Sky TV Sports commentary team where his inimitable "cheeky northerner" persona has earned him a cult following world-wide. He is universally known as 'Bumble' and cannot resist a wind-up. Cue Jimmy.

The scene is an England tour of Sri Lanka, where the only way to get from one venue to another is by coach on narrow, clogged, twisty roads on which brakes and horns are in constant use. England have to make the trip from the capital, Colombo, to their hill-top hotel retreat in the jungle near Dambulla. The journey is about 70 miles, but takes six hours on the one main road towards Kandy from the coast. The journalists and commentators tend to travel by cars or mini-buses, which are quicker than a lumbering team coach, and we arrive at the hotel first, slip into something casual for a fruit punch by the pool and await the players' arrival. Jimmy stumbles off the coach looking frazzled by the experience of six hours of pushing and shoving on the roads of Sri Lanka.

Bumble (sipping cocktail): "Where you been, Jim lad?"
Jimmy: "Six hours on the bloody bus, that's where?"
Bumble: Six hours? Never. We did it a little more than two!"
Jimmy: "Impossible, with that traffic. You must have flown."
Bumble: "No lad, we came by the new highway, barely a soul on it. Straight through once you're past the toll booths."
Jimmy: "I don't believe it We've had six bloody uncomfortable hours stuck on the coach. You telling me there's a quick way here?"
Bumble: "Aye lad, if you're prepared to pay the toll. About 20 quid – but well worth it."

At this stage Anderson stomps off to find Phil Neale, the England team operations manager, who is in on Bumble's joke with Anderson. Neale informs Jimmy, who by now has recruited an indignant Kevin Pietersen to the cause, that, yes, the management knew about the new road, but, no, the England and Wales Cricket Board were not prepared to stump up the toll charges. By this time, Jimmy and KP are reaching for their wallets and offering to pay the toll charges for the return journey themselves, but Bumble and Phil Neale can keep up the pretence no longer and crack into hysterical giggles.

As efficient as ever, Rebecca, our benefactor at Lancashire, has done her job of organising our rooms as promised. The hotel reception is expecting us, even the men on the security desk are expecting us, and they open up a back door into a large passage where we can stow our bikes beside the kit bags of the players. Having an hotel room each, it is an opportunity to delve into the far recesses of our panniers, empty everything, hang what few possession we have in the wardrobe and do some much needed laundry before our night out.

That evening we are being met by a journalist colleague named Myles, and his partner Emma. Myles, who has recently bought himself a bike as part of a fitness campaign, had threatened to cycle a leg or two of the ride with us, but instead decides to take us out to his favourite Manchester curry house instead. Not much difference, really.

Tom has left us for the evening to meet up with an old school friend, who is at university in Manchester, but the rest of us are picked up and chauffeured to a restaurant that, what it lacks in space and décor, makes up for on flavour and size of portions, much to Alan's approval. It must be good because there in one corner is our host from a few nights ago in Monmouth, Matthew Engel. He is in Manchester to cover the Labour Party Conference for the Financial Times. It is, as they say, a small world.

Curry is not the most advisable dinner to have the night before a long day in the saddle – and tomorrow is going to be a long day – but there are times when it just feels the perfect meal to have. This was one such occasion as the poppadoms kept arriving and the gassy lager kept flowing. It reminded me of the time when in a restaurant on a cricket tour in India, a colleague asked the waiter to bring poppadoms while he and his colleagues studied the menu. The waiter inquired as to whether the group required plain or spicy poppadoms, to which he was told "50-50". The waiter returned with 100 poppadoms, 50 plain and 50 spiced.

Alan could have certainly eaten that many had the same confusion in communication arisen in our Manchester curry house, but instead he made do with a mountain of rice, several towers of nan bread and whatever the rest of us could not manage to get through. I was glad I was not sharing a room with him – or any of my other fellow cyclists, come to that – tonight.

Myles and Emma drove us back to our hotel in their cars, collecting Tom from his mate's student digs en route, and we headed for a night of blissful isolation in the knowledge that the next day was going to be one of our biggest challenges. What we did not know, however, was that it was going to get off to the worst possible start.

Day Nine Route: *Stafford town centre, B5066 to Sandon, Hilderstone, Meirheath. Join A50 to Stoke on Trent, get lost, rejoin A50 to Kidsgrove. A34 to Congleton, Alderley, Wilmslow. B5166 to Styal past Manchester Airport to Gatley. B5167 towards Didsbury. Left on to A5145 towards Stretford and follow signs for Old Trafford Cricket Ground.*

String Distance: 55 miles
Actual Distance: 58 miles
Time in saddle: 4hrs 42 mins
Average speed: 12.3 mph

Overall string distance: 533 miles.
Actual mileage to-date: 594 miles.
Time in Saddle: 49 hrs 47 mins.
Average speed: 11.9mph

CHAPTER ELEVEN

The Viaduct Velo

...from Manchester to Hawes

IT IS, of course, a fallacy that Manchester is the wettest place in Britain. It is not even the wettest place in England (several small villages in Cumbria vie for that honour). Manchester is, come to that, not even the wettest city in England – Plymouth earns the urban umbrella award – but unfortunately for Mancunians, it just feels like it is always rainy in Manchester.

Perhaps it is the fact that the Manchester sky-line can look so bleak when the clouds roll in off the Irish Sea that makes it seem that if it is not actually raining, then it will not be long before it is. And when the rain sets in it is difficult to shift. Manchester has steady, unrelenting rain, as I can verify from long days sitting in the press box at Old Trafford waiting for play to begin. Some days it never did stop.

Sure enough, when the curtains of the Red Rose Lodge were thrown back on Monday morning it was pitter-pattering down. The expanse of tarmac car park in front of the hotel glistened wet while the sky above was a mass of brooding grey cloud.

Oh well, we could not complain. After nine days of dry weather, we knew this had to happen at some stage of our ride, and anyway, we had to put on a cheery smile this morning for Rebecca, our friend from Lancashire County Cricket Club, who had organised our free accommodation in the Lodge at the ground. An Aussie with indefatigable enthusiasm for her job in promoting Lancashire cricket, 'Becs' had arranged to meet us at 8.30am, us with our bikes, her with a camera, for a 'photo shoot' with the pavilion as a backdrop. She wanted to publicise our sponsored slog on the county website, and all publicity is good publicity. We happily obliged. It was the least we could do before retreating back into the warmth and shelter of the hotel café for breakfast.

We are at a stage of the ride where we can cope with a bit of adverse weather, even if we would rather have rain on an open country road than on the grimy streets of a city where the buses and vans constantly throw spray up from their tyres into your face. In fact, the clouds are lifting and the rain has virtually stopped as we pull out of the cricket car park although the road still glistens wet, warning us not to take liberties.

On a long ride, you build up fitness as you go: leg muscles get visibly bigger and firmer, lungs no longer feel like they are bursting on the long climbs. We all have a few aches and pains but learn to manage them. Alan has to be careful with his knees, which he swathes in elasticated bandages each day; Tom was forced to pull out of our trip around Ireland for the last few days because he aggravated an old rugby injury in his knee and now takes care on the climbs; David and Toddy can be susceptible to nose and throat complaints and were particularly unwell on our French trip; I have chronic backache from being bent forward over the handlebars for six hours a day, which I alleviate by changing position on the bike, sitting up whenever possible and even exercising shoulders while on the move, although this last bit can earn curious stares from motorists.

Everybody makes jokes about cyclists having a sore bum, but that is usually the least of our worries – and for the record, it is not the bottom that takes the strain, anyway. It is the perineum, that bit between your bottom and your dangly bits that rests on the saddle and tends to feel bruised in the early days of a ride.

After nine days of riding and with more than 500 miles behind us, we are feeling comparatively fit, but we know we shall need all of that fitness for the day ahead, which promises to be the toughest yet as we head north from Manchester, through the industrialised valleys of Lancashire, into the Pennines and across the exposed moors of the Yorkshire Dales National Park. The last thing we need is a puncture, but after cycling just seven tenths of a mile that is what happens.

We have just passed Manchester's less important Old Trafford and 'Lou Macari's Fish and Chip Shop' and swung into Bridgewater Way when Jack dismounts on the side of a thundering dual-carriageway packed with commuters and commercial traffic, and glares at his useless front tyre. There is no pavement or quiet side road to retreat into, just a narrow grass verge with crash barriers and thorny bushes. The only saving grace as David and Alan get to work is that the rain has relented.

A new inner tube fitted within 15 minutes, we are back in the saddle and looking for our way out of Manchester, a justifiably proud city that the urban planners have done their best to ruin. Our route north is a veritable Who's Who of Football League clubs as we are heading towards Bury, which is sandwiched between Bolton and Rochdale and just beyond Oldham. A little further on our road takes us through Accrington and near Burnley, which is a stone's throw from Blackburn, whose other near neighbours are Preston.

The textile industry which once made this a thriving area has now virtually disappeared, but the old red-brick mills and terraced housing on the hillsides still make this one of the most evocative places in England for me. It is a fascinating place to cycle through even though the terrain is tough and the road surfaces neglected.

Far away from the madding crowd, we also have a date later today at a place for the privileged: Giggleswick School, near Settle, one of the oldest and most famous independent schools in the country. A schoolteacher friend, who taught at Tom and Jack's school in Kent, once worked at Giggleswick and insisted they would be delighted to host us for tea on our journey north. It was no more than a mile out of our way and seemed like too good an offer to turn down, so they were primed to receive us in late afternoon.

Manchester proved as simple to get out of as Birmingham. In a car, an unfamiliar city can seem like a nightmare to the motorist, who feels pressurised by the BMW travelling six inches from his rear bumper and the female partner in the passenger seat whose map reading technique involves turning the book upside down and then suggesting you stop to ask for directions from the group of youths dismantling the nearby bus shelter. On a bike, you have more time to take in road signs and even pull over in the Bus Lane to check the map. Our target on the ring road is the distinctive Manchester Evening News newspaper offices, where we take a sharp left on the A56 to Prestwich and Bury.

Instantly, the boys are impressed not only with my navigational skills at identifying our turn off so clearly, but also by the help I have arranged from the Manchester Constabulary. Lining our route now are police officers spaced at intervals of about 200 yards just to ensure there is no crowd trouble, while all parked cars and vans have been moved to give us a nice clear run. My colleagues' admiration, however, lasts only a few minutes before they realise the real reason for police presence when Prime Minister Gordon Brown's cavalcade comes wailing through on its way to the Labour Party Conference.

Manchester behind us, we begin to encounter some serious climbs after we pass under the M66 and on to Ramsbottom and Rawtenstall, while up ahead, the rain clouds are re-grouping over the hills that are our destination.

Ramsbottom is a splendid spot, much cherished by those who do not dismiss it as "just another northern town." Like most of the places on our route, it has a history worth delving into, evidence of which can be seen in the monument on a nearby hill and is visible from virtually everywhere in the town.

The monument is in memory of Sir Robert Peel and was erected on Holcombe Hill in 1852 thanks to public subscription, which raised the not insignificant sum of £1000 in honour of Ramsbottom's most famous citizen. Peel was Prime Minister for two terms of office in the 1830s and 40s, but is most famous for founding our police force – hence the nickname Bobby or the now less common Peeler for a police officer. Law and order, though, was not what the good folk of Ramsbottom had upper-most in their minds when they collected their subscriptions. Peel had introduced the textile industry into the area and turned Ramsbottom into a thriving community. He had also been instrumental in repealing the hated Corn Laws, which had greatly inflated the cost of bread, the staple diet of the working man. The local people had much to be thankful to Peel for and they showed their appreciation with the 128ft stone pile on top of a hill.

Every Good Friday, local folk indulge in egg rolling down Holcombe Hill, quite why, no-one seems sure, but it is one of those curious British traditions that is rooted in some distant belief. Busy place that it is, Ramsbottom is the home of another idiosyncratic pastime: the World Black Pudding Throwing Championships, which is not, as yet, an Olympic Sport, although there are those who are keen to get it on the rota for 2012 in London. Black pudding throwing (which is probably the best thing to do with a black pudding) involves hurling the little meaty devils underarm at a tower of Yorkshire puddings, knocking over as many as possible.

Britain, God Bless her, has surely cornered the market in odd-ball events? In nearby Morecambe, locals indulge in an annual 'Railway Trespass' on Christmas Day, walking along the line. Just up the road from Ramsbottom you will find the 'Bacup Nutters' who every Easter Sunday black up their faces and dance through the town.

In Bourton-on-the-Water, Gloucestershire, they play football every year. Nothing unusual in that you might think, except this footy match is in the Windrush River which flows through the village, with the bridges used for goalposts. In nearby Chipping Campden, they stage an annual 'Olimpick Games,' which includes the treasured sport of shin-kicking. From nettle-eating in Dorset to worm-charming in Cheshire to cheese rolling just about everywhere, this truly is a wonderfully potty nation.

None of it, though, is half as daft as trying to cycle around 18 county cricket grounds with your worldly goods packed into two panniers.

Our switchback road is beginning to sort out the men from the boys, and one of the men, yours truly, is beginning to feel the strain. The Pennines rising to our right make for breath-taking scenery but it is something else that is taking my breath away as I labour up yet another long climb and drop off the back of the pack. What makes the going tougher is the knowledge that this is only the start of a long day that is going to become more demanding, not easier.

At least the climbing is generating plenty of body heat that keeps out the chill of the wind off the hills. The temptation is to remove my outer jacket, and cycle in just a tee-shirt, but I know this would be counter-productive because on the down-hill section, the extra speed and wind would instantly chill the sweat and start me shivering. Traditionally on the big climbs in the Tour de France, riders, while still on the move, accepted newspapers from spectators at the summit to stuff inside their cycle tops to keep out the cold winds on the descent, dispensing with them when they reached the bottom. As my copy of today's

Daily Express is wedged inside one of my panniers, I have to make do with zipping up my jacket before the descent into Haslingden, where we have agreed to re-group for our morning break.

Haslingden is a pretty little town with two tea shops a few yards apart. One owner wants to serve his customers, the other apparently does not. Having stood for what seemed an eternity at the counter of the latter while everyone else was getting served ahead of us, we cut our losses and left. The next one served us instantly. If you visit Haslingden, I hope you chose the right one. For us, the minutes wasted in the first establishment were frustrating as we were already slipping behind schedule. Standing on the pavement drinking our coffees, I feel it is only right to ring the number I have been given for Giggleswick School and leave a message with the secretary of the master, who is to be our host. I explain that we may be a little after 4pm instead of before 4pm. Fingers crossed.

There seems to be solidarity in the peloton today. Perhaps it is the feeling of working class togetherness you get in these northern towns, perhaps it is the knowledge that we still have plenty of tough cycling ahead and we are all in this together. The frequency of the towns on our route with their pedestrian crossings, traffic lights and roundabouts slows down our progress and it is beginning to rain again as we free-wheel down the hill into Accrington and past the home of its famous football club Accrington Stanley, a name redolent with all that is good about lower league football despite the mickey-taking of those who attach themselves to the likes of Manchester United, Liverpool, Chelsea and Arsenal.

Re-born two years after going defunct in 1966, "Accy" were saved again recently by a local businessman, who paid off their bills as administration loomed. They are run on a shoestring and mean a lot to the people of the town.

I have never been to see a match at the Crown Ground (capacity 5,057) in Accrington, one of about 30 grounds I still need to visit to complete the set of all 92 Football League club grounds. Joining the 92-Club used to be a proud boast of some fanatics. It meant something, but these days it seems a rather pointless exercise with teams moving to new grounds at the drop of a hat and fresh teams joining the league structure from the Conference every season. It is impossible to keep up with all 92 venues.

By the time we exit Accrington's town boundaries, it has stopped raining and we head for Clayton-le-Moors and Whalley, towns that just seem to merge into one another. We skirt around the towering Pendle Hill and on towards Clitheroe, reputedly the most central town in Britain and where, Ian informs us, is found one of the most famous independent wine merchants in the country, D Byrne and Co, a family run business. Alan's ears prick up and he breaks off from his head-down rhythmical cycling to learn more.

Alan has a love – some might call it a weakness – for most things alcoholic, but, in particular wine. Even on a cycle ride where the amount of weight you carry is so important, he would be prepared to buy a couple of bottles to put in his panniers. When he and his wife Diane have cycling holidays in France, he deliberately makes sure her panniers have plenty of spare room to accommodate the wine he intends to buy. We, however, convince Alan that we do not have time to stop for shopping. We must still have 40 miles ahead of us and it is nearly lunch time. To ensure Alan is not tempted, we by-pass Clitheroe on the main A59 and then cut westward for our cross-country route alongside the River Ribble which will lead us to Settle and Giggleswick School, and then the formidable Ribblesdale, our major climb of the day.

We stop on the verge of the main road at our small turn-off for Sawley to make sure everyone is together. David is handing out the rations of sweets to keep us going, but we are in need of something more substantial than a jelly baby. We had targeted Wigglesworth as a potential lunch stop, but that is still about ten miles away. Our quiet country lane, however, looks likely to be short of suitable stopping places and we are in need of food again.

We halt briefly on an ancient stone bridge over the River Ribble to admire the view before pushing on to Bolton-by-Bowland. As we arrive in the village, our excitement at seeing a sign for a pub restaurant is soon replaced by disappointment when we see the next sign :'Closed'. It is after 2pm. We are just beginning run out of hope when we crest another gentle climb and see a sign for a garden centre with a café accompanied by the word 'Open'.

The proprietor is rather taken aback to have six hungry customers asking for lunch at this time of day. Whatever next? The kitchen staff are washing up the dishes from the lunch rush. She goes off to see if the cook can still rustle something up and comes back to inform us that we are in luck. After a large order of soups, pies and sandwiches, we are feeling better – and so is our café owner when we hand over a generous tip on top of the large bill we have run up.

Just before we set off I ring my contact at Giggleswick School once again and offer sincere apologies. I am afraid that we are running so late that we will not be able to drop in. It is a pity, it would have been some experience to have scones and tea in the staff refectory at such an esteemed establishment.

Revived, we make short work of getting to Wigglesworth, eating up the miles of gently rolling moorland along narrow lanes and on to the flat approach to Settle. I have been looking forward to getting to Settle. Not only does it signal the beginning to the most exciting part of our ride across the Yorkshire Dales, but it is the starting point for a spectacular stretch of railway from the town, north to Carlisle. Whole books have been written about this 72-miles of line that is an astonishing feat of Victorian engineering over some of the bleakest terrain in the country. I have travelled on the Settle to Carlisle line more than once and the haul out of Settle up to Blea Moor is called the Long Drag for good reason. It is tiring enough by train, feeling the engine labour up the hillside, but now I was to make the same climb by bike.

Road, river and railway line follow the same path up Ribblesdale through a handful of farming communities to Horton in Ribblesdale. It is slow, hard going. To use cycle jargon, each of us 'bury ourselves' to make the climb the best way we know how. It is a gruelling, unrelenting ascent on which each twist of the road reveals yet more tarmac pointing upwards. The only thing to do is to find the right gear and a steady rhythm, 'bury' yourself in your thoughts and not look up too often. The scenery is sensational, of course, but it is only when you can sit up on a flat section that you get that wonderful feeling of achievement and drink it all in.

Kirkby Fell rises steeply to our right, the hill criss-crossed by dry-stone walls until it becomes too sheer even for the sheep, who are our constant companions on this section of the ride. Most of them stay obediently behind their walls but there are always a few who think the grass on the other side is greener and wander onto the verge beside the road. They have clearly seen cyclists before on this remote road because they pay us little heed as we crawl by. One farm we pass is offering "Well Bred Lamb For Sale." It probably went to Giggleswick School.

Disappointingly for me, we do not see a train rattling along the line that keeps us company through Stainforth, Helwith Bridge and Horton in Ribblesdale, where we re-group at the village store to buy chocolate bars and sit on the seats outside watching the evening sun touch the tops of the hills to the west. Fatigue is creeping in, but that is no excuse for what can only be described as Alan's bizarre behaviour at this stage of the day.

In the store, he spies some bottled beer named after Yorkshire Dales' landmarks. He assumes they are produced by a local 'micro-brewery' and purchases the set: four pint bottles. Four heavy pint bottles. Alan announces that we will crack them open when we arrive at our digs tonight, which is the Hawes Youth Hostel, to celebrate the completion of a tough day.

Tom shakes his head in disbelief as Alan adds two bottles to each pannier. We still have an awful lot of climbing to do. To take on board extra weight at this stage of the challenge seems insane to the rest of us. "I'll be having the last laugh when we enjoy the local brew later on," Alan confidently informs Tom, who has never developed a taste for beer – unlike his younger brother Jack, who is impressed by Alan's devotion.

We set off again. It is beginning to get cold as the evening approaches, and the sweat on our backs is turned chill by the winds heading down the Dales directly from the Arctic Circle. High to our right on Horton Moor is the Pennine Way, a walk that must be a challenge for all but the fittest. Down at road level, even the dry-stone walls offer little protection from the north-easterly blowing into our faces that makes the going tougher still. Even on the flat, I find myself changing down to the lower gears just to keep plodding along at 10mph. As a group, we soon split up, Tom and David setting the pace, with Alan and his boozy cargo surprisingly not far behind. Toddy, who is contemplating his second mid-tour break, is in the middle while trailing behind in our familiar position are me and Jack, whose mood is growing darker with every mocking look from the sheep we pass by.

Ribblehead Viaduct is a magnificent sight. A quarter of a mile long, built on a gentle curve, its 24 arches carry the Settle to Carlisle line across Chapel-le-Dale 100ft above the moorland. The dale is a windgap where the gales off the Irish Sea can touch 100mph. They have been known to be so strong that they have brought steam trains to a halt on the viaduct. We are there just as the sun is setting between its arches, casting a mellow evening haze across the rolling moorland creating a scene that would be an artist's dream. Jack, though, is not in a creative mood as he rolls into the gravel car park at the road junction and throws his bike on to the ground followed his cycle helmet and cycle gloves. He has clearly had enough of this arduous day.

This is where I started our story: with Jack abusing the sheep, the scenery and his bike, which lies discarded in the stony lay-by, front wheel spinning, as he sits down on a boulder with the air of someone who has had enough and will not budge another inch.

I feared before we left home that, while Jack's teenage body would stand up to the challenge, his mental resolve might not. Up to now he had proved me wrong, but he would clearly have been close to abandoning here and now had there been an alternative method of transport. As it was, we were as close as you can get to a wilderness in England.

What tipped Jack over the edge was the signpost at our junction with the B6255 which said 'Hawes 11' and pointed to a road that reared up across Blea Moor and the appropriately named Gayle Moor. Our photo-stop is a quick one and no-one dare say to Jack: "Smile, please."

We trudge on into a wind that appears to be reaching the aforesaid gale-force and Alan concedes quietly as he labours up the incline that buying the four bottles of ale might not have been such a good idea after all. As we re-group at the remote summit, we estimate that we have another five miles to go, and it looks as if it could be downhill all the way. By now the odd car that meets us on the road has its lights blazing and we realise that it is rather dark and we are not the most visible of road users in our cycle coats on this unlit exposed piece of highway.

We need lights for safety's sake but only David and Alan are sensible enough to carry them, so we decide to ride in strict convoy: David at the front illuminating the way, Alan at the rear with his red tail-light glowing brightly for any traffic approaching from behind. The next five miles turn out to be the most exhilarating jaunt of the whole trip as we swoop along the twisting moor road like a closely knit professional team leading out a sprinter near the finish of a stage of the Tour de France. There is never more than a couple of yards between each of the six bikes in our train and we eat up the miles on what for us is a dangerous descent in the dark. It is, indeed, downhill all the way into Hawes and the benefit of cycling as a pack carries us along at around 20mph. We arrive at the Youth Hostel at five minutes before eight, our longest day in terms of time and our latest arrival yet. The distance covered from Manchester, however, was a mere 72 miles, three miles fewer than my piece of string had suggested. Its credence had been restored, in my eyes at least.

Before the ride I had read a cycle tour book about a middle-aged guy who went from southern-most tip of England to the northern-most. On the way he stayed in youth hostels but explained that they were inappropriately named these days. What had been intended as cheap, basic accommodation for intrepid teenagers, the hostels have become the refuge of the middle-aged adventurer. Not so much Youth Hostels as Long-in-the-Tooth hostels. The bunks are hard, you have to make your own bed and the breakfasts are basic. But they are fun. I can recommend them. You will also get to meet an eclectic group of fellow travellers.

At Hawes, we had a party of charming tourists from somewhere in the old Soviet Bloc, none of whom spoke a word of English. There was a young Australian couple cycling from Land's End to John O'Groats in 10 days, which is going some. We spent more than two weeks covering the 900 miles on the End-to End, a snail's pace put alongside the record of 44 hours on a conventional bike. Also staying at our youth hostel were two very hairy and very gay motorcyclists, a rather odd Scottish couple, whom we assumed to be father and daughter walking the Pennine Way, and two soldiers doing the same thing. We must have been the sanest people there...particularly Alan, who in our bunk room triumphantly produced his cherished bottles of beer from his panniers, chilled to perfection by the Yorkshire night air. "We'll save these for later," he says furtively, not sure if booze is allowed on the premises.

This evening is rather special for Toddy. He is meeting up with his son Martin and daughter-in-law Gina. Martin is a Lieutenant Colonel in the Army and is the Commanding Officer of the Queen's Royal Lancers, a tank regiment stationed at nearby Catterick. At 39, Martin is one of the youngest in the Army to achieve such an exalted rank. Ian is understandably a very proud father. Martin and Gina have come to Hawes to have dinner with us and Martin has, being a good military man, done a recce of the local hostelries. He has chosen the Crown Hotel and booked a table, but is growing rather anxious. He has telephoned his father to inform him that last orders for food are 20.30 hours – only 20 minutes away, and we are barely pulling off our cycle shorts in the hostel having just locked our bikes in the bike-store.

There is a mild panic. Alan is so intent on not missing his dinner that declines to have a shower, yanks on a clean shirt and heads off into the night to find the Crown, which is, we are informed, a 10-minute march away. The rest of us tumble down the hill into the town just in time to find the landlord poised with pen and pad at the table to take our orders. Never has wholesome pub food and real ale tasted so good as it did that evening. The glow even returned to Jack's cheeks as he insisted on a second bottle of Rioja.

Martin and Gina are delightful company, and the presence of a lady at the dinner raises the tone of the conversation several notches above the norm. Martin even insists on paying for us all, but beside his generosity, there was a concern about his father that was to manifest itself the next day.

Back at the Youth Hostel, tired and happy, we let ourselves in and repair to the lounge, which is deserted. Alan disappears upstairs and returns a minute later carrying a laden pannier trying desperately not to let the bottles inside clang together and giggling when they did. We still did not know if alcohol was allowed in the hostel. I knew, however, that my Swiss Army Knife would come in handy at some stage, particularly as among its tools were a corkscrew and a bottle opener, and this was the moment.

Alan ripped the top off the first bottle with such eagerness that the metal cap took an inch of glass with it. Crestfallen, he decided we had better not risk drinking it in case the odd shard has dropped inside. The second bottle opens cleanly and he pours five glasses (Tom declined) of what looks like fizzy pale ale. It is pleasant enough, but not quite the unique real ale brewed locally with Ribblesdale water that Alan had imagined. The contents of the third bottle, although it also has an exotic name along the lines of

'Blea Moor Ferret Chaser', tastes and looks much the same as the previous one. It is only then that Alan turns the bottle around to read the small label on the back to discover that what we are drinking has been produced in the largest brewery in the country and stuck into a bottle with a fancy label on the front.

All that effort on Alan's part for a glass of mass-produced pale ale. The fourth bottle remains unopened on the table. We just could not summon the energy to drink it after falling about laughing at Alan's expense.

Day Ten Route: *Manchester ring road onto A56 to Prestwich, Bury, Ramsbottom and Rawtenstall. A680 to Haslingden, Accrington, Clayton-le-Moors, Whalley and Clitheroe. Minor roads to Sawley, Holden, Bolton-by-Bowland, Wigglesworth, Rathmell and Settle. B6479 to Langcliffe, Stainforth, Helwith Bridge, Horton in Ribblesdale and Ribblehead. Right on to B6255 to Hawes.*

String Distance: 75 miles
Actual Distance: 72 miles
Time in Saddle: 6 hrs 54 mins
Average speed: 10.4mph

Overall string distance: 608miles.
Actual mileage to-date: 666.
Total cycling time: 56hrs 41mins.
Average Speed: 11.7mph

GETTING ANGRY AT SHEEP...
By Jack Bateman

Back in the spring when my father asked if I would like to join him on his next cycle ride that autumn, I was shocked. Until then, I had been nothing but a bystander during his previous tours, staying at home, getting on with day-to-day life and waiting for news from wherever they were, on how things were going and how they all were.

Until Pa suggested I join them, I never dreamed I was capable of such a feat and, to be perfectly honest, I didn't think I had it in me physically or mentally. Between you and me, I don't think my father did either.

Then after a week or so of stalling, I thought, why not? I can do this, and that was it: I was going to attempt to cycle approximately 1,100 miles in 16 days..... Shit!

When we set off on Day One I was full of confidence, excitement and energy, physically and mentally. As we raced through London's streets on the first leg of our journey, weaving in and out of grid-locked traffic, it felt great.

As a motorist I knew the frustration of being in those nose-to-tail jams, but not today. Today was so much better and I found myself smiling and chuckling away, thinking what a great feeling it was to travel in five minutes the same distance a car would travel in the best part of an hour.

That feeling would soon end, though, and for the majority of the cycle ride I found myself cursing the traffic as it flew past at 60mph. What am I doing here? I'd ask myself. Why the hell did I agree to do this?

On one particular day in the Yorkshire Dales I found myself getting angry at sheep. This may sound stupid, but, as I battled against the unforgiving head wind and endless undulations, I could have sworn the Dales sheep were taunting me and mocking me. I know this is totally ludicrous, but at the time, because I was alone, I used them to vent my anger, and it worked. But those feelings would all go away at the end of each day when we arrived at our digs and soon sunk that first pint in the nearest pub.

This brings me to Larry, who was not a figment of my imagination. No, far from it. Larry was a small rubber lizard, which I found at the bottom of the drive as we were leaving our B&B in Romsey. I decided to pick him up and wedge him in between my front brake cable and handlebars, and that is where he would live for the remainder of the tour.

There were times when I would look at him half way up what would seem like an endless climb to find his lifeless rubber eyes staring back at me, and I'd say something like: "Why don't you do some bloody pedalling for once?" or "I'd like to see you do better!" It was similar to the sheep in Yorkshire, I guess. I knew it was pointless and totally mad, but it gave me a peculiar sense of satisfaction having someone or something at which to direct my anger and frustration.

Other times, Larry would be my best friend and I'd give him a little high-five when I was in good spirits and things were going my way.

By now I probably seem crazy to you, but I think that fellow cyclists who read this will probably relate to what I have said and went through. Maybe not to such an extreme degree, but I am sure there are those cyclists out there who do something similar to get them through the tough times.

On a bike, cycling alone, you find yourself thinking about all sorts of curious things: where you would like to go on holiday, how you would like things to change at work, how you are going to make a relationship work, what's wrong with your football team, why do sheep look so stupid? Anything to keep your mind off the physical and mental task ahead.

One thing that I have decided from all of this is that on my next cycle tour, I will definitely take my MP3. ...as well as Larry.

CHAPTER TWELVE

Top Of The Country

....Hawes to Chester-le-Street

Martin and Gina Todd had been alarmed to see how fatigued Ian appeared the previous evening over dinner in the Crown Hotel in Hawes. While we all feel fighting fit after ten days in the saddle, the rigours of the road have clearly taken their toll on all of us. No doubt, we all look a bit haggard to outsiders. Unshaven, buffeted by the wind and showing the effects of our hard days, late nights and disturbed sleep in unusual beds, we are probably quite a sight in our scruffy, crumpled clothes. Seeing Ian, who is normally immaculately turned out, looking somewhat dishevelled and drawn had convinced Martin to persuade his 71-year-old father to take a day off from the ride and spend it with them and his grandchildren at the army home in Catterick.

Toddy had always had this option in the back of his mind. He did not see enough of his family during the normal course of life so it seemed too good an opportunity to miss as he was virtually cycling past their front door. He had mentioned to us that he might bail out of the final hike north up to Chester-le-Street and the home of Durham County Cricket Club to spend 24 hours catching up with his family before re-joining the *peloton* on our route south through Yorkshire.

Martin had thought of being a guest rider on this day's leg but instead it was arranged that Gina would drive to the postcard-pretty town of Leyburn to pick up Toddy on our route, and take him and his bike back to their home. Gina had also very kindly offered to do our laundry, no doubt taking pity on us having seen us (and possibly smelled us) at close quarters the night before. While we washed our cycle gear through every day, our civvies for evening wear rarely got to see soap and water, becoming more crumpled and disgusting as the trip went on. We were concerned that this really was beyond the call of duty for Gina, but Toddy informed us that officers had staff to do such menial tasks and the British Army would take care of our smalls. Our gear, tied up in supermarket bags, was to be handed over today and returned to us, all creases present and correct, when we were re-united with Toddy tomorrow. Gina's offer was too good to turn down.

The day begins with a cold youth hostel shower. I am not sure whether this is YHA policy to cool the ardour of the teenagers for which the hostels were originally designed or whether the other guests have simply used up the one tank of hot water before we had stirred. Whatever the reason, it is a bracing start to the day and one I would not recommend. Breakfast is equally austere. The group from the Soviet Union Bloc had invaded the sausage and bacon trays and laid the scrambled eggs to waste, but there is still just enough baked beans and toast to go around.

The Australian couple are heading north on their Land's End to John O'Groats ride and were keen to know what to expect in Scotland. We tell them to wrap up warm and beware the haggises grazing on the roadside as they are likely to dart out in front of any passing traffic. I think they believe us. They are certainly in for the most spectacular and rewarding part of the End-to-End ride, which is one of the reasons, as well as the prevailing wind, that it is always best attempted from south to north.

As for us, we are in the middle of what I anticipate is going to be the most exhilarating two days of our Odyssey. While I could not be certain, I am confident we have climbed to the highest part of our journey. Passing over the Pennines was always going to be a major challenge, but I felt we had accomplished it. Our route to Hawes had taken us past a series of peaks topping 1500ft, which, while hardly mountainous, is still challenging enough. We had skirted Widdle Fell, Cam Fell, Dodd Fell and crossed Blea Moor. It felt like we had conquered the hump that runs down the middle of England.

Hawes is at the head of Wensleydale. The rolling Yorkshire moorland and sturdy stone buildings, built to withstand the tough winters in these parts, makes it feel like we are extras in 'All Creatures Great and Small', the television and film series based on the 'It should not happen to a Vet' books written by James Herriott. In fact, we are on the set, because our route today takes us by Askrigg, the village used for the fictional home of the Herriott practice. The set used by the BBC for the interior of the Herriott surgery is in the museum in Richmond, which is also on our route.

There is, sadly, no time to linger and appreciate the local attractions, of which there are many for the tourist. The good thing about being on a bike, however, is that you can admire the view as you cruise along. You can also hear and smell nature when you are riding, something you miss ensconced in a car with windows shut, CD playing and climate control switched on. The noises and, yes, even the odours of the countryside add to experience that makes cycling – and walking, come to that – such a rewarding thing to do.

There is, however, one spot of sightseeing that we have agreed to stop for at the renowned Aysgarth Falls. They are hardly in the same category as Victoria Falls, but are pretty enough all the same as the River Ure tumbles down over a triple set of stony out-crops. Aysgarth is about 10 gentle miles out of Hawes and clearly a major stop on the tourist route, as the large sign on the A684 points to the left and declares 'Aysgarth Falls Café Car Park.' Ideal. The road down to the falls is particularly steep so it makes sense to park up the bikes and do the last few hundred yards on foot.

The car park is tucked in behind the white-painted café that is closed on this Tuesday morning at around 10am. The parking area is a large, gravel affair, big enough to accommodate several tourist coaches as well as cars. There is a small wooden sentry box at the entrance that is, no doubt, the home of the car park attendant who collects the parking fees in high season. But this is late September and the car park is deserted. The sentry box is locked and there is not a soul in sight. Given the name of the car park, we assume this is where we should park for Aysgarth Falls.

We dismount and are pushing our bikes towards the fence at the far edge of the car park when living, breathing proof that the British Tourist Industry has a shotgun aimed at both feet appears from the café.

"You can't leave those here," barks the middle-aged man, who could genuinely have been a left over extra from All Creatures Great and Small when they sent out to central casting for a 'dour Yorkshireman.'

To add to the theatrical nature of this encounter, Yorkie is wearing a raincoat over what looks like striped pyjama bottoms, indicating he has hurried from his bedroom to accost us. He has a mop of wild, curiously red hair that suggests he has mixed up his 'Away-with-the-Grey' hair dye with Chinese Red food colouring.

We start to explain that we are here to see the Falls, but he tells us we are trespassing and had better move our bikes immediately. We ask why, this being the 'Aysgarth Falls Café Car Park.'

"The Café's closed and your bikes will be in the way later," says Yorkie.

I look at him incredulously: "In the way? There's nothing here and, anyway, how can they be 'in the way' chained up against the fence over there. And we were thinking of using the café when it opens later." This last bit is a lie, but he is not to know that.

"I don't care, you can't leave them here. The car park will be full in five minutes. Bugger off," says the Aysgarth representative of the British Tourist Industry.

"My. My, we are happy in our work, aren't we?" I tell him, wondering if sarcasm can deflate this preposterous man.

"I don't need to be happy because I'm rich." he says.

Stunned by the irrefutable logic of his argument, we shrug and push our bikes a yard out of the car park and leave them leaning on the wall by the road as Yorkie slams the door of his money-making emporium behind him. Now, I know most Yorkshire folk are good-natured friendly souls, but I can assure you there are still a few that are determined to maintain the image of the gruff northerner who would not give a southerner the time of day, or a space in his car park unless there is a fee to be collected.

Alan and Jack, armed with cameras, head down the 1-in-4 incline to the falls while the rest of us hang around our bikes munching on snack bars. We have quite lost our appetite for sight-seeing. We are also keen to witness the predicted rush of coaches, cars and mini-buses crammed with tourists into the café car park, which remains stoically empty throughout our 15-minute stop. Serve Yorkie right if global warming dries up the Falls and he loses all his business.

Our easterly route follows the tumbling River Ure down Wensleydale to Leyburn , where the river heads south-east for York and eventually the North Sea, while we veer north again, but not before we have had a delightful stop in the busy town centre, sitting on benches in the sun and eating buns and drinking coffee from the local bakery. Gina is there to meet us as arranged. She takes our laundry bags and we help pack Toddy's bike into the back of her car. Toddy is a strong character and his fitness belies his years, but he does look in need of a rest. Perhaps we had all underestimated the draining affect of the dental treatment he had had in Bristol. For the second time on the trip, we are down to five in number and I secretly wonder if Ian will fancy resuming the ride in 24 hours time or opt to call it a day and have a holiday with his family. No-one could blame him if he did.

Our ride from Leyburn takes us past the Catterick Garrison, where Toddy will be by now comfortably holed up, and into Richmond, another tourist haunt with its castle, abbey and pretty streets. So far, the cycling today has been comfortable, but we still have a mini-break outside the abbey for bananas and energy bars. We know the next stretch is not going to be easy. It is here we can leave the main road and take the country route north through the villages of Melsonby and Aldbrough St John, where very little appears to have changed in the last half century judging by the cottages around the village greens, the odd pub, church and reassuring red telephone box along the way. The only sign of the 21st century is the mobile phone mast just outside Melsonby.

At Aldbrough St John, we turn left on to the B6275, or Dere Street as the Romans called it when they constructed it more than 1500 years ago. It runs, arrow straight for much of the way, from York to Edinburgh and parts of it now form the A1 and A68; some sections are cart tracks across fields, while other sections have become by-roads, much like the stretch we are now on, heading for Piercebridge, where we are planning to stop for another pub lunch.

The large, cavernous inn there is hardly crowded but the lady behind the bar gives us a grim-faced welcome all the same. You would have thought she would have been pleased to see some customers, but she has clearly been to the same charm school as our friend from Aysgarth Falls, and grudgingly takes our order for cooked food. A few minutes later, the place is full of smoke and alarms start ringing. Alan looks appalled at the thought of his lasagne and chips going up in flames, but we are told not to worry: the smoke is from the two large fireplaces which have just been lit and which often suffer from down-draughts. It seems this is a regular occurrence and one the locals put up with despite the no-smoking signs all over the bar.

The food, when it appears from the veil of smoke, is surprisingly good and we are in no rush to get back on our bikes. The fires that have been lit in the giant hearths are now throwing out plenty of heat instead of smoke and it is a real effort to drag ourselves away. Before we can set off, David's mechanical expertise is required again for some running repairs to Tom's right pedal, which is still working loose and threatening to drop off.

We have now left Yorkshire, England's largest county, behind, and enter County Durham, the northern extremity of our adventure and another milestone to tick off, although we still have another 25 miles or more to go to reach Chester-le-Street, the home of Durham County Cricket Club, and then 15 back south again to our hotel for the night.

You can say what you like about how the further north you go in our country so the folk become more careful with their money. From my experiences, it is a myth perpetuated by those living south of Watford Gap.

We had contacted all 18 county cricket clubs about our fund-raising efforts before the ride and which three arranged free accommodation for us? The northern three, that's who. Lancashire, Yorkshire and Durham. We also had free accommodation in Canterbury because the manager of the hotel there had a personal reason for backing our cause, and a free night in Bristol because the England and Wales Cricket Board wanted to show their support, but it was the three northern-most counties that put themselves out to support us – so let's not be hearing anything more about tight-fisted northerners!

During our lunch stop in Piercebridge, I ring Yvette, the media officer at Durham County Cricket Club, who has made the arrangements for us to stay at the Honest Lawyer Hotel, which sounds like an oxymoron if ever there was one. She has some bad news. The Lawyer has been struck off the list because of flooding. The rooms they had expected to have been refurbished by now are not finished and there is no room at the inn for us. The county club, has, however, provided us with alternative digs at the Premier Inn at Durham Motorway Services about eight miles to the east of our planned route. Although this is a motorway service area, it is accessible by A roads so we can cycle there, but we have misgivings about where we will be able to leave the bikes in safety overnight at a place that is in use 24 hours a day. Still, beggars can't be choosers, so we have to do some quick re-routing and once again we are dropping well behind schedule.

Straight Roman roads serve their purpose in that they get you from point A to point B in the shortest distance, but against that is the fact that they take the steepest route up hills instead of going around them, plus you can see the hilly road ahead from miles away. It is becoming tough going on this the second of our two long days north from Manchester to Chester-le-Street and the prevailing north-easterly wind is not making life easier. It is also getting cold, which saps the energy as the body uses more fuel just to keep warm instead of diverting it into muscles to push the pedals around.

I am beginning to feel the strain today. On a few of the long climbs I have very quickly slipped down into one of my lowest gears and simply crawled to the summit. Looking up at the others pulling further away from me, I know I would abandon if I was cycling on my own. The legs are feeling like jelly, the resolve is fading fast. The week ahead is a daunting prospect right now and I seriously start to wonder if I am going to make it.

My sons Tom and Jack, I am pleased to see, are coping well, though. Riding together at the front this afternoon they look quite the part: Tom in a blue and red team shirt of Cofidis, who were one of the major European cycle outfits, Jack in his *Credit Lyonnais Maillot Jaune*, the official yellow jersey of the Tour de France.

Tom's suspect knee is not proving too much of a problem. A few times, as happened yesterday just outside Settle, he has stopped to ask me to for a couple of painkillers and some Ibuprofen cream, which eases the joint, but so far the knee is not giving any indication that it will force him to abandon as he did on our tour of Ireland a few years earlier.

Jack, on his first long ride, is now confident that he can last the course and while he is often full of grumbles (which he normally shares with his plastic lizard, Larry) he is coping well and enjoying the sense of achievement at the end of each climb and each day. He likes being out of doors, which is one reason he never really embraced school work. He is not sure yet what he wants to do with his life but he has his eye on forestry work, which, of course, would mean he would be a Lumber Jack.

After a long stint through the sparsely populated countryside, we arrive at Bishop Auckland and a much more industrialised area. Although the coal and iron works that brought the town its wealth have long gone, there is still a great deal more heavy traffic on the roads, especially as we arrive at the start of rush hour. Stan Laurel, the British half of the famous comedy duo Laurel and Hardy, grew up in Bishop Auckland, where his parents owned the theatre. Needless to say, we had gotten ourselves into another fine mess.

Our planned journey to the Honest Lawyer in Croxdale, our original overnight stop, was to take us through Spennymore then on the direct road north, the A167, but we had to navigate our way east now towards the A1, which is a motorway in these parts, and then up to Bowburn, where we were told we could slip into the motorway services on a back road. The roads were now very busy and not intended for bikes, but there is nothing for it but to battle on, head down into the wind and ignore the occasional blast of a horn.

The A688 from Bishop Auckland to Spennymore is getting particularly busy as we approach the end of another working and school day. Everyone seems in a hurry to get somewhere and the streams of traffic in both directions are virtually continuous. It is here I have one of my (thankfully) few scary moments when a green bus brushes past my right shoulder and makes me wobble. I do not suppose for a second that the bus did actually 'brush' me, but the draught from these large vehicles can have quite a destabilising effect when you are on two wheels less than an inch wide. For a second I feel as though I am going to topple into the side of the bus or just behind it into the path of the next vehicle but I recover my balance and pull into the kerb. Taking a swig from my water bottle and a deep breath, I glare at the bus, which has pulled into the bus stop a short way ahead. I would like to think the driver might feel chastened if he glances in his mirror as he sees my accusing stare. But I doubt it somehow.

Battling through the traffic that is both leaving and joining the motorway section of the AI, we crawl into Bowburn and the Durham Service Station quite frazzled. Our original plan had been to dump our panniers at the Honest Lawyer and then cycle to the ground at Chester-le-Street and back with unladen bikes. We stick to the first half of this scheme by checking in at the Premier Inn, where a life-sized cardboard cut-out of a grinning Lenny Henry, greets us in the lobby instead of Andrew Flintoff.

With a 30-mile round trip to Chester-le-Street still ahead of us, we are facing a mini-crisis. Even without our panniers on our bikes, I know I will not make it. Jack is equally convinced that he is almost spent. Then there is the problem with the daylight, which is fading fast. It stays light longer in the north of the country, but even so, we realise we will be cycling home in the dark without lights if we do our trip to Durham's county ground and back this evening. We may have done this on the trip to Hawes the previous night, but the roads around here are much busier.

We discuss the options. I favour the lazy one of simply staying at our hotel and doing the extra miles the next morning, although that will mean tomorrow will be a 100-

plus mile day. Alan wonders about cycling to Chester-le-Street and catching the train back to Durham with our bikes, but that would result in us not having cycled the whole way around the 18 counties, which would ruin our quest. David is the one with the brainwave. He suggests cycling to the ground, finding somewhere there to store our bikes and getting a taxi back to the hotel. In the morning, we would get the taxi back to the ground to retrieve the bikes and continue our journey. That option would mean we would still be cycling every yard of our route but have only one more leg to navigate this evening. Brilliant.

With renewed optimism, we set off through the traffic jams and over the cruel hills around Durham back to the main A167, a fast dual carriageway with a cycle lane all the way to Chester-le-Street. The cycle lane is not quick going, but it is safe. Along the way, we pass through the appropriately named village of Pity Me. There are many suggested derivations for this curious name including it being a translation of the French for a small lake (*petit mer*). There is another line of thought that suggests the name came from monks who sang for pity from God here during the Viking invasion. There is also a much more straightforward theory that it is simply a whimsical local name for what was a desolate area that was difficult to farm. Pity Me for living there. Whatever the origin, Pity Me felt appropriate enough this evening as we cycled through.

We arrive at Chester-le-Street's Riverside Ground at 6.30pm and with barely enough light to take our photographs. Yvette is there to greet us long after she should have gone home from work. She is a real star when she hears about our problems with our late arrival and the need

213

to leave the bikes at the ground for the night. She arranges for them to be stored safely in one of the gyms not in use that evening, organises our taxi back to the hotel for us and then buys us a round of drinks at the club bar while we are waiting. People like Yvette restore your faith in human nature at the end of a long day, which had started with our collision with the absurdly inhospitable – but apparently very wealthy – car park owner at Aysgarth Falls.

Durham, it should be said, are one of the success stories of English county cricket. They are the youngest of the 18 full-time counties having been granted First Class status in 1992 and invited into the Championship. They played at the beautiful University Ground beside the River Wear in Durham for a few years, a few ageing stars such as Ian Botham, John Morris, Simon Hughes and David Graveney seeing out their careers at a county that struggled to win a match. Then came the move to the Riverside ground, and Durham came of age. They were about to become County Champions for the first time when we visited the ground and had a highly successful production-line of players who have proved good enough to move up to international cricket, such as Steve Harmison, Paul Collingwood, Liam Plunkett and Graham Onions.

We have done 70 miles today, five fewer than estimated by my trusty piece of string, but that is misleading as we are not returning to the hotel by bike as planned. The bikes are left in Chester-le-Street, which would add about 15 miles to the next day's journey. That, though, was tomorrow.

Our taxi back to our hotel by the motorway costs £30, but it is worth every penny. It is a happy group that settles into the modern comfort provided by Durham even if staying at a motorway service station is an unusual experience. There is no restaurant or bar at the Premier Inn, but next door is the services café. It is hardly cordon bleu dining, but the chicken curry followed by Ben and Jerry's ice cream goes down a treat. A night without alcohol will do us no harm either – at least, that is what we tell ourselves. There is the added bonus for me of a room on my own again. With no Ian, one of us has to strike lucky with the three twin rooms and my colleagues sense that I probably needed the extra pampering most.

This has, for me, been a horrible day in terms of coping with the physical challenge. By the end of the next day, though, it would be another of our number who would be thinking seriously about calling it quits.

Day Eleven Route: *Hawes A684 to Aysgarth and Leyburn. Left on to A6108 to Richmond. B6272 to Gilling West. Minor roads to Melsonby, Aldbrough St John. B6275 (Dere Street) to Piercebridge. B6275 to Shildon. A6072 to Bishop Auckland, A688 to Spennymore and Bowburn. A177 to Shincliffe and Durham. A167 to Pity Me and Chester-le-Street.*

String distance: 75 miles
Actual Distance: 70 miles
Time in Saddle: 6hrs 25mins
Average speed: 10.9mph

Overall string distance: 683 miles.
Actual mileage to-date: 736.
Total cycling time: 63hrs 06mins.
Average speed: 11.6mph

CHAPTER THIRTEEN

The Long Haul

....Chester-le-Street to Leeds

The taxi to take us back to our bikes at the Riverside Ground in Chester-le-Street is ordered for 8.30 this morning after an early breakfast in the Durham Motorway Services, where our cycle gear attracts curious looks from the truckers and commercial travellers. We know we need this early start because leaving our machines at the cricket ground the night before means we have added about 15 miles to our ride today, which will now certainly be the longest leg of the trip and, for most of us, take us into uncharted territory.

Alan has done plenty of 'long 'uns' of 100-plus miles in a day before. He is a regular on the annual Action Research 100, a Bath to London ride that does exactly what it says on the tin and covers 100 miles. As if that was not enough, Alan sometimes adds another dozen miles on to that by starting out from his sister's home in Bristol.

We are not about to crack three figures today, but it will not be far short. The morning starts with feelings of trepidation over the distance ahead but also some excitement over the thought of finally heading south again, the first time we have done so since the second day when we rode from Canterbury to Brighton. That was ten days ago yet it seems like an eternity since we stopped for spaghetti bolognese in the back garden of my home in Kent. We are now at Wednesday of the second week and convinced we can achieve our goal of cycling around the 18 cricket grounds provided we avoid injury or illness on the last five days.

I have since read a book called 'The Man Who Cycled the World' by Mark Beaumont, who cycled not 18 counties but 18,000 miles on his own around the world with his tent on the back of his bike. It is an astonishing tale of human endeavour and adventure and puts our little jaunt into perspective, yet on another level I reckon we can emphathise with him: swinging your leg over that saddle at the start of every day can be a chore but at the same time an exhilarating moment, whether you are heading for Northampton or the Nullarbor in Australia. The feeling of freedom of being on a bike for a long ride with only your own thoughts for company is difficult to explain to those who cannot see the sense in it.

The Riverside looks much more attractive in the morning sunshine than it did the previous evening, and on the hill above the ground, which was shrouded in gloom yesterday, we can see Lumley Castle in all its glory. Built in the 14th century by Sir Ralph Lumley, it is now an official part of strategic planning to bring success to the England cricket team, who play internationals at the Chester-le-Street ground most summers. Let me explain:

The castle passed through the hands of several wealthy owners and in the 19th century became the residence for the Bishop of Durham. It was later turned into a spectacular halls of residence for students at Durham University, but when cash was needed to build a more sensible student block in Durham, the castle was sold to an hotel group and converted into four-star accommodation. This is where the ECB come in. They encourage touring teams to stay at the hotel as it is so handy for the Riverside ground, which is less than a mile away. There is, though, another attraction for having the opposition spend a night or two at Lumley.

Like all good castles, Lumley is haunted. The resident ghost is that of Lily, Lady of Lumley and wife of Sir Ralph, who met a rather grisly end, being murdered by local priests who dumped her body down the castle well. It is said that Lily now wanders the hotel corridors at night showing scant respect for 'Do Not Disturb' signs hanging from bedroom doors.

It was all too much for the touring West Indians in 2000, three of their players checking out and moving to another hotel. They lost the match against England at the Riverside the next day. Five years later, one of the touring Australian side, Shane Watson, was so spooked, that he refused to sleep alone and spent the night on the bedroom floor of team-mate Brett Lee. The story caused much glee among England's players on the field the next day and Watson was the target for plenty of mickey-taking, but even that could not prevent another Australian victory.

We wheel the bikes out of the gym at 9am and, with the wind at our backs at last, head back on the cycle path beside the dual carriageway towards Durham. As on our leg from Newport to Cardiff, we do have to cover ground we have already cycled, but this time the going is easier as it is the start of a day and we are not on congested roads.

After skirting Durham, another place worth a stop that we cannot do, we cycle through Croxdale and past the Honest Lawyer, which does, indeed, look to be in a sorry state in the aftermath of the flood which had aborted our planned stay. We now have more than 30 miles on the same main road, the A167. As the route is straightforward there is no need for the front-runners to keep stopping to wait for the slow coaches to catch up. We have agreed Darlington should be our first stop so it is a good opportunity to get the head down, give it a blast and get a chunk of miles behind us early in the day, which is always a good tactic.

This is a surprisingly flat part of the country through the Tees Valley, the Vale of Mowbray and then the Vale of York with the Yorkshire Dales to the west and the Cleveland Hills to the east. We are on an A road but the traffic is light. After a tough battle across the Pennines over the past two days, this is fast cycling by our standards and even Jack and I are able to keep in reasonable touch with Alan, David and Tom at the head of the pack.

Our route takes us through the village of Aycliffe, another of those places in England with an astonishing story to tell. During the Second World War vital ammunition factories were built here on the low lying land around the River Skerne that was frequently shrouded in evening mists and therefore difficult for the German Luftwaffe to locate and bomb. The factories gave rise to the legend of the Aycliffe Angels.

Some 17,000 women from the neighbouring towns and villages undertook incredibly dangerous tasks at the munitions factories here producing bombs and bullets for the troops. There were many accidents killing some, leaving others horribly disfigured, although the facts were always hushed up under the Official Secrets Act so as not to damage war-time morale.

The Aycliffe Angels earned their nickname from, of all people, William Joyce, the Irish-American who joined Germany's war cause and broadcast Nazi propaganda over the radio to Britain under the name of Lord Haw-Haw.

During one of Haw-Haw's infamous 'Germany Calling, Germany Calling' broadcasts, he said: "The little angels of Aycliffe won't get away with it." But they did and the name stuck. The Luftwaffe bombs never found the factories in Aycliffe despite many raids, and the women played a huge part in the Allied victory in World War Two. For years, their efforts remained unrecognised until a newspaper campaign by the Northern Echo in 2000 led to a memorial being erected in their honour in neighbouring Newton Aycliffe.

Our rapid journey takes us over the A1M and into Darlington and our coffee stop at probably the scruffiest café of the whole trip so far on the main drag through a fairly scruffy town, if truth be told. Who cares? We are making sensational progress and have covered around 25 miles in less than two hours. We are actually having our coffee break at the traditional mid-morning time instead of the wrong side of midday. Carry on like this and we will be too early for our rendezvous with Toddy in Northallerton, where we are also to be re-united with our laundry. David calls Toddy to tell him of our progress and the meet time is brought forward 30 minutes.

Darlington is one of those towns there is little reason to visit unless you have relatives living there or your football team has an away fixture against The Quakers. It does, however, house the Darlington Railway Centre and Museum to remind everyone what an important part it played in this country's transport history. The Robert Stephenson Company built the famous Locomotion One nearby and in 1825 it hauled the world's first steam passenger train from Shildon in the west to Stockton-on-Tees in the east via Darlington. These days, you cannot make the 25-mile journey by rail without changing. There's progress for you.

Out of Darlington, our route takes us through the Vale of Mowbray with its wide expanse of gently undulating arable fields. We snake over the River Tees again in the village of Croft-on-Tees. These roads were made for cycling: reasonably flat, a good surface under tyre, little traffic and enough twists and turns to make it interesting. Jack and I take each other's wheel, taking it in turns to spend a minute in front before the other moves to the front for his stint. This makes the going easier as you gain from the leader's slip-stream, and encourages both of you to maintain a good momentum. We are cruising along at speeds between 15-20mph without breaking sweat and wondering why these Tour de France riders make such a fuss about their outing on a bike.

We have already covered 40 miles as we glide into Northallerton, another of those prosperous-looking Yorkshire market towns, and even the dreaded word 'puncture' cannot deflate our mood today.

Toddy has arrived in Northallerton and as he hauls his bike out of the back of Gina's car, he discovers he has a puncture. Quite how he has picked up a puncture staying overnight in Catterick, he is not sure, but fortuitously, Gina has decided to unload her father-in-law in Halfords' car park. We have yet to arrive so Toddy wheels his bike into the store, explains his situation and receives their immediate attention. It is astonishing how many bike shops – even big chains such as Halfords – are run by enthusiasts, who will do all they can to help a fellow cyclist. Much like Masons and Mormons, there appears to be a Brotherhood of the Lycra – but without the dodgy handshake.

By the time we five arrive, the tyre is almost fixed. Gina hands over bags of sweet-smelling clothes and wishes us well as she leaves, and Toddy seems genuinely excited to be back in the group, which is pleasing.

There is a market in town. The place is packed with pedestrians and stalls, most of which are spilling over with local produce such as cheeses, preserves, pickles, smoked meats, sweets, cakes and vegetables. There is no chance of cycling through the throng, so Jack, Tom and I wheel our bikes through the market stalls to find a suitable place for lunch while the others wait for Toddy's tyre to be re-fitted with new inner-tube.

We find a pub with a secluded back patio, but our lunch of baguettes takes longer than it should. This being a busy market day, though, we cannot really complain. Although we have made good time, we are still not half-way through our journey to Leeds, which I know will involve some tough climbs towards the end when we are all feeling the effects of a long day.

Following the main East Coast rail line that links London with Edinburgh, we continue south out of Northallerton and into the Vale of York along the gently undulating A167.

David and Tom are in full racing mode now, go down on to their dropped handlebars and put their heads down for the next stretch of open road. Alan responds and that is when near disaster strikes. This is how Alan tells the story in his tour diary:

"I keep an eye on my cycle computer, and as we hurtle along the road I exclaim to David that after only 38 minutes we have already knocked off another ten miles. But you know what they say: pride comes before a fall. I may be going well but without realising it, I am pushing myself a little harder than is sensible. Just two miles before Topcliffe, I feel a sudden twinge in my right knee. I know this is my weak point, and indeed I have been wearing knee support bandages throughout the ride as an insurance policy. But it is too late to ease off now, and I dread that the damage has been done. I slow down and try to ride using the minimum effort, but I know only too well that the pain won't go away."

We have been fortunate with injuries on this ride to date, so we cannot bemoan our luck over Alan's setback. On two of our three previous rides, one of our number has been forced to pull out altogether, but up to now the only problem we have had on this venture has been Toddy's troublesome tooth, and that was hardly likely to force him to abandon the ride for good.

On our first venture from John O'Groats to Land's End, David had to drop out after three days in Scotland because of the death of his father-in-law, rejoining us in Chepstow for the last four days. On our circular tour of Ireland, Tom had to abandon two days before the end because he had aggravated an old knee injury suffered playing rugby. On our trip from the top to the bottom of France, illness swept through the *peloton*: Alan could barely get out of bed on the first day while Toddy and David, suffering from a chest infection, spent several days in the second week swathed in mufflers and dosed up to the eyeballs well beyond the limit of any drug test imposed during the actual Tour de France. It was probably the sheer fact that it was not so easy to get home that made everyone soldier on all the way to the Mediterranean coast.

Not that we were aware of Alan's problems at the time on our journey to Leeds. Like a good stoical cyclist, he soldiers on in silence and we assume his dropping down through the pack to cycle with us back-markers is simply a supportive gesture on his part.

The road takes us into the River Swale valley, another expanse of rolling countryside, and the village of Topcliffe, where we re-group for more snack bars, but not a word from Alan about his fears concerning his knee.

From Topcliffe we have to endure a short stretch of dual-carriageway that takes us to the roaring A1 – we are back on Dere Street again – but fortunately we do not have to join the trunk road. The up-grading of the Great North Road over the years has left the original single-track highway along the same route virtually redundant. Running cheek-by-jowl with the A1, this is now a quiet, country lane used only by local traffic, tractors and cyclists. Our route takes us over the River Ure at Boroughbridge, the river we had followed down Wensleydale 48 hours earlier, although by now it is no longer a cascading stream but a fully-fledged deep, meandering river. We also pass 'The Devil's

Arrows', three standing stones dating back to the Bronze Age, the tallest of which is more than 20ft high. Apparently, there were more arrows in the devil's quiver originally but they were broken up to build bridges over the river.

Our plan is to head into Harrogate via Knaresborough on the A6055 and treat ourselves to a very special ritual in these parts: tea in Bettys Café Tea Rooms. Bettys (always written without the apostrophe, before you write in and complain) is one of those establishments that is quintessentially English and resists the pressure of change. It is packed with ladies of a certain age and tourists most afternoons, the queue for the tea-room often snaking through the shop area and out of the double doors on to Parliament Street in the swish part of town.

Although Bettys appears to be as English as Colman's mustard and Melton Mowbray pork pies, it was, in fact, started by a Swiss confectioner who emigrated to Yorkshire early in the last century. There are now six 'Bettys' dotted around the country and they serve up traditional afternoon teas including, of course, Swiss Roll. We, though, are to be disappointed.

By the time we arrive in Harrogate, Bettys is closed and we have to make do with the very traditional English custom of tea in a Pizza Hut with 'American Style Blueberry Cheesecake' instead of scones and jam. It is a let-down but we need an intake of calories for the last 12-mile push to Leeds.

Harrogate is one of the very attractive spa towns in this part of Yorkshire. It was immensely popular with the elite in the Victorian era and still exudes a rather snobby air. It looks down its nose at those scruffy former mining towns in the county, and caters for tourists and visitors to its International Conference Centre. It also used to be a favourite haunt of cricket journalists, who stayed at one its quaint hotels for matches in Leeds. That is why David and I know the area so well and are keen to try our 'secret' back route from Harrogate to the ground at Headingley, the home of Yorkshire County Cricket Club and two rugby teams.

There is a busy main road from Harrogate to Leeds past the stunning stately pile that is Harewood House, but our back-doubles avoid the traffic, although they do take in a few sharp hills. Dusk is beginning to close in as we swing off the main road on to our single track country lane for Eccup and its pub that was a familiar watering hole on our way back to Harrogate after a day at the cricket. There was no time to stop today, sadly. The climb up to the pub is more vertiginous than I remember and it is a long, weaving slog in a low gear to reach the summit. We have now done 80 miles, and counting, today and Jack's patience is wearing thin again as I hear him muttering something about me and my piece of string as he hangs on to my back wheel up the incline.

I pretend not to hear because I know that once at the top, it is an easy cruise down to Headingley, a suburb in the north of Leeds, with only a busy ring-road crossing our path to slow us down. We roll up to the security barrier at the ground shortly after seven and our contact at Yorkshire, Shaun, has done us proud by organising three free rooms at the on-site hotel, the White Rose Lodge. Our bikes also have a cosy little lock-up in one of the groundsman's storerooms underneath the stand.

To give the ground its full name, it is now Headingley Carnegie, the Carnegie being added after financial investment from the Leeds Metropolitan University. Like that other traditional home of cricket in the north, Old Trafford, Headingley is badly in need of bulldozers and brick-layers, and work on the up-grading of the ground was to start the year after our ride. It is also unique among cricket grounds in that it is home to three major sporting teams: Yorkshire cricket team, the town's Rugby League side, the Rhinos, and the Leeds Tykes Rugby Union side. They share the same venue but not the same pitch. The rugby pitch is alongside the cricket ground with a double-fronted stand separating the two playing fields. One side of the stand looks out over the cricket field, the other side looks out over rugby posts, and underneath the same changing rooms and tunnel serves both.

It is only when we get to our room in the Lodge that I learn the full extent of Alan's problem with his knee. He asks me what pain-killers I have (he knows my wife Brenda, a nurse, keeps me well stocked up on medical supplies to cover most eventualities on the ride) and confides that he is not sure if he will be able to carry on the next day.

Alan retreats to our bathroom for a well-deserved long hot shower as I slump on the bed from where I witness one of the potentially most embarrassing moments of our ride involving Tom and Jack and their impersonation of Alan making a telephone call to his wife Diane.

We all have our own curious little ways, of course, particularly when it comes to talking to our nearest and dearest, and Alan is no exception. Like the loving husband he is, he rings home on a daily basis from our rides, but instead of his usual manly matter-of-fact baritone, he slips into a sing-song voice when conversing with Diane, sliding up an octave or two. It is very endearing but also open to mimicry – as Tom and Jack have discovered.

Knowing it is that time of evening when Alan normally rings Diane, unaware that Alan is suffering from a very sore knee and believing he is in another room sharing with David tonight, the two very naughty boys burst into my room through the door, which I have left ajar. Tom is holding a mobile to his ear and doing his impersonation of Alan calling home while Jack is almost wetting himself in fits of giggles. I wave frantically at them pointing to the bathroom door and putting a finger to my lips to hush them, but still they carry on with their imaginary phone call to Diane about the day's ride. I am convinced Alan will hear through the thin hotel walls but the noise of the shower still gushing may have drowned out their mimicry and saved them from acute embarrassment.

By the time Alan emerges a few minutes later wrapped in a hotel bath-robe, scrubbed and glowing, Tom and Jack have departed and decorum is restored in the room. I think we have got away with it, although to this day I do not know whether he heard his naughty cousins sending him up.

One of the delights of Leeds is the fish and chip shops. They are rightly proud of their chippies in Yorkshire and there are two close to the Headingley ground that are more than simple takeaways. We opt for the closest called Bretts, a favoured haunt of that great cricket commentator of old, the late John Arlott. Situated in a pretty ivy-covered cottage and with a licence to sell wine and beer, it is no ordinary chip shop. The speciality of the house is haddock (deep fried in beef dripping not cooking oil) the size of a baby whale and served with a mountain of chips. It hits the spot tonight after our long 87-miles haul on which we have touched our highest daily average speed of 13.2mph, and even Alan's limp appears to be easing as we walk back to hotel. Tomorrow, though, will tell whether this has been his last day or whether he will be able to carry on.

Day Twelve Route: *Chester-le-Street, A167 to Durham, Croxdale, Spennymoor, Newton Aycliffe, Darlington, Northallerton, Topcliffe. A168 to Boroughbridge. A6055 to Knaresborough and Harrogate. A61 to Pannal and Harewood, right on to A659 then minor roads to Eccup and A660 towards Leeds and Headingley.*

String Distance: 70 miles
Actual Distance: 87 miles
Time in Saddle: 6 hrs 36 mins
Average Speed: 13.2mph

Overall string distance: 753 miles.
Actual mileage to-date: 823.
Total Cycling Time: 69 hrs 42 mins.
Overall Average Speed: 11.8mph.

CHAPTER FOURTEEN

Industrial Industry

....Leeds to Derby

The anaesthetic effect of Brett's *sauvignon blanc* and a couple of pints of Tetley's Best have worn off by the morning and, while I have a slight pain in the head, Alan has a severe one in his right knee. He tests it gingerly on the bedroom carpet and it does not feel good. Six hours of pushing pedal through what is going to be a stop-start day of mainly urban cycling is not an enticing proposition for him. Alan does not give up easily but he is thinking about abandoning our ride here in Leeds on this suitably overcast Thursday morning.

We know his mood is not good because he can barely be bothered with breakfast, although, to be honest, the food on offer in the canteen that serves as an eatery for those who work and study at the ground and the guests from the lodge is pretty unappealing as it congeals in its stainless steel trays looking rather tired. Still, we need to fuel-up for the day and we force something down.

Outside, on a gloomy Yorkshire morning, we do our regular photo-call to prove we have been here, our 12th county cricket ground out of the 18. The back-drop is the Headingley outfield, but instead of being a lush green meadow as it should be at this time of year with the cricket season still going on, it is a muddy morass with piles of earth and JCB diggers dotted around. They are laying a new drainage system at the ground and the only green patch is the playing square in the middle, which is roped off from the bulldozers. There are many batsmen down the years who have felt this bit should have been dug up too, the Headingley pitch being notorious at times for being helpful to the bowlers.

The sporting nature of the pitch combined with the conditions that can help swing bowling has made Headingley a ground where many memorable matches have been played, none more so than the famous Ashes Test of 1981 – 'Botham's Test' – when England somehow beat Australia after being made to follow-on. It was said a few of the Aussies had been to the bookies mid-match when they were in a totally dominant position to put money on an England victory at 500-1 for a laugh. A few years later, match-fixing and player involvement with bookmakers was to throw the world game into crisis, but there was never any suggestion that England's success in 1981 had been down to anything other than two outrageous performances from Botham with the bat and Bob Willis with the ball.

Just up the road from Headingley in Pudsey lives Ray Illingworth, one of the great characters of the game and, many believe, one of the greatest post-Second World War captains England have had. I would not demur. While many regard Illy as an old curmudgeon, I know him to be a kind individual who was always willing to help a young journalist who knew precious little about the game of cricket. I was Illingworth's 'ghost' for a few years on the Daily Express, which meant that I wrote down his thoughts in suitably short, pithy sentences for his columns in the newspaper. To be honest, it did not take much journalistic expertise as Illy tended to speak in short, pithy sentences anyway.

Illingworth became England's chairman of selectors and head coach for a while and regularly clashed with the then captain Michael Atherton. The problem was that both were mule-stubborn opinionated northerners, who, if they had only been willing to back down an inch or two to see the other's point of view occasionally, might have got along famously. Illingworth speaks more good sense about cricket than anyone I have come across in 20-odd years working in the sport, while Athers has become one of the most insightful commentators on the game, who at times (although do not say this in his hearing) can sound as trenchant as old Illy in his pomp.

Alan, with the help of some more pharmaceuticals from my medicine bag, doses himself up and does not let on just how concerned he is about his knee and the day ahead, which is to take us through what looks on the map to be a never-ending string of towns connected by ring-roads and by-passes. At least we shall not have any problem finding places to stop to eat.

Our first challenge is to get out of Leeds. It is difficult enough by car, with the town's road planners coming up with what they have called the 'The Loop'. It is more like a noose that strangles the centre of the city. Motorways abound around Leeds so battling your way out on a bicycle is not straightforward and we spend a hugely frustrating hour before we finally find the right road south. At one stage, totally exasperated, we end up at the railway station and ask a policeman, and even he does not appear to have a clue how to find the A61 to Wakefield.

The tiresome stop-start beginning to our day is, in fact, a blessing for Alan who can ease himself into the cycling, and by the time we hit the open road, he is feeling more confident that, with the aid of tablets, cream, knee bandages and the occasional pint, he might be able to get through the 70 miles ahead.

Our early tour concerns about town cycling have long disappeared for all of us apart from Ian, who remains nervous about squeezing in and out of tight lines of traffic and constantly having to be aware of vehicles pulling out, pedestrians stepping out and car doors being opened into his path. There is, in fact, much satisfaction to be had in town cycling as, more often than not, the biker's progress is quicker than that of the cars you pass on the inside while they queue at traffic lights.

Jack and Tom have formed a union today and are going strong at the front with David while Toddy, Alan and I form a second group not far behind, often catching up at roundabouts and traffic lights, or when they are not certain which way to go and have to wait. It is good to see my sons Tom and Jack enjoying the ride so much. I knew Tom would cope well as he had been part of our France and Ireland adventures, but Jack adds a new dimension to the group. He gets on well with his brother, but, more significantly, genuinely seems to enjoy the camaraderie between the different generations on the road and over the dinner table in the evenings.

Just outside Leeds, we are surprised to find ourselves going through a village called Robin Hood. We are not that close to Nottingham, or Sherwood Forest come to that, but apparently our folk hero with a bow and arrow was probably a Yorkshire lad from Loxley near Sheffield. His robbing-the-rich-and-giving-to-the-poor escapades have been claimed by Nottingham, but there are plenty of stories to suggest he had links over a wide area as far north as the River Aire, which runs through Leeds.

The congested route south on the A61 takes us through what is known as the Rhubarb Triangle, an area of around nine square miles between Morley and Rothwell in the north and Wakefield in the south that until recently produced virtually all of the world's forced rhubarb during the winter months. They are potty about the stuff around here. In Wakefield – 'The Rhubarb Capital' – they have an annual Rhubarb Festival. There are Rhubarb Tours of the forcing sheds and rhubarb cookery demonstrations for visitors. They have even erected a statue in Wakefield to King Rhubarb, and after seeing that you can go for a pint in the Rhubarb Triangle pub. There is a saying in cricket that when a batsman is dominating the bowling "he could play it with a stick of rhubarb." They probably do at Wakefield Cricket Club.

We are cycling through what was also once the heart of the Yorkshire coal mining industry, which was decimated during Margaret Thatcher's reign as the Conservative Party Prime Minister in the 1980s. There are remnants of the mines and slag heaps everywhere in an area that saw some of the most bitter demonstrations during the national miners' strike of the time. The irony was that while the miners fought to keep the pits alive, very few of them wanted to see their sons follow them down the pits. The National Mining Museum is a few miles away at Overton at the Caphouse Colliery, one of the pits that had been closed down.

Deep beneath our wheels there is a grim reminder of just how dangerous mining can be. It was in this area that England suffered its worst mining disaster at the Oaks Colliery, which was part of the rich Barnsley seam. In 1866, a series of 18 explosions caused by ignited methane gas left 388 men and boys dead, some of them members of rescue teams sent down the mine after the first explosion.

Barnsley is to be our first stop of the day, a café in an Asda store half way up another steep climb providing us with some respite. Having given Tesco a go earlier in our trip, we thought it only right to let Asda have some custom. The hills are frequent and demanding in these parts but Alan appears to be coping well. So does Toddy, whose day off has clearly given him a second wind. He may be wary of town cycling, but he is having no trouble keeping up with the pace and has even been darting off to the head of the pack at times to prove there is still plenty of life in the old dog yet.

Barnsley has a rich cricket heritage, it being the home of one of the game's most charismatic cricketers of recent years Darren Gough, a Yorkshire and England fast bowler who gained even wider fame by winning the BBC television show Strictly Come Dancing. Vying with 'Goughie' in the nation's affections is another Bansley product: Harold

'Dickie' Bird. A modest county batsman, 'Dickie' became the most recognisable umpire in the game, renowned for being pernickety over the weather. He so infuriated the normally staid members of the MCC with his reluctance to allow play to start in the 1980 Test against Australia at Lord's that he needed a police escort to get through the Long Room on to the out-field when play did eventually get under way.

Leaving Barnsley behind, our road takes us parallel to the M1 through a string of small towns and villages that all seem to merge into each other. One is called Jump, the residents of which are presumably called Jumpers. Finally we are able to slide off the A61 onto a B road which takes us through the village of Thorpe Hesley, where we glimpse a few fields and horses, but the countryside is not going to last as we are about to tangle with the urban sprawl that is Sheffield.

The rider among us who surprises me most today is David. Not because he is coping easily – I always thought he would – but because he confides he has never enjoyed a ride as much as this one. Working and travelling together as journalists on the cricket circuit, we probably spend as much time in each other's company as we do with our wives. As well as seeing a lot of each other during the summer season at home and going abroad for England cricket tours every winter, this is now our fourth long road trip together on our bikes over the last eight years. David says it is the best yet. Despite the frustrating delays waiting for me to catch up, he is relishing the challenge of each day plus the added enjoyment of seeing the cricket venues we normally associate with work not play.

He has really caught the two-wheel bug, far more than me, and regularly cycles in the lanes around his Hampshire home carefully logging his miles. Since we started riding together at the turn of the century, he has kept a careful note of miles ridden and is determined to do more each year than in the previous year. As this trip alone will add 1100 to his tally, that will raise the bar even further for him next year. If he ever does complete the ride he hankers after – a 4,000-mile epic around Australia – then the year after that will be interesting.

On the road, David is probably the most considerate of our pack. While we have a certain fraternity in the *peloton*, the battle ahead of us each day is a very individual one. David, however, is genuinely concerned about how his colleagues are doing, which is not something I can always claim. Perhaps that is why he has adopted the mantle of being our chief mechanic. If ever anything goes wrong with one of our machines, David is always prepared to get his hands dirty, quite literally.

There are, thankfully, no such problems today as we pass the sign that welcomes us to 'Sheffield, the Steel City'. Sheffield could well have been one of our county stops as this was, for a while, the home of Yorkshire County Cricket Club before it decamped to Leeds. The county used the Bramall Lane ground, which it shared with Sheffield United Football Club, and there was even a Test match played here against Australia early in the last century. Sharing the same field as a football team never really works though (as Northamptonshire and Nottinghamshire have also discovered) and in 1973, Bramall Lane became a dedicated soccer stadium, and first class cricket left Sheffield.

The hills of Sheffield do not make cycling easy but the road signs do. The City is surprisingly simple to cross and in the southern suburbs we find a greasy spoon café that provides the perfect lunch stop. Strange how the people who run these unpretentious cafés tend to be much more obliging and welcoming than those in charge of grander establishments. There is one such greasy spoon outside the Headingley Carnegie cricket ground called Ugly Mugs, and it seems we have stumbled across Sheffield's equivalent this afternoon.

We are behind the clock once again, partly due to the amount of urban cycling we are doing, but also because I feel everyone is feeling the effects of the previous three tough days since leaving Manchester. We averaged close to 80 miles a day on those three days, but as well as the distance, it was tough cycling terrain. Energy levels are low and today's battle through industrialised south Yorkshire is not the most inspiring of rides. We sit in the café in fairly reflective mood. The ride has become a bit of a slog, and today is to be endured rather than enjoyed. Yorkshire is the largest county in the United Kingdom and, boy, does it feel like it today. From Croft-on-Tees just south of Darlington in the north to Sheffield in the south, we have covered more than 100 miles cycling through a county, many of whose inhabitants would like nothing more than to declare independence for what they regard as 'God's Own Country.'

Just outside Sheffield we slip into Derbyshire and are able to escape the A61 for a while to use side roads through the villages of Dronfield and Hundall before hitting the Chesterfield dual-carriageway, which skirts what is a fine town with one of the sweetest little county grounds on the circuit at Queen's Park. Derby is the main home of Derbyshire County Cricket Club, our next port of the call, but Chesterfield has what is called an out-ground. Having been dropped from the rota for a few years, Queen's Park is happily back on Derbyshire's fixture list. It was at one time also a velodrome, but the banked cycle track around the ground has long gone.

The Chesterfield ground is overlooked by the famous 228ft twisted spire of St Mary and All Saints Church. The spire, which has come to symbolise the town, leans more than 9ft and looks as if it is going to topple over any day. There are several theories as to what has caused the twist, the principal one being that when it was built in the 14th century, there was a lack of skilled craftsmen following the Black Death. Poor workmanship allied to the use of unseasoned timber saw the spire warp when heavy slate tiles replaced the original wooden ones and hence the spire's precarious crooked appearance.

There is another theory, though, and one that I am inclined to believe: so shocked was the spire to learn of the marriage of a local virgin in the church below that it bent down to take a look at this most rare of occasions and twisted itself. It is said that the spire will only straighten up again when another Chesterfield virgin gets married in the church. It has been a long wait.

South of Chesterfield, we find relief from the traffic on more country by-roads that take us to Tibshelf, where the village signs welcome us to the home of Britain's first productive oil-well. While Tibshelf Crude may not exactly have caused a mass out-break of nodding donkeys across the Derbyshire countryside, it was a significant find.

Aware of the strategic importance of oil during the First World War (1914-18), the Government in 1915 ordered that exploration start in Britain, and Derbyshire, where oil seepage had been found in underground coal seams, was one of three sites to be drilled. Four years later in 1919 black gold was struck in Tibshelf. Six barrels a day flowed from the gusher at first and although production dropped steadily, it was not until 1945 and the end of the Second World War that it closed. The site is now a garden centre but the old well-head still seeps a little Tibshelf Crude.

Wells of a different kind have a far more active part in Derbyshire life these days. It is in the county that the custom of well-dressing, that sees springs and wells decorated with flowers, is thought to have originated. Just how it started is unclear although there are suggestions that it was a sign of giving thanks for pure water during the Black Death in the 14th Century. The custom has spread far and wide, and now involves elaborate framed pictures made of flowers, seeds, nuts and cones depicting a religious theme being placed by sources of water from the local well to a common or garden tap. Of course, there are now well-dressing associations and competitions in these days when getting one up on the neighbouring village is all-important.

Getting one up on my fellow cyclists would be nice, but it rarely crosses my mind as I grimly hang on at the back of the *peloton*, grateful if I am still in the same county as the rest of them, although, to be fair, on this ride I have almost always had Jack for company. The group reassembles at the petrol station in the little town of Alfreton in the Amber Valley just north of Derby for our last snack break and breather of the day. Our main route south, the A61, merges into the busy, dual-carriageway of the A38 here, but there is a quieter back route into Derby via Ripley, home of the Midland Railway, one of those heritage railways that keep steam trains puffing around our country.

The town also has grander links to railways in that the local engineering company, Butterley Engineering, made the magnificent arched roof of St Pancras Station in London. Under the Butterley works is one of those great feats of engineering from the days of the Industrial Revolution in England, the Butterley Tunnel. It runs for almost two miles carrying the Cromford Canal, an underground wharf serving the works above. The narrow tunnel had no towpath and the crews had to propel the barges by lying on their backs and 'walking' on the sides of the tunnel to push the vessel along. The tunnel was so long that a barge could even hire the "registered leggers" stationed at either end to walk the vessels through.

From Ripley we speed through Denby and past its famous pottery works as the light starts to fade again. We still have a few miles to do before Derby, and then we have to find our rather remote guest house on a back road somewhere on the way to Nottingham. It looks like we shall need lights again and have to travel in convoy, particularly as these roads are much busier than when we rode into the night in the Yorkshire Dales.

The rush hour traffic is stacking up on the A38 as we enter Derby and start searching for those little brown signs that will indicate the way to the cricket ground. I have been to the Racecourse Ground (The racecourse is no more, alas) many times, but always from the direction of the M1. Finding it from the other side of the city is likely to prove quite a challenge, although I know if we pick up signs for Nottingham, we will not be far away, as the ground is beside the main road linking these two rival East Midland cities.

We find the home of Derbyshire County Cricket Club surprisingly easily thanks, I have to say immodestly, to my sense of direction – and a few brown road signs. The ground is deserted, which many in cricket might say is nothing new. Even on match days there can be a distinct lack of atmosphere at the Racecourse Ground. For me, I think Derbyshire gets an unfair rap from the cricket fraternity. It tends to be the butt of jokes about the last place you would want to be, whether as a player or spectator. The county is neither glamorous nor wealthy, and has had little success. But it is part of the fabric of the professional game in this country – and if there were no smaller teams, the big teams would not be…well, big.

One of the county's more famous players of recent vintage is John Morris, who, after a time as a players' agent, is back at the county as Head of Cricket trying the reinvigorate its fortunes. Morris was a talented batsman who played a handful of matches for England. He was also a bit of a lad, which may or may not have held back his international career, although he did reach dizzying heights, so to speak, on the 1990-91 Ashes tour of Australia.

David Gower, one of the great batsmen of his era and a former England captain, was a well-known *bon viveur*. On that trip to Australia it surprised no-one when Gower, who had been left out of the team for an up-country practice match in Queensland, decided to relieve his boredom by taking a pleasure flight from a local air-strip in a Tiger

Moth biplane, paid for by a loan from the unsuspecting tour manager. Gower's plan was to water-bomb his mate Robin Smith, who was batting at the time, but the pilot outlawed such naughtiness, although he did agree to fly in low between the floodlight pylons and scare the living daylights out of the players. Just behind was a second Tiger Moth doing exactly the same thing, but it was Gower, of course, who collected all the headlines and notoriety for the fly-past. In that other plane was Morris, whose international career was soon grounded. He had played three Tests for England before then but never appeared again. The moral of the story is: if you are going to take liberties, make darned sure you have enough clout to get away with it.

Photographs done at the Racecourse Ground to provide a record of our visit to venue No. 13, we head off into the rush-hour traffic again and by this time the yellow neon street lamps are burning brightly. We have to find a small village called Draycott, which is about five miles away in the strip of countryside that separates Derby and Nottingham and carries the M1. It is agreed we should travel in convoy again with David and his light at the front, and Alan at the rear, but it is not so easy to stay together on congested roads with roundabouts and traffic lights. Those in front have to be aware of those behind, but that message does not seem to have got through.

At a large roundabout that goes underneath the A52 dual carriageway, Jack and I are dropped at traffic lights on the approach as the other four pull out into the traffic ahead of us. There are at least six exits off this roundabout, three of which are obscured by the pillars carrying the flyover.

When Jack and I finally join the roundabout there is no sign of the others so we stop and wait. Still no sign, so we wait a bit more. I think it is the responsibility of those leading to make sure they have everyone in tow, while clearly those leading think it is the responsibility of the stragglers to find them, and so we have an impasse in the Derby rush hour on this chilly Thursday evening.

Jack and I wheel our bikes into a lay-by and make a phone call to David, who as ever, has remained calm and is perfectly reasonable. I, though, am somewhat tetchy and wonder out loud if they have any idea where they are going. As tonight's accommodation has been booked by David, I have washed my hands of arrangements altogether and suspect they are hopelessly lost without recourse to 'The Master Itinerary.'

David has received directions from the owner of the farm where we are staying, but they are far from clear and by now it is authentically dark and I sense a little panic creeping in to the group. Jack and I do, finally, re-join the other four, who are waiting on the far side of the roundabout by an exit they believe (hope?) will take them to Draycott. The road takes us through some anonymous suburbs with a row of shops and two pubs then back under the A52 and out into the pitch black of unlit country lanes. It is time to stop to ring the farmhouse again to check on directions. It appears we are still heading the right way so we set off again barely able to see the bike in front, let alone the road ahead. Finally we spy a pub we have been given as a landmark and then, another half mile on, the five-bar gate that is the entrance to a long gravel drive up to the farmhouse.

Our welcome is most warm and our accommodation among the most curious we have had all trip. The bikes are put in a workshop and then we are shown to our two rooms, which are in a converted out-building that my grandmother would have described as "looking like a tart's boudoir." Clearly, plenty of money has been spent on the conversion, but not all of it is in the best possible taste. It is the bathroom that is the most exotic – or erotic, depending on your taste – feature with an enormous walk-in bathing pleasure-dome that doubles up as a shower or a Jacuzzi, with flashing coloured lights and built-in waterproofed television.

Fortunately, I am sharing with Tom and Jack, and, being youngsters, they can get the hang of the various remote controls that turn the thing on. In the other room I can hear cries of frustration from middle-aged men just wanting a quick shower and to get down to the pub. Toddy has had the first attempt to use the ablutions but managed only in turning on Emmerdale Farm. David offers to help out with the end result that Coronation Street is now accompanied by pulsating blue and red lights while the Jacuzzi section starts to fill with foaming water. When Alan takes command of the remote control at least water does emerge from the shower-head but it comes out in short rhythmic bursts, alternating hot and cold while someone on Masterchef is blanching his almonds.

Tom and Jack are summoned for help and explain that Alan has clicked on 'Danish Massage' or some such button. They managed to stop the Jacuzzi and silence the television, but are unable to work out how to stop the disco lights show. They do, though, get the shower operating like a normal shower and at the right temperature. Relieved, Alan, Toddy and David decide they had better not turn the thing off until they are all done so they shower in quick relay (though, not at the same time) before calling for Tom and Jack to return to "turn the damned thing off."

I am weary and still a little fed up with the 'roundabout episode' so I decide I am going to spend the evening in and watch the football on television. There comes a time on all these trips when you fancy a little solitude and want to get away from the group, and tonight is it for me. The nearest village with a pub that serves food is just over a mile away and our host has kindly offered to drive us there to save the walk. Jack says he would also like to watch the football with me and suggests he travels in with the others, picks up some Indian take-away and returns with our host. It is the best possible solution for an early night, which I am in need of. As Jack also returns with a Threshers' bag full of chilled lager, the decision to stay in is a winner.

Tomorrow should be a good day, it is one of those I have been looking forward to since the ride was in the planning stage, but unfortunately it is to get off to the worst possible start before we have even laid a tyre on tarmac.

Day Thirteen Route: *Headingley to Leeds, A61 to Wakefield. B6132 to Royston and Barnsley, A61 to Worsbrough, Hoyland, then A6135 to Sheffield. A61 and B6158 to Dronfield, B6057 to Whittington, A61 to Chesterfield. B6039 to Holmewood, Tibshelf and Alfreton. A61 and B6179 to Stanwick, Ripley, Denby, Little Eaton. A61 into Derby for Derbyshire County Ground. A52 towards Nottingham then A5111/A6005 to Borrowash, B5010 to Draycott.*

String Distance: 76 miles
Actual Distance: 81 miles
Time in Saddle: 6 hrs 49 mins
Average Speed: 11.9mph

Overall string distance: 829 miles.
Actual mileage to-date: 904.
Total cycling time: 76hrs 31 mins.
Average Speed: 11.8mph

CHAPTER FIFTEEN

The Fox Chase

....from Draycott to Moulton

We have just completed two of the biggest days of the trip and although the legs are weary, it feels like we are almost home and dry. The 87 miles we cycled from Chester-le-Street to Leeds was the longest day of our ride and there is nothing ahead of us on the last three days that will come close to that unless my piece of string has been horribly deceitful. Yesterday from Leeds to our East Midlands hill-top farmhouse was not a great deal shorter at 81 miles. Only one other day on the trip has been more than 80 miles – Bristol to Monmouth – so from now on we should be in our comfort zone. Comparatively speaking.

Breakfast at the farmhouse cooked by our host's wife is of a high standard. I hesitate to call her a farmer's wife because I don't get the feeling the couple do a great deal of farming. There are few muddy boots around and the pristine beige carpets are hardly in keeping with a working farmhouse. There is little sign of agricultural machinery or livestock either, apart from a couple of horses in the paddock out front. In daylight we can now see that behind the outbuildings that housed our bedrooms are a few containers – the sort you see on the back of lorries – a caravan or two and an expensive-looking customised American motor-home. We cannot see what is across the fields because they are shrouded in the early morning fog but I don't suspect our host is up early and out there somewhere at a milking parlour or on his combined harvester. Still, it has been a good place to stay even if the steamy Jacuzzi with its disco lighting was wasted on six blokes with greasy hands and stubble.

We push our bikes along the 150 yards or so of the stony drive. Our slim road tyres are not made for this sort of surface and it would be silly to take chances before we have set off. Unfortunately, Toddy's back wheel rebels all the same. We are just closing the five-bar gate behind us when Toddy announces that he can hear a worrying rubbing noise. This is usually caused by a tyre rubbing on a pannier that has not been carefully clipped back on the rack above the back wheel. This is easily sorted by a quick adjustment of the pannier, but in this case it appears Toddy's rear brake blocks are sticking on one side. David is summoned and lays out his tool bag on the grass bank with precision much like I imagine a surgeon would spread out his instruments before removing something nasty. After a few efforts to free the block with his bare hands, David tells Toddy this may be a major operation. Toddy has to remove his panniers and turn the bike upside down, so David can get at the recalcitrant brake block more easily.

The wheel is not aligned properly, it seems. Just how it got like that no-one is sure, but David removes it, which is not straightforward with the chain and all the gears on the rear, re-aligns it and tightens everything up. By the time Toddy has packed all his possessions back on to the bike again and David has cleaned his oily black hands on a some dock leaves, we finally hit the road at 10 o'clock, almost an hour late already.

Our first stop is not far away. It is less than 10 miles into Nottingham and the home of Nottinghamshire County Cricket Club at Trent Bridge. The road that was pitch black when we arrived the previous evening turns out to be a wide lane with high hedges on each side. Our host for the night has told us to turn right out of his gate and we cannot miss Nottingham, which is a gentle downhill spin away. He is right, and we are soon back among houses, traffic and on the Maid Marian Way in the city centre that leads us to Trent Bridge, which for me is the most attractive of all the Test grounds in England and Wales. Although big enough to stage international matches, Trent Bridge has retained the feel of being a welcoming county ground. It is also a good place to work as a journalist with great facilities for the media, friendly staff and a car park just a short stroll away.

The origins of the ground are delightful, too. In the 1830s, William Clarke, a bricklayer and keen cricketer, met and married Mary Chapman, the landlady at the Trent Bridge Inn. William ran a nomadic cricket team while Mary had a large field stuck on the back of her inn going to waste. It seemed perfectly good sense to turn it into a cricket field so that William's team had a permanent home and Mary had a regular supply of thirsty customers. By 1840, the first county match had been played on the ground and for many years the grand red-brick pub, which is still a big feature of

Trent Bridge today, served as the dressing rooms and pavilion until they were relocated on the opposite side of the ground. It was another of those grounds that shared with football – Notts County were the tenants – until early in the 20th century when the footballers moved to Meadow Lane just the other side of the River Trent.

I would have liked to have taken pub-loving Alan to one of my favourite watering holes in Nottingham, but it is too early in the day even for him to sink a pint of ale and, anyway, we do not have the time to spare. The pub in question claims to be the oldest inn in Britain and, although it has become something of a tourist haunt, is still a thoroughly good boozer with no pretentions to serving posh food. Ye Old Trip to Jerusalem – 'The Trip' to its regulars – is literally built into the sandstone rock and caves at the foot of the hill on which sits Nottingham Castle. The date 1189AD is painted on its white exterior walls and there is no doubting the feel of history in the little bars that are part of the cave network under the hill. The pub's curious name is derived from the knights of King Richard I (Richard the Lionheart), who were said to have stopped here for a few jars for the road before setting off on the Crusades to the Holy Land to quell the troublesome Saracens. And it still sells a thoroughly good pint.

Nottinghamshire County Cricket Club lives up to its reputation of being one of the most friendly around as we bowl up to the wrought iron gates alongside the Trent Bridge Inn. There is due to be a match going on against Hampshire. It is the third day of the four-day Championship game, the last of the season, but the autumn mists have delayed the start, making it too gloomy to play. I did wonder if the gatemen might be wary about letting us in on a match day. They might think six blokes turning up and saying they were on a charity bike ride to all the county grounds was simply a novel ruse to get to see the cricket free, but it took only a few words of explanation for them to open the gates and allow us to wheel our bikes to the boundary edge between the stands.

With no cricket taking place yet, we become quite an attraction for the crowd already in the ground, and the head gateman takes great delight in ushering us through as if we are celebrities. He is so taken with his new role that he even poses with us for our photographs against the misty backdrop of the playing area. Our arrival was probably the high spot of the four days for the local fans as Nottinghamshire blew their chances of winning the Championship in that match, losing by 203 runs to allow Durham to take their first title.

Pictures taken and with the chill of the mist already beginning to creep into our legs after just a 10-minute stop at the ground, we head out of Nottingham through West Bridgford on the A60 towards Loughborough, a non-descript English county town that has gained recognition for its famous sporting university, and which is where the England and Wales Cricket Board has its Centre of Excellence, which is another name for an Academy.

The cycling is easy through the gently rolling countryside and as the sun burns off the morning mist, it turns out to be another glorious September day in the heart of England. Spirits are high as we eat up the miles heading south through the villages of Bunny, Costock and Hoton. We are now touching a part of the country called the Vale of

Belvoir, which my colleague Jonathan Agnew, the BBC cricket correspondent, has made it his personal mission to promote whenever possible. On air during commentaries on Test Match Special, 'Aggers' will not miss an opportunity to mention The Belvoir, where he and his wife now live.

Aggers might tell listeners that it was "pretty damp in The Belvoir" when he woke up that morning. Or he might say: "The Belvoir is looking particularly glorious at this time of year." He has even been known to suggest that he "cannot wait to get back to The Belvoir this evening." This gratuitous name-dropping, of course, has nothing whatsoever to do with the fact that Belvoir is pronounced "beaver" – and that Aggers has a rather naughty sense of humour.

Hoton marks our entry into Leicestershire and the opportunity to get off the main A60 and head south on minor roads, avoiding Loughborough. As usual, we had studied the maps over breakfast to identify likely places to stop and our planned mid-morning break this morning is at the village of Barrow upon Soar, where we find a pub prepared to serve coffee after some sweet-talking to the landlady and her rather reluctant barmaid.

Our flat route to Leicester follows the meandering River Soar and the Midland main-line railway, and the going is easy until we hit the city suburbs. Leicester is one of those places that appears incredibly difficult to navigate to me. It has no obvious landmarks, hills or rivers to relate to. One busy road looks much like another, unless, that is, you are in the Asian quarter, where it would feel like India if it was warmer, dustier and had a few cows sat in the middle of the road chewing the cud. There is a large Asian population in this part of the East Midlands and their influence is unmistakable on our journey into the city. The exotic smells from the Asian supermarkets, the rows of textile shops, the gaudy frontages, the Indian restaurants and the general hubbub of activity give this area of Leicester a distinct feel of the subcontinent. Close your eyes and you could be in Chennai or Chandigarh, two places I know well from my tours following England's cricket team. It seems a reasonable place to ask the way to the local cricket ground given Asia's love of the game.

As soon as we pull up by the kerb we are surrounded by helpful and inquisitive passers-by who are only too happy to point us in the right direction. Unfortunately, they do not all point the same direction. We get the general idea, though, and once we stumble across the railway station, I have my bearings at last. We weave our way around the giant one-way system and find the road to Grace Road, home of Leicestershire County Cricket Club – and, for a couple of weeks during the summer of 2009, the Australian team.

Australia found themselves in the unexpected and unwanted position of being eliminated at the early stages of the 20-over World Cup being held in England that summer. As they had a full Ashes tour in the country still to come, Australia were left with close on two weeks to kill before their programme resumed, so they decamped to Grace Road, which led to much hilarity in the 'Pommie Press.' While the facilities at the cricket ground may be ideal for training, the city itself is not known for its glamorous attractions, and the British media had a field day making helpful suggestions as to how Ricky Ponting's Australians might fill their hours. A trip to the local theatre, where The Full Monty was showing, was high on the recommended list, as well as a tour around the local Everards Brewery. There was, of course, the National Space Centre to visit, which is always a good bet on a wet afternoon, or (Jonathan Agnew's favourite) they could spend a day at Belvoir Castle

There is cricket on at Grace Road when we arrive and, as at Trent Bridge, the gatemen are more than happy to wave us in to the homely ground where the local team, The Foxes, are ripping East Midlands' rivals Derbyshire to shreds in their last match of the season. Tom and Jack are keen to linger to watch the game and have lunch at the Foxes' chip and pie emporium, which is imaginatively called 'The Meet', but we persuade them that we really should be on our way. With Leicestershire ticked off, we have just three more of the 18 grounds to go.

We are heading next towards ground No.16 at Northampton, but our journey today is to stop a few miles short of the town at a small village hotel booked by David. We have only another 30 miles to go and the prospect of a reasonably early arrival is appealing. We decide to make our lunch stop a short one and on the way out of Leicester find a petrol station for sandwiches, flapjacks and coffees that we consume sitting on a low brick wall by the road. When I say 'we', though, I do not include Alan, who is most unimpressed with the idea of a snack stop. Alan is not to be denied. He informs us that this is not a proper lunch stop and stalks off across the road to a pub he has seen for his mandatory pint.

Our route now is a simple one: straight down the A5199 to Moulton, our overnight stop. The flattish, agricultural countryside of south Leicestershire was made for cycling and we eat up the miles without really trying on our quiet main road through the villages of Arnesby and Husbands Bosworth, where we cross the Grand Union Canal, the once vital link between London and the coalfields of Derbyshire and Nottinghamshire.

At Welford we cross the River Avon, which marks the border into Northamptonshire, and pass the site of the Battle of Naseby, the key battle of the English Civil War in 1645 when the Royalist army of King Charles I was put to flight by the Parliamentary New Model Army of Oliver Cromwell. Today, the only battle going on is between Tom, Jack and David as they vie for front wheel in their little breakaway group.

The road is straight as we run parallel to, and a few miles east of, the M1, and even the break-away group cannot get too far ahead of Alan, Toddy and me in the second pack. It is one of those rhythmical rides on which the pedals almost seem to turn themselves and it is simply a case of ticking off the miles at each road sign we pass and maintaining the good momentum. A few more villages and a lot more fields later and we stop in Chapel Brampton to re-unite so that no-one misses the sharp left turn on to a little side road that will take us to our hotel in Moulton, a village of narrow streets, quaint buildings, a sprawling agricultural college and several pubs. Things are looking up for the evening, which gets off to an impressive start when we check in at the Poplars Hotel. There waiting for us is a bottle of white wine left as a welcoming present by the brother of Matthew Engel, whose charity fund in memory of his son Laurie we are supporting.

Being a small hotel there are also plenty of bedrooms and as the inn is far from full, the temporary landlord has given us two single rooms as well as two twins, which means I strike lucky again with a room to myself. The privacy gives me a chance to phone home and catch up on the news. On rides like this, it is easy to lose touch with the real world in which people work for a living. All is well back in Cranbrook, and my wife Brenda is relieved to hear that Tom and I have settled our differences and are getting on famously again. It appears Tom has been using her as an agony aunt, seeking advice on how he should react to his father's unreasonable complaints. He really should have known better.

The only disappointment at our cosy hotel is that the restaurant is closed. The owners and head chef are away on holiday, and the place is being run by a locum, who is a dab hand behind the little bar but whose talents do not stretch to cooking. So we traipse the village streets in search of a recommended pub but, this being a Friday night, when we get there all the tables are booked. Our last resort is another hostelry with a very English feel to it, but also with a Chinese restaurant attached to the rear. It is surprising how often the unplanned can work out so well. The food is excellent and Toddy has us all hugely amused with his assertion that the very attractive oriental waitress has her eye on Jack for far more than a tip. We tell, Jack, however, that it is not a takeaway and we should head off for a reasonably early night.

Tomorrow has something very special in store for all of us: we are about to pass 1,000 miles on the road.

Day Fourteen Route: *Draycott to Nottingham B5010 and A52 to Trent Bridge (Nottinghamshire CCC), A60 to West Bridgford, Ruddington, Hoton. Minor roads to Barrow upon Soar, Sileby, Cossington. A607 to Leicester. A426 to Leicestershire CCC, A5199 to Wigston, Arnesby, Husbands Bosworth, Welford, Thornby, Creaton, Spratton, Chapel Brampton. Minor roads to Boughton and Moulton.*

String Distance: 65 miles
Actual Distance: 70 miles
Time in Saddle: 6hrs 7mins
Average Speed: 11.4 mph

Overall string distance: 894miles.
Actual mileage to date: 974.
Total cycling time: 82hrs 38 mins.
Average Speed: 11.8mph.

THE ART OF TIMEKEEPING...
by Alan Dracey

One would have thought it a fairly simple task for six blokes on a bike ride to be able to synchronise such little things as taking breakfast together, setting off on the road each morning together, cycling together, and finishing each day together.

You must bear in mind that we are recreational cyclists, unencumbered by the need to develop racing tactics where you might find a lone breakaway, or a lead group pulling away from the peloton. By contrast, all we needed to do was to ride together as a group of friends, stop for refreshments or rests when the mood took us, and enjoy the company.

Well, that's the theory. In practice though, this probably took as much work to get right as it did to cycle 70 or 80 miles a day.

The first thing we discovered was that whatever time we might agree to meet up for breakfast the next morning, when it came to it, some people were better at getting up than others. So while David and Ian would usually be sitting down with their cornflakes and the morning papers, Tom and Jack were generally found trying to eke out another half hour or so in bed, in the hope that they could catch up by eating and packing their panniers more quickly than the rest. Of course, this rarely worked as they might have hoped, and it became a recurring theme of the ride to find Colin chivvying them up and berating them for their tardiness. The departure from Monmouth in particular comes to mind, when Jack ran the real risk of being left behind at the start.

But time and timekeeping had not finished with us yet. For having negotiated this first obstacle of the day, we would still have the whole day ahead of us for time to play its little tricks. It quickly became apparent that some of us liked to start riding at a faster tempo and then slow down as the day went on, while others would start slowly and then speed up as they grew into the day's riding. Others were just too bloody fit for their own good, and left the rest of us behind from the word go.

For the most part, David and Tom would leave the rest of us in their wake after a mile or so, and wait whenever they got to the top of a hill until the stragglers had caught up, before repeating the process. Generally speaking, this was an approach that worked well, but when the ridiculously fit and athletic Steve James entered the equation (I could argue that he wasn't weighed down by panniers like the rest of us, but somehow I don't think it made that much difference) synchronicity went straight out the window.

Steaming off at a pace that had me suspecting EPO abuse only encouraged David and Tom to try to match him, and suddenly the whole thing became a race. OK, so we had an agreed route plan in mind, but what they really wanted to do was to get from A to B in the shortest possible time. If this meant sticking to the main road that was more direct, rather than taking a scenic detour along some pleasant country lanes as had been planned, then so be it. Of course, now that we were taking two completely different routes, it did make it a bit more difficult to establish a rendezvous for our late morning coffee.

This brings us to the next thing that time had in store for us. As well as maintaining some sort of a schedule each day to ensure that we arrived at our destination before nightfall, we also had to reach consensus as to what time our bodies wanted to eat and drink.

It strikes me as interesting that the longer the ride went on, the later we would stop for lunch, and the shorter the lunch breaks became. In fairness, this might have been borne of necessity, as our daily mileage seemed to increase quite noticeably in the second half of the ride, and we could no longer afford the luxury of a leisurely meal.

For the most part, it was a pretty easy decision to make when it came to discussing when and where to stop. However, there comes a point when a sandwich and a coffee just won't hit the spot, whereas a pie and a pint of local ale is just what the doctor ordered. Now you might consider me a bit of an old soak, but I do recall on one occasion feeling more than a little distressed: in the delightful town of Wigston just outside Leicester we had chosen to stop at a petrol station to buy sandwiches to go, even though there was a perfectly good looking pub on the other side of the road. Everards it said, and Everards it was for me.

I'm sure the others enjoyed their polystyrene cups of tea or coffee, but you can't tell me a pint of ale didn't win hands down.

Of course, we still had to finish each day together, as there was no guarantee we'd have otherwise all found our way to our accommodation for the night. Which leads us to the last of the treats that time and timekeeping had in store for us. It was a fact that out of the six of us, only two of us had come equipped with lights for cycling in the dark.

That might seem reasonable enough given that we were riding for pleasure, and not expecting anything too arduous (or in my case, anything that might keep me from the pub after opening time) but we hadn't allowed for the possibility that some days might take longer than others if there were (a) a surfeit of hills, and (b) a persistent headwind from start to finish.

I am thinking here of our day to Hawes, when the sun had set a full eight miles before we had reached our destination. In a way though, this gave us a new and not entirely unpleasurable experience. *In order to negotiate the last few miles in the dark, we had to ride in convoy, with one light at the front, and one at the back. There were not many occasions when we rode as a unit for a significant length of time, but this was one of them.*

After all this, there was still one final reminder of the impact that time and timekeeping had on ride and riders. When we came to the end of the whole event, and swept into Lord's, there was Old Father Time himself presiding over all, to tell us that our time together was up, and that tomorrow life would be back to normal. But hey, that also means there will be a next time!

CHAPTER SIXTEEN

The Penultimate Push

....Moulton to Bishop's Stortford

Autumn is closing in. On the last few mornings it has been misty when we have set off but today it is positively foggy in our Northamptonshire village. Visibility is down to no more than 20 yards and the air is damp and cold. Judging by the foggy nature of my head, we probably had slightly too much to drink last night, too. The wine with the food was sensible but it was the few pints of local brew in the noisy bar before and after eating that may not have been so advisable. The bikes have been locked up against a fence at the far end of the beer garden at our hotel, so they are feeling damp and chilly too. Alan is looking snug in his long trousers, but the rest of us still insist on riding in shorts confident that the sun will soon break through again.

It is only five miles to our 16th cricket ground, Wantage Road, the home of Northamptonshire County Cricket Club, another of the more modest venues on the circuit like those at Derby, Leicester and our penultimate port of call, Chelmsford. As we make our way through the streets of terraced houses, Wantage Road is still shrouded in mist and the main gates to the car park are closed. To be honest, there is not much to see inside. Northamptonshire have never won the County Championship and the ground reflects the club's modest means and achievements. Northampton Town Football Club shared Wantage Road until 1994 before moving to a new stadium.

The county has produced its share of fine players, two of the most colourful whose careers burned briefly and brightly were Colin Milburn and Frank 'Typhoon' Tyson. The rotund Milburn was a buccaneering batsman in the 1960s but played only nine Tests before a car crash cost him the sight of his left eye, and he never played effectively again. Tyson, as his nickname suggests, was a fearsome fast bowler in the 1950s but played only 17 times for England before emigrating to Australia.

The current coach at Northamptonshire is another former England player, David Capel, one of the most engaging men you could wish to meet at any cricket ground. As the cricket correspondent of the Daily Express, I remember touring with 'Capes' in his early days as an England player, and in particular one trip to Amsterdam, which is not the most likely of cricket venues. Cricket is a popular amateur pastime in the Netherlands, nothing more, but the paternalistic English authorities saw it as their duty to encourage the Dutch, and in 1989 sent out a strong England XI to play them, with Capel in a squad that was to play two one-day matches.

After the second game, that England had won to cancel out their embarrassing defeat in the first, the players were allowed to let their hair down and enjoy Amsterdam's nightlife, which was slightly more Bohemian than Capel's local in Northampton. Very much the innocent abroad, 'Capes' loved nothing more than talking cricket and my abiding memory is of him in a bar trying to explain the intricacies of swing bowling accompanied by the full range of hand movements to a group of bemused leather-clad moustachioed locals who looked as if they had just left an audition as back-up singers for Village People. It is possible that they got hold of the wrong end of the stick when 'Capes' said he could make it swing both ways.

Our route out of Northampton takes us south-east on the A428 and, with the sun on our backs now, we are making rapid progress towards Bedford, which is 20 miles away. The cycling is easy and pleasant across rolling countryside and through pretty villages such as Denton and Turvey. The journey also takes us through Yardley Chase, a forested area used by the military as a bomb store during the Second World War. The giant reinforced bomb huts were seen as potential shelters in the advent of an atomic war in later years but that idea was abandoned. The area, though, is still out of bounds to the public and used for 'military training'.

This morning, for some reason, I am in the lead pack and able to keep up with David and Tom. With no big climbs it is easier to get into a good rhythm and we ride as a pack, taking it in turns to lead and give those just behind some respite. Alan's knee appears to be holding up well, Toddy is gaining in confidence and strength as he always does the longer these rides of ours go on. Jack is busy talking to his plastic lizard, Larry, which he found on the fourth day of the ride and who still resides on his handlebars tucked under the brake cable. If Jack is feeling in a good mood, he regales Larry with his thoughts on Arsenal's chances in the Premier Division this season, the weather or last night's dinner. If Jack is in a grumpy mood, Larry catches the rough edge of his tongue and is blamed for everything under the sun and even, at times, is squirted with water from Jack's bottle. We all have our own curious ways of getting through the day.

Bedford on the Great Ouse, which we have already crossed once this morning, seems the ideal place for our mid-morning stop and we wheel our bikes through the pedestrianised shopping centre where we find the perfect coffee shop with tables outside in the sun. Our stop is made even more enjoyable because the two charming ladies running the place tip us instead of the other way around. When they hear what we are doing they make a £5 donation to the two charities for which we are collecting. Yorkie, our friend from the café at Aysgarth Falls, would no doubt tell them he did get not as rich as he is today by making daft donations to every passing stranger who bought a cup of coffee and a Danish.

By David's reckoning on his bike computer, Bedford marks the spot where we have reached 1,000 miles. Alan does not think this is the case and believes we still have about another 15 miles to do before reaching that landmark. The problem with bicycle computers is that they are only as accurate and reliable as the person who fitted them, and in my experience no two ever appear to give exactly the same reading. I, though, am happy to go along with David's Grand Assertion.

We were tempted to linger longer in Bedford but this is no time to get complacent about the ride. You literally never know what is around the next corner, so we push on taking the A600 out of the town and through Harrowden, birthplace of John Bunyan, who wrote his famous allegorical novel The Pilgrim's Progress while incarcerated in Bedford Gaol for 'illegal preaching'. Our progress is serene and I feel so good that I have broken away at the front, like a lone rider on the Tour de France. I have left the peloton for dead, none of them anticipated my break and they are gasping at the sheer brilliance of this tactical move when fate sticks a nail in my revelry.

PUNCTURE.

I look down at my rear wheel in dismay as I hear the slight change in tone of the slowly deflating rubber on the tarmac and feel the tyre start to cling to the road. Just when I was about to grab the yellow jersey off Jack's back, fate has put me back in my place. Oh well, it could be worse. It is a lovely day, there is a good-sized verge to pull on to and my mechanic is puffing up the road less than a minute behind me.

By now I get the feeling David is almost wishing punctures to happen, so expert has he become at whipping wheels off and changing inner tubes. I am sure he gets an enormous amount of satisfaction at being able to take charge and resolve our problems, so who am I to stand in his way. I unclip my panniers and turn my bike upside-down as David dismounts and lays out his tool-kit with the assurance of a neuro-surgeon. Even an awkward back wheel is not going to delay us more than 15 minutes and we are soon on our way again.

That is five punctures – two for Toddy, two for Jack and now one for me – among 12 wheels over 15 days, which is not bad going. Let's hope it is the last.

Now that I have let the others catch up and catch their breath, we move on as a tight-knit group on our pretty route to the villages of Shefford, Henlow and our lunch stop in Baldock, which, legend has it, was named after Baghdad by the Knights Templar, who founded the town. Disappointingly, there is no 'Bagdad Café' here, but there is a greasy spoon with outside tables in the wide High Street that will do just fine. We had already tried two pubs on our way into town but they were showing live football and were not prepared to serve food. I have never understood why people want to watch television in a pub; surely the whole point of going to a pub is to get away from the television?

Opposite the café is an up-market bakery that does all sorts of fancy buns and cakes, ideal material to stock up on for the Saturday afternoon ride through the Hertfordshire countryside. This area lays claim to having its very own version of Robin Hood. A giant of a man called Jack o'Legs (he was reputed to be about 8ft tall) is said to have roamed these parts in the 14th century robbing the wealthy traders of Baldock and distributing his ill-gotten gains to the peasants. To add to the legend, there is a Jack's Hill nearby and in the parish churchyard in the village of Weston are two stones standing eight feet apart which are said to mark either end of Jack's grave.

Ten miles out of Baldock, we reach the small market town of Buntingford and by Alan's calculations, this is the 1,000-mile point. As we are also crossing the Prime Meridian in Buntingford at the same time, this seems just too good to be true. Even my piece of string could not have worked out such a clever landmark for the 1,000-mile point of our ride. Alan, who remains loyal to that lovely old tradition of writing and sending postcards home, insists we stop for a moment so he can pop into the post office-cum-village store to buy one to mark the occasion.

Here we leave the A507 and cut across country on quiet lanes that roll around arable fields. The afternoon's cycling is as easy as the morning's although we do have one minor delay and – on my part – panic. For some reason, Tom and Jack are hanging back, possibly because they are trying to ride and listen to the Saturday afternoon football reports via an ear-piece from a radio. Normally I am at the rear of the field and if there are any mis-haps I soon come across them, but today I am near the front and keep looking back, fretting about my sons as though they are still at primary school and on their first day out on the roads on a bike. We reach a T-junction where we have to turn right so I wait to make sure they head in the right direction. I wait and I wait, and still no sign of the stragglers apart from Toddy, who says he has seen them a couple of miles back.

They should have been here by now so I set off back along the route I have taken growing increasingly anxious. There is little traffic on this B-road but that does not mean there are never any accidents on it. So far on our long rides we have been remarkably lucky and no-one has come a cropper on the road. There have been one or two hairy moments when lorries, coaches and the dreaded caravans have cut in too close for comfort and caused a wobble, but none of us have come off our bikes because of a collision.

I try phoning the boys, but there is no answer, which, in itself, is no cause for alarm as it is often impossible to hear a ringing mobile phone when you are on the move. I am imagining all sorts of unpleasant scenarios when the pair of them trundle around a corner coming towards me, side-by-side and chatting away seemingly without a care in the world. They look astonished to see me heading back towards them and Tom explains their delay had been caused by them having to go back to retrieve Jack's wind-jacket after they had noticed it had fallen off the rack behind his saddle.

With everybody present and correct again, we cruise at a leisurely pace along one-track country lanes and through a few hamlets before coming to the quaintly-named Furneux Pelham. The village has a ford that is more than a half-a-mile long, the road and the stream flowing along the same route. It is popular splashing place for teenagers on mountain bikes and grown ups in their four-by-fours, but it is not part of our route so we stay well clear. Alan looks up at the church clock, not to study the unusual inscription below a picture of the grim reaper which reads 'Time Flies, Mind Your Business', but to confirm that it is five o'clock: time to stop for a pint and listen to the football results.

With perfect timing, we find the village pub, which has a beer garden and plenty of room for us and our bikes to spread out. It is an idyllic setting but one with a link to a chilling and still unsolved murder that put Furneux Pelham on the national news a few years ago.

Every Friday, retired Lieutenant Colonel Robert Riley Workman used to pop into the pub to buy a packet of small cigars and a portion of fish and chips to take away. The 83-year-old, who suffered from arthritis, was a familiar figure in the village where he had lived for several years caring for his invalid wife up to her death.

An Oxford graduate, he had served in the Second World War and then gone into the antiques business before retiring to the Hertfordshire countryside. It appeared he had no enemies, yet early one evening in January 2004 he answered a ring on the front door of his home, Cock Cottage, and was shot dead by single gunshot to the chest.

Fatally wounded by a large cartridge normally used for hunting animals, Mr. Workman was left to die in his hall. Nothing in his house was touched including his antique collection of silverware. At 5 o'clock the next morning a 999 call was made from a local telephone box asking for an ambulance to go to Cock House. Police believe that the man making the call, who had a local accent, may have been the murderer, but no-one has ever been arrested despite several appeals and the case – Operation Sacristy – being featured on the BBC's Crimewatch. The case is still listed on the Hertfordshire Constabulary website and the recording of that chilling 999 call can be re-played. Some villagers fear that the killer still lives among them.

Unaware of the village's dark history, we enjoy our rest in the evening sunshine in the beer garden and get excited about more mundane matters: Lewes have beaten Oxford United to win their first match of the season in the Conference Premier, but our other two main concerns, Bristol City and Arsenal, have both lost, taking the gilt off our last few miles into Bishop's Stortford and our final overnight stop.

On the way, Jack speeds ahead armed with my camera. He wants to take some more pictures of us on the road for posterity. As this is still a quiet country lane, he has instructed us to spread out, five-abreast, and pedal slowly so he can take a group photo of us coming towards him like a gang of desperados in a spaghetti western. Sure enough, around the next corner, Jack is crouched in the road clicking frantically as we approach. As we pass him, he topples over backwards in his excitement. The mood could not be happier.

After cycling through the town centre of Bishop's Stortford, we find our bed and breakfast down a quiet residential road on the outskirts. Most of the guests who stay here are people looking for overnight accommodation before using nearby Stansted Airport. Bishop's Stortford is hardly on the regular tourist route but is a town with a special attraction for us, it being our last night together. Alan and I are sharing the 'family suite' with Tom and Jack, who are in an adjoining room with the shared bathroom in between. One bathroom between the four of us makes it even more cosy, but we are at the stage of the ride where no one really cares. There is a feeling of euphoria that we have made it even though we still have one short day to go to take in our last two cricket grounds at Chelmsford and then Lord's in north London.

Bishop's Stortford town centre is a 20-minute walk away, which is a good way to loosen up the muscles after a long day in the saddle, and we are determined not to compromise on our dinner this evening. We find an Italian restaurant called Zizzi's that serves rather good Italian wine, and raise a glass "to six blokes and their piece of string."

Day Fifteen Route: *Moulton to Northampton and Northamptonshire County Ground on minor roads. A5095 through Abington, A428 to Denton, Yardley Hastings, Turvey, Bedford. A600 to Harrowden, Shefford, Henlow, Baldock. A507 to Buntingford. B1038 to Hare Street, minor roads to Furneux Pelham, Little Hadham, A120 to Bishop's Stortford.*

String Distance: 65 miles
Actual Distance: 68 miles
Time in Saddle: 5hrs 46mins
Average Speed: 11.8mph

Overall string distance: 959 miles.
Actual mileage to-date: 1042.
Total Cycling Time: 88hrs 24mins
Average Speed: 11.8mph.

PSSST...THE MECHANIC'S TALE...
by David Lloyd

Picture a Formula 1 pit lane with highly trained mechanics gathered around a gleaming car, each person knowing precisely what they're doing: old tyres off, new tyres on and away – and all before Murray Walker could say "and there goes Rubens Barri...."

Now visualise, if you will, a gravel-strewn hard shoulder alongside the A2 late on a Saturday afternoon with the chequered flag (or, at least, a hot shower and a pint of beer, though not necessarily in that order) still a dozen or so miles away and six blokes looking at yours truly with expressions which said: "Come on then, you've got the tools – stop messing about and fix the ruddy puncture."

To be honest, three of them – tour leader Col, map reader extraordinaire Alan, and master of just about every subject under the sun, apart from sodding bicycle maintenance, Toddy – should have known better. Were they not with me in France a few years earlier when, having confidently told them to step aside and leave the first blow-out of the tour to Monsieur Mecanicien, it took me half an hour to remove the little nut thing which holds the valve in place? Of course they were (although thankfully none were present when, having pedalled down the road and knocked on a door in search of additional tools, I suddenly remembered I couldn't speak a word of the lingo).

Anyway, when we had left South London a few hours earlier for stage one of our 18 Counties epic I was optimistic, having sorted out a few more punctures between tours, that I could deal with any mechanical misfortune that might hit us – just so long as it was nothing worse than a 'flat' and no-one was in a hurry. Chain splitter? I don't think so.

I would not say, then, that I was pleased exactly to hear Toddy's cry of "Sorry lads, I think there may be something wrong with my bike" but neither did the sight of a pancake-flat rear tyre send me into a state of panic. Which it probably would have done before I stumbled on a magic piece of kit.

Remember that scene from *Fawlty Towers* in which Basil sets about his car with a tree branch because it will not start? I've been there! Out on the road, miles from home, I have become so frustrated with my inability to refit a tyre that I've given my dear old Dawes Super Galaxy a damn good thrashing as though it is his fault that the last two inches of rubber will not be pushed, pulled, stretched or levered over the wheel rim. There are many annoying words in the English language but right up there in the Premier League, so far as I'm concerned, is 'simply'. As in "simply roll your hands forward to stretch the last bit of bead over the rim" as the manuals say. Yeah, right.

And then (and here comes the advertising plug in the hope I will be showered with free gifts) I discovered something called a Crank Brothers speed lever. If you have no problem refitting your tyres, then fine. But if it is a nightmare for you then all I'll say is spend a fiver or so on the aforementioned and the chances of you throwing your bike over a hedge and catching the bus home will be greatly reduced.

No piece of kit, however, can overcome one major problem: sheer incompetence. As in losing things. In roughly the time it takes a Tour de France mechanic to change a wheel (then watch his man ride the second half of a long mountain stage), I had removed Toddy's tyre, taken out the inner tube, replaced it with a new one and put the wheel back into what I believe are called the drop-outs. *And do you know what? I barely even flinched when one of the crew asked ever so politely, if a tad belatedly, whether we should have found out what caused the puncture. "Well, of course, you CAN do that if you want to but on this occasion I'm blowed if I'm going back to square one just because I forgot, under intense pressure caused by a large audience, to do the bleeding obvious..."*

"Trust me. It will be okay this time." And so it was – once those of us who hadn't made an excuse to nip off to Canterbury in order not to miss a very important radio interview (Col!) had spent a further 10 minutes searching among the gravel, broken glass and gawd knows what else for the nut which I'd managed to drop and was important only in that it prevented Toddy's wheel from falling off.

Still, as I told the boys in what I hoped sounded like a voice of experience, it is always good to get the first 'mechanical' of the tour out of the way. "And when we get to Canterbury I'll give all the bikes a good once-over to make sure everything is fine."

Well, a quick squirt with the WD40 and a prayer to the patron saint of bicycle travel, anyway.

CHAPTER SEVENTEEN

Lords Of The Road

...Bishop's Stortford to Lord's

One bathroom between four people with adjoining doors from two different bedrooms that are being opened simultaneously lends itself to scene from a Whitehall farce. Some of the moments in Coral's Guest House in Bishop's Stortford do not bear repeating but suffice it to say, there is little room for bashfulness. We are all keen to get ready to tackle the last day. I feel a genuine sense of excited anticipation at finishing what had seemed an improbable challenge nine months earlier when the plan was hatched. There had been times when the venture looked like it would never get off the ground, times on the ride when I cursed the day I thought of it, times when I thought my legs would not get me up another hill.

But here we are in our digs in Hertfordshire with just two more cricket grounds and – according to my trusty piece of string – only another 52 miles to go. It is Sunday morning and the roads for the first half of the day, at least, will be quiet. There is excited chatter over the breakfast table and even Jack, who is hardly a 'morning person' is

277

larking around. There will be a small welcoming committee for us at Lord's cricket ground, apparently. The wives and a few siblings will be there plus former Test batsman Hugh Morris, who is now a big wheel at the England and Wales Cricket Board and patron of the Heads Up charity, one of the two causes we are supporting on the ride.

The weather is suitably sunny and crisp for our final day and as we wheel our bikes out of the garage at our guest house, our landlady makes us feel even better by handing us back £10 towards our fund raising. Small gestures such as these can have such an uplifting effect and prove that not everyone in Britain is out to grab as much as they can and keep it for themselves. Far from it, in fact. The most rewarding part of this whole venture has been the generosity of people we know, and many who we do not. There is a financial crisis brewing in the world but so many people are still prepared support so many genuine causes in the UK.

We cycle back into the centre of Bishop's Stortford and are due to cross over the traffic lights on the main A120 but are halted by 'Road Closed' signs propped up on the tarmac in front of us. So often these signs do not actually mean that the road is closed. What they should read is 'Road Closed to Vehicles'. We could see there were workmen and tar-laying machines up ahead so we ventured forth, pretty certain there would still be a way through for pedestrians – and cyclists. Sure enough, our way is clear and we head out of Bishop's Stortford on the A1060 as planned for the 20-mile ride to Chelmsford, the home of Essex County Cricket Club.

Without anything being said, we ride as a six-strong

team into this final day with a great feeling of togetherness. We have come through a lot together, had our fall-outs and problems along the way, but rightly decide to finish this thing as a group as we leave Hertfordshire and whistle through the quiet roads of Essex. We pass under the M11 at Little Hallingbury and soon arrive in Hatfield Heath, another pretty commuter village that has barely woken up this Sunday morning.

I take a dim view of cyclists riding along talking on their mobile phones, it is probably even more dangerous than motorists who think they can cope with one hand on the steering wheel and another up to their ear, but this morning I am happy to turn a blind eye to Tom and Jack making excited calls home to their mother to tell her we are on our way.

Our deserted A road takes us into White Roding, one of nine settlements in this small area of Essex that share the name 'Roding'. It is the largest group of villages in England to share a common name. The Roding family consists of: White Roding, Abbess Roding, Aythorpe Roding, Beauchamp Roding, Berners Roding, High Roding, Leaden Roding and Margaret Roding with Morrell Roding, which is officially a hamlet and not a village, making up the nine. It is believed they took their name from an Anglo-Saxon tribal leader called Hroda, who sailed up the local river – now named the River Roding, of course – and settled in this area. In comparison, there are only three Batemans in the area and none of them intend to stay that long.

We breeze through two other members of the Roding Clan – Leaden and Margaret – and close in on Chelmsford, where Alan will take the lead wheel, it being the town of his birth. On the Tour de France, a rider passing through his home town or village is allowed to lead the pack and, if it is not too late in the day, stop and give his wife and children a kiss, while the *peloton* slows down. Alan has no-one to embrace him in Chelmsford today but we are happy to accord him the honour of leading the way when we get to the outskirts.

Alan spent the first 14 years of his life in Chelmsford before moving to Somerset and still has strong ties there. He suggests we leave our main road at Writtle and take a more picturesque back route into the town. Writtle these days is a quintessentially pretty English village with its duck pond and green where nothing much appears to happen, but it has played a central part in broadcasting as we know it today.

It was here that the country's first licensed radio station, 2MT, was set up in 1920, backed by the Marconi Wireless Telegraph Company a couple of miles away in Chelmsford. The town's signs as you approach Chelmsford proclaim it to be 'The birthplace of Radio.' Writtle was made famous by the call sign from the pioneering broadcaster at 2MT, Peter Eckersley: "This is Two Emma Toc, Writtle testing, Writtle testing," he would say. Two years later the station became part of the commercial British Broadcasting Company, which in turn was wound up in 1926 and became the British Broadcasting Corporation, which is today the largest broadcasting organisation in the world. Eckersley became the BBC's chief engineer, but after a couple of years was sacked because he divorced his wife. Those running the Corporation did not approve of such scandalous behaviour.

Alan's father Brian used to work for Marconi and he was also one of the reasons Alan wanted to take this route into town as it took us past the crematorium where Brian is buried. "I think he would be proud of his son for doing this ride," Alan wrote later in his tour diary.

Chelmsford is an easy town to navigate, particularly when you have such good local knowledge to call upon, and we arrive at a deserted County Ground off New Writtle Street at 11am. The Essex ground is best described as cosy. It can neither claim to be grand nor glamorous but that does not seem to stop the county's youth network producing a long line of cricketers good enough to play for England. Essex has provided England with a string of good captains, too. Keith Fletcher, Graham Gooch, Nasser Hussain and Alastair Cook, have all led England with various degrees of distinction over the last 40 years.

The ground is one of the smallest in the country with a capacity of 6500 and has little room for expansion, it being hemmed in by the River Can, a major town centre road and residential flats. There is no-one around this morning but the gates are open and we bowl up the long drive that becomes the scene of major traffic jams on match days. We sit on the white bench seats in front of the utilitarian pavilion for our photo-call and a rummage in the panniers for snack bars and sweets that we are not going to have much use for after today.

Back at my home in Kent stuck somewhere in the understairs cupboard is one of my favourite cricket souvenirs, which I came by courtesy of one of Essex's former England players, fast bowler Neil Foster. 'Fozzy' was a good old country boy from Colchester, and he and I were both callow young men on England's tour of India in 1984-85. For some reason, we hit it off, which can often happen between players and press when you are away touring together for three months. He was a good fast bowler although prone to injury and bouts of self-doubt, and had convinced himself he would not play a single Test on that tour. I assured him he would and we struck a bet. I am not sure what my side of the bargain was, but if Foster played he promised to give me one of his bespoke Gray-Nicholls bats. He did play two Tests on what was a successful tour and I still have the bat at home, little used but much treasured.

That tour of India, my first overseas assignment for any newspaper, proved to be my big break in journalism. The morning after the day we arrived, we awoke in our Delhi hotel to find the country in turmoil. The Prime Minister, Mrs Indira Gandhi had been assassinated, shot 31 times by two of her Sikh bodyguards. She was a major figure in world politics and suddenly this eager young sports hack found himself covering the biggest news story of the year.

A state of emergency was declared in Delhi and all foreigners ordered to stay indoors. Back in England, plans were already being made to fly the England team to Sri Lanka for the period of mourning in India. Unaware that America was being accused of being behind the assassination plot – Mrs Gandhi had strong links with the Soviet Union while the U.S. backed neighbouring Pakistan – I ventured out on to the streets with three colleagues driven on by journalistic instinct and oblivious to the dangers.

Seeing three white men with notebooks and another

with a camera, the mobs, which had just torched a rickshaw and beaten up its Sikh driver, turned on us assuming we were American, and chased us down the street hurling stones and threats. Fortunately, our brave hotel taxi driver was still waiting around the corner as arranged – I would not have blamed him if he had shot off – and we escaped unharmed.

Our individual story plus what was happening all around the city and the country that day made front page news, and my name was up in lights on the first three pages of the newspaper the next morning instead of being buried away in the games section at the back.

There were to be more incidents on that troubled tour which made me a favourite of the news desk back home. I had to cover another assassination, this time of Britain's Deputy High Commissioner in Bombay (Mumbai), Percy Norris, and then the Bhopal Chemical Factory disaster which left 10,000 dead at the time and has been blamed for a further 25,000 deaths since, and thousands of birth defects.

The Union Carbide pesticide plant in the town released toxic gasses that killed many in their sleep and polluted water supplies. The news desk at the Daily Express was soon on the telephone to my hotel in Bombay (the Taj Palace, which was to be attacked by terrorists in 2008) telling me to forget the cricket and get myself to Bhopal, 500 miles away. The prospect of venturing into an unknown city supposedly overcome with a deadly gas was not appealing, but I did go to the airport to try to catch a flight.

Indian airports are chaotic at the best of times but the clamour to get to the desk for Bhopal was like a surge at the stage of a rock concert. All flights were crammed with relatives and emergency service personnel trying to get to Bhopal. I did try half-heartedly but after 30 minutes of attempting to queue in an orderly British fashion, I found myself even further from the flight desk. I was not too disappointed, gave up trying to get to Bhopal and hurried back to my hotel.

In the mid-80s, overseas telephone connections were not easy. There was no mobile network, while landline calls had to be booked through the hotel operator, often several hours in advance. There was no way I could make instant contact with the Express in London so, feeling rather panicky because I had failed in my task of getting to Bhopal, I did what I was trained to do and used what resources I had. I monitored events on Indian television, spoke to a few local journalists that I knew and checked on the stories coming out of the international news agencies.

With what I had gleaned, I pieced together an "eye witness" account of the scenes of horror in Bhopal and sent my story to the London office via telex (no email in those days). Then I placed my call through to the Express via the hotel operator. Before the call came through, I received a 'hero-gram' telex message in return from the office, from the Editor-in-Charge congratulating me on a magnificent job. When I did eventually get to talk to the office, I did not have the courage to admit that I had not actually made it to the scene of the devastation that I had described so vividly in my report. My reputation was made and the full story of my 'non-trip' never came out as far as I know, although my cricket-writing colleagues on the tour knew the truth, and the nickname of 'Bhopal' stuck with me for several years after that.

Sitting in the sun on the benches at the Chelmsford County Ground, we almost have too much time on our hands. We have arranged to arrive at Lord's at 5pm and have just a shade over 30 miles to go. We dallied at the ground for 30 minutes, working our way through our last reserves of snack bars and biscuits before the final leg of the 18 counties.

The main A12 from Chelmsford to London is a beast of a road, made even more unpleasant for driving because much of it is concrete instead of tarmac. It is not fit for cyclists and we were going to avoid all but a short section of it.

Our route out of Chelmsford towards Galleywood took us past the hospital where Alan was born and I express my surprise that there is no blue plaque on the wall commemorating the momentous event. Alan nods in agreement. From Galleywood we find minor roads to take us through Margaretting (which always sounds like a cocktail to me), through Heybridge and Mountnessing into Brentwood, a non-descript satellite town of London that witnessed one of the most significant events in British history.

It was here, in 1381, that the Peasants' Revolt had its first birth pangs. The Great Uprising that followed was the most extreme insurrection in English history and marked the beginning of the end of serfdom for the lower classes. Down the road at the village of Fobbing on the Thames Estuary, the locals had refused to pay the latest poll tax imposed on them and when a representative of the justice system, Robert Belknap, was despatched to sort out the unruly mob, he was waylaid and attacked in Brentwood. The down-trodden populace responded to this act of defiance in other parts of the country, notably Kent, and there were mass marches on London by common people demanding change. The names of the leaders, Wat Tyler, Jack Straw and John Ball, went down in English folklore and although the initial rebellion was quashed, it marked a sea-change in the country's history because the revolt also won support from influential sections of the ruling classes and led eventually to change.

There was no rebellion in the *peloton* today, just harmony, although David did have one break-away moment when a rude club cyclist, no doubt on his regular Sunday morning outing, sped by us without acknowledging our existence. David, and then Tom, gave chase briefly but soon sat up and drifted back to rejoin the rest of us. We had nothing to prove to anyone today.

We rolled into Brentwood looking for a coffee stop and found a swish Italian bar decorated with Lambretta scooter memorabilia that was just opening up. There was no room for our bikes on the patio area so we had to leave them outside near the road and took great care locking them together. This was no time to have a bike pinched and it takes only a second for an opportunist thief to hop on an un-tethered bike and cycle off. Perhaps unnecessarily, we also felt there was more likelihood of this happening now that we were back in the Home Counties and near London. Alan, as was his way, even unclipped his panniers and took them into the Italian bar, a precaution none of the rest of us bothered with, reasoning that if a pilferer wanted our dirty washing, he was welcome to it.

The last day of the Tour de France is always a procession with the leaders sharing a glass of Champagne in the saddle until the final dash for last-day glory up and down the *Champs Elysées* by the sprinters. So it was for us on our last day except there would be no sprint along St John's Wood Road for Lord's at the finish. Leaving Brentwood, we cruised along the A1023 for our next big landmark: our return inside the M25. Having escaped London's 117-mile orbital motorway at Dartford on our first day, we were cycling back underneath it 15 days and 1060 miles later. It felt like quite an achievement.

For about two miles, we had to follow the A12, but thankfully there were cycle paths to take us to Harold Hill and the delightfully named Gallows Corner, once a quiet country crossroads where the condemned were hanged, but now a thundering road junction where six cyclists were dicing with death trying to find the right route to Ilford on the A118.

The Sunday afternoon traffic was astonishingly heavy. Just where was everyone going? People in Britain appear to have this unquenchable desire to drive anywhere rather than stay at home. The shops, the pub, the cinema, or just cruising around; the national psyche seems to demand that people get out and about in their car otherwise they feel deprived. As well as causing mass pollution and being an awful waste of money, it is a national trait that is not good for us cyclists.

Despite the lemmings in their cars, we are still making good progress. Too good, in fact, if we are not to be too early for the Lord's welcoming committee. We have told them five o'clock and it would be a shame if we rolled through the Grace Gates early to find no-one there.

We decide to look for a lunch stop and pull into a pub in

Ilford that has tables and chairs in the car park and a large sign announcing 'Hot Food'. It is a con, of course. Having sold us a round of drinks, no one seems keen to take our food order on the basis that the kitchens are busy and cannot really be bothered. It is nice, though, to have a break and kill some time, and it does give us an opportunity to give Alan the treat he has been waiting for all trip.

Alan's aversion to fast food is well known to us. On previous tours he has eschewed fast food joints and take-aways of any description. Top among his list of no-go areas are McDonald's, which, for those who do not frequent the golden arches, sell meat patties served between a bun with deep fried chipped potatoes among other culinary delights. David and Tom have been extolling the virtues of McDonald's burgers to Alan for several cycle tours now but he has not set foot inside one in more than 30 years...until today.

Less than a mile after our pub stop, we pass a McDonald's with plenty of empty tables outside and so the lead group of Tom, David and Jack swing in, presenting Alan with a *fait accompli*. This is to be our lunch stop. At last, after four long tours together, we have got Alan inside a McDonald's. It is with great delight that we watch Alan look mournfully at the menu of meaty treats on the wall over the tills and then try to place his order with the girl-in-a-hurry at the counter.

"No, Sir, we are not serving roast beef with Yorkshire pudding and new potatoes today. Now, is that large fries or regular on your BigMac?"

When Alan settles down at our table for his sumptuous lunch, we all have cameras at the ready to provide photographic evidence for his wife Diane. She will not believe it otherwise.

From Ilford we head for Manor Park and as we arrive at the North Circular Road we are astonished to find the traffic absolutely grid-locked. It does not look as it will move for hours and there is no obvious cause for the jam. Even on a bike, it is difficult to pick our way through the nose-to-tail rows of cars, buses and coaches that are going nowhere in a hurry. Our progress is painfully slow and for the first time today there is a danger of us being late for the welcoming party. Our snail-paced route eventually takes us to the heart of Cockney-land – Bow – where my parents hailed from, and Mile End, where Tom now lives and goes to university.

Being an urban cyclist these days, we suggest to Tom that he takes the lead to get us from here to Kentish Town, a journey he has done many times as his girlfriend lives there, and then on to Regent's Park. He knows the road well, but because we are keen to stick together, it is slow going. Toddy especially, is not enjoying this battle with the London traffic. Bus lanes do afford us some space and protection but even these are frequently blocked by parked cars and, heaven help us, buses. We know now we are going to be late so we stop briefly at a petrol station to telephone ahead to warn our families that we are at least half an hour behind schedule – and to use the facilities. There are no convenient bushes in this part of London even for Tom.

Tom leads us to Old Street, past the Angel, along City Road and into Marlybone Road where we swing into the relative tranquility of Regent's Park and to the traffic lights by the mosque that is just a six-hit from Lord's Cricket

Ground. It is here that the others pull over and stop at the kerb. I look at them. Surely we have not suffered another puncture here? David informs me that they insist that I lead them home for the last few hundred yards. I protest pretty lamely. I have, after all, been the *lanterne rouge* – the back-marker – for 80 per cent of the ride and say it would be wrong for me to cross the line first. But David very kindly insists, pointing out that this whole daft idea was mine in the first place.

The feeling, cycling along St John's Wood Road as we pass the back of the Mound Stand and then the Tavern Stand and then swing in through the Grace Gates at Lord's, is a mixture of huge satisfaction tinged with a little relief and regret that it is all over. The MCC gatemen, famed (these days unfairly) for their obstructiveness to anyone without a membership card, have been primed and wave us in past the up-raised barrier, and there to greet us is a small but tearful gaggle of friends and relatives. It has been some trip for them as well, I guess.

The story should end here but for Tom, Jack and me, there is one postcript: we cannot get home. Dead beat having done 1,099 miles over the past 16 days, the great British railway system was going to scupper us at the very last. My wife Brenda informs us that trains to our local station in Kent, Staplehurst, have been replaced by a bus service because of engineering works on the line. And, of course, you cannot take bikes on a bus. The closest we can get by train from Charing Cross is Sevenoaks, still 20 miles from our home and where she has left her car.

We do, of course, get home, but not before much delay and help from a friend of Jack's, who comes to meet us at

Sevenoaks to ferry us home, while our bikes and panniers are crammed into the back of my wife's Renault Clio. Long before we reach Cranbrook late on that Sunday night, Jack is sound asleep. Dreaming of sheep, no doubt.

Day Sixteen Route: *Bishop's Stortford A1060 to Hatfield Head, The Rodings and Writtle. Minor Roads into Chelmsford and to the Essex County Ground. B1007 to Galleywood, minor roads to Margaretting, B1002 to Heybridge, Mountnessing. A1023 to Shenfield, Brentwood. A12 to Gallows Corner, A125/118 to Ilford, Stratford. A11 to City of London, various local roads to St John's Wood and Lord's Cricket Ground.*

String Distance: 52 miles
Actual Distance: 57 miles
Time in Saddle: 5hrs 53mins.
Average Speed: 9.7mph

Overall string estimate: 1011 miles
Actual Total Mileage: 1099
Time in Saddle: 94hrs 17 mins
Overall average speed: 11.65mph.

AFTERWORD

We did all make it back in one piece and when the totting up was done we reckoned we had cycled through 26 counties, covered 1099 miles and raised close to £8,000 for the two charities. The '18-Counties' is hardly likely to become a rite of passage for long distance cycling in Britain as Land's End to John O'Groats has, but I believe it could catch on among the cricket fraternity. If anyone wants the route, they can contact me at the address below.

Since the ride, David has given up full time journalism and has really caught the touring bug. He is currently planning a 4,000-mile ride around Australia. Toddy is as active as ever and hoping to join David Down Under. Alan is still pedalling furiously to work in Brighton and is keen to organise another French cycling adventure taking in a few gastronomic delights and a couple of famous Tour de France climbs.

Tom is in his final year at University and too busy to cycle! Jack is a fully-fledged, busy tree surgeon and desperately keen to go on another long ride. He still has Larry, who will, no doubt, come along too. Rupert, my youngest son, is contemplating joining us for the next one, while Brenda, my wife, says she will enjoy the peace and quiet while we are all away.

As for me, I am still writing about cricket. But there will be another long ride. Just where and when I am not sure. My piece of string is ready and waiting.

BIBLIOGRAPHY

Grounds of Appeal by Aylwin Sampson, The Top 100 Cricketers of All Time by Christopher Martin-Jenkins, Eleven Minutes Late by Matthew Engel, Settle to Carlisle in Colour by David Jay, The Highway Code, Myles' Text Book for Midwives, Construction News, Canterbury Cathedral Archive, The Peak District Holiday Guide, The Northern Echo Archive, Wisden Almanack, Fovant Badges Society website, Fauld Explosion website, Wikipedia website, BBC archive, Guardian Archive, Times Newspaper Archive, and a host of city, town and village councils' websites.